[印度] 阿维纳什·迪克西特 著 陆赟 译

牛津通识读本·

微观经济学
Microeconomics
A Very Short Introduction

译林出版社

图书在版编目（CIP）数据

微观经济学 ／（印度）阿维纳什·迪克西特著；陆赟译．
—南京：译林出版社，2021.8
（牛津通识读本）
书名原文：Microeconomics: A Very Short Introduction
ISBN 978-7-5447-8730-7

I.①微… II.①阿… ②陆… III.①微观经济学
IV.①F016

中国版本图书馆 CIP 数据核字（2021）第 095222 号

Microeconomics: A Very Short Introduction by Avinash Dixit
Copyright © Avinash Dixit 2014
Microeconomics was originally published in English in 2014.
This licensed edition is published by arrangement with Oxford University Press.
Yilin Press, Ltd is solely responsible for this bilingual edition from the original work and Oxford University Press shall have no liability for any errors, omissions or inaccuracies or ambiguities in such bilingual edition or for any losses caused by reliance thereon.
Chinese and English edition copyright © 2021 by Yilin Press, Ltd

著作权合同登记号　图字：10-2016-181 号

微观经济学　［印度］阿维纳什·迪克西特／著　陆　赟／译

责任编辑	陈　锐
装帧设计	景秋萍
校　　对	王　敏
责任印制	董　虎

原文出版	Oxford University Press，2014
出版发行	译林出版社
地　　址	南京市湖南路 1 号 A 楼
邮　　箱	yilin@yilin.com
网　　址	www.yilin.com
市场热线	025-86633278
排　　版	南京展望文化发展有限公司
印　　刷	江苏扬中印刷有限公司
开　　本	635 毫米 × 889 毫米　1/16
印　　张	17.25
插　　页	4
版　　次	2021 年 8 月第 1 版
印　　次	2021 年 8 月第 1 次印刷
书　　号	ISBN 978-7-5447-8730-7
定　　价	39.00 元

版权所有·侵权必究

译林版图书若有印装错误可向出版社调换。质量热线：025-83658316

序 言

郑江淮

人们通常把微观经济学视为研究经济体系中消费者、企业等当事人个体（agent）经济行为的学问。经典的看法是将微观经济学描述为价格理论。从这两种定义中不难看出，微观经济学实际上是从个体行为出发，关注众多具有经济资源和能力的当事人个体如何在市场、组织等特定环境中共同发生作用，如何形成特定的经济结果。例如，对商品或服务的供给和需求如何在市场上汇聚，似乎在"看不见的手"的指挥、协调下形成价格，反过来，又应对价格的变化，对商品和服务的供给量、需求量进行适应性调整，尤其是通过竞争机制在个体之间、行业之间、地区之间进行重新配置，最终达到更有效率的均衡。

然而，随着现代经济学研究的进步，人们也在不断拓展微观经济学的知识边界，将信息、激励、博弈、组织、产权、制度等涉及经济主体之间"多样化互动"的经济行为基本原理纳入研究之中。这些新纳入的基本原理，解释了市场交易安排的多样性及其有效运行的制度条件、企业边界和内部激励机制、应对外部性与公共品供给失灵的多样性制度安排等诸多非市场性组织活动,让人们更全面深入地理解了经济运行除了受到"看不见的手"指挥,还受到"看得见的手"、"帮助之手"、"攫取之手"等制度性力量的影响,并从中揭示了这样一个基本经济规律,即正是这些与特定环境相适应的有效率的非市场组织或制度的存在和创新,才能最大限度地发挥市场配置资源的基础性作用,才能最大限度地激发经济当事人个体的活力,从而转化成经济发展和增长的源泉。

本书的作者阿维纳什·迪克西特教授是当代著名经济学家,他出生在印度,在美国麻省理工学院获得经济学博士学位,在微观经济理论、博弈论、国际贸易、产业组织、增长和发展理论、公共经济学以及新制度经济学领域均有丰硕的研究成果,他的《经济政策的制定》《法律缺失与经济学》《策略思维》《策略博弈》等多部著作均已在国内出版了中文版,并且成为很多高校相关专业学生的必读书。这本《微观经济学》则是迪克西特教授献给普通读者的经济学通识读物,他用极其简洁、生动的语言向我们介绍了截至到当代的微观经济学基本原理。例如,对于消费者的经济行为,该书揭示了其理性、非理性行为的特征及其背后一系列的基本逻辑,其中一个普遍的基本逻辑是,消费者在特定约束限制下应该如何对机会成本努力做出最好的权衡。在分析生产者的基本行为逻辑时,该书则着重分析了一个基本原则,即"只要生产的数量增加所产生的额外收益超过(额外的、边际的)供给成本,那就继续扩大经营规模"。这一点在软件、人工智能等信息技术领域表现得尤其明显,随着边际成本的持续下降,甚至几乎为零,这类企业的经营规模可以达到"巨无霸"的水平。

有学者说，经济当事人个体作为受市场力量支配的竞争者时，总是"怀揣着成为垄断者的梦想"。事实上，他们会付诸将产能提高到足够大的规模、不断进行产品或技术创新、利用外包和一体化获取多渠道的低成本投入等手段，在很大程度上或者在较长时间内形成垄断势力。

但是，当一个经济体中的多数行业充斥着从竞争者成长起来的垄断者时，那么该经济体也就进入了"极盛"时期。本书用很大的篇幅论证了垄断所带来的社会损失，比如"牢固的垄断可能会削弱创新动力"，即使达到了帕累托效率，其结果也可能造成极为不公平的福利分配。更有甚者，垄断者作为巨大利益集团通过特定的政治联系还会引致政府失灵。迪克西特教授在本书中坚决地表达了"反对任何一种形式的垄断"。可以推断，当经济体进入"垄断梦"盛行的"极盛"阶段时，若不能有效地反垄断，将很难逃脱"盛极而衰"的命运。迪克西特教授在本书中指出，破解垄断的唯一手段是保持进入市场的自由，即保持市场的竞争性；而政治竞争作为一种纠错机制，则可用于制约权力滥用，纠正严重的判断错误。他也由此认为"混合经济是组织微观经济活动的最佳方式"，因为这是一种能够将克服市场失灵的政府和其他社会组织与市场竞争有效结合的经济模式。

多年前，我曾翻译了迪克西特教授的《法律缺失与经济学：可供选择的经济治理方式》一书，当时对他极力论证"市场只有得到足够的治理制度支持，才能获得成功"这个命题印象很深刻。他在该书中明确指出，转型国家照搬照抄西方正式法律模式并无必要，而且有些时候是不适当的，甚至会带来损害。

迪克西特教授在这本通识读本中特别强调了混合经济是组织微观经济活动的最佳方式,这也给我们创新地思考、分析和探索适合各国国情的经济治理模式提供了强有力的理论支持!

2021年6月27日
于南大安中楼

目 录

前　言　1

第一章　何谓微观经济学　1

第二章　消费者　6

第三章　生产者　29

第四章　市　场　51

第五章　市场失灵与政策失灵　68

第六章　制度与组织　100

第七章　什么才是有效的？　117

索　引　120

英文原文　127

前　言

在非专业人士看来，经济学的研究对象是失业、通货膨胀、经济增长、国家竞争力，以及与整体经济有关的其他问题（或者，用经济学的专业术语来说，是**宏观经济**）。他们很少提到，甚至可能不知道，在宏观经济背后选择和交易的复杂关系。比如，人们要选择在哪里生活和工作，要选择储蓄所占收入的比重，要选择购买哪些商品，等等。公司要在地点、投资、雇佣、解雇、广告和许多其他商业领域做出决定。政府也要在基础设施、行业监管、商品及服务的税收结构和税率等方面制定政策。公民对于经济的细微层面（或者说，**微观经济**）了解较少，甚至可能会忽视上述问题。原因在于，经济运作在微观层面通常非常顺畅；即便偶尔出现故障，和宏观经济遭遇的麻烦比起来，也显得微不足道。但这样的小故障一旦累积到一定数量，就会造成巨大的经济损失，并且可能在宏观经济层面产生巨大的影响。因此，我们需要弄清楚，为什么在微观层面经济运作大多数时候都非常顺畅；为什么经济运作有时会出现小故障，有时会遇到大麻烦，以及如何来防范和应对这些问题。在本书中,我尝试提出这样一种关于经济学的思考方式,并由此得出一些结论。我希望能说服非专业读者,让他们明白微观经济学非常重要,与他们的日常生活有着密切联系,其重要性不亚于失业和通货膨胀。我希望能带给他们一些顿悟的时刻。他们会说:"我经常看到这个话题,现在我终于明白这是怎么一回事!"不仅如此,我还希望能给他们提供一些微观经济分析要用到的基本概念和工具,供他们在自己的思考和行动中使用,并且促使他们想要继续阅读我推荐的书目。

进入正题前,我先强调三点。首先,本书只是通识读本,不可能对这个领域进行全面介绍。我不得不排除许多话题、想法和方法,不是因为它们不重要,而是因为我想把通识读本的篇幅留给其他内容。如果你是专门研究微观经济的学者,并且本书没有涉及你最喜欢的话题,还请谅解。

其次,经济学必然涉及定量研究,需要读者具备一定的数据分析能力,比如阅读表格和图表。我尽可能用最简单的方式来处理这些话题,如果有些读者在理解图表或数字方面偶尔会遇到麻烦,可以跳过这些内容,直接阅读剩余部分。

最后,我希望本书能吸引读者,希望我的写作方式易于理解,但读懂本书并不轻松。如果你对微观经济学完全陌生,那么我建议你不要一次性阅读太多内容。我想借用P.G.伍德豪斯在他的吉夫斯故事集序言中所说的一句话作为我的建议:不要试图一次性读完本书。虽然这完全可以做到——我在校对时就是一口气读完——但是阅读效果并不好。如果你只是想告诉别人你已经读完了,我觉得这样做不值得。放慢节奏。把书翻开。

逐步去理解。每次只需读懂一部分内容。如果偶尔失眠,那就在夜里增加一点额外的阅读量。

既然这本书是面向非专业的聪明读者,那么就应该请这类读者来审读草稿。我很幸运,在"小世界"咖啡馆有一群定期和我共进早餐的朋友。我非常感谢弗兰克·卡拉普莱斯(物理学家)、朱莉·杰滕(律师)、比尔·谢弗(财务顾问)、康妮·谢弗(高中法语教师)和凯西·史密斯(催眠治疗师)。他们很有耐心,乐于助人。读完书稿之后,他们告诉我哪些内容需要说明、重写甚至删除。另外,牛津大学出版社的安德里亚·基根和她的同事就文体和内容提供了宝贵的反馈意见。

经济学同行也拨冗阅读书稿并提出建议。他们不仅纠正了我的小错误,还提供了更好的例子和解释。卡拉·霍夫既是出色的经济学家,又是目光敏锐的编辑,我对他的建议深表感激。我也非常感谢迪利普·阿布勒、保罗·克伦佩雷尔和约翰·维克斯的敏锐评论和有用建议。

最后,我尤其要感谢的是我的老师、同事和学生,在整个职业生涯中,我一直从他们那里学习并提高我对于微观经济学的理解。本书的优点归功于你们,不足之处由我本人负责。

第一章

何谓微观经济学

引　子

每天早晨我会选择喝咖啡的具体方式。我有多个选项，可以在家里自己制作，可以去全国性的连锁咖啡店（比如星巴克），或者去普林斯顿当地的"小世界"咖啡馆。如果我决定外出，我可以选择步行、骑自行车或开车。喝咖啡的同时，我还可以吃有益健康的麦麸和浆果，选择含有大量碳水化合物和脂肪的松饼，或者改吃鸡蛋和培根来摄入脂肪及盐分。

我的选择取决于诸多因素。比如：下雨还是下雪；我是否在前一天晚餐时饮食过度，需要锻炼；我的朋友是否聚在一起，并且我是否觉得当天早晨应该参加社交活动；当天我是否突发奇想，或者纯粹渴望新的花样；另外，还要考虑不同地点吃喝需要支付的价格和享受的品质（如果我在家自己制作，还要把时间成本计算在内）。鉴于这些条件每天或每月都在变化，我的选择也随之发生变化。但是，每当我来到咖啡馆，店员从不会说："对不起,我们今天不提供咖啡。"当我去超市购物,想买一些咖啡回家自己制作时,也不会遇到断货的情况。他们怎么知道我会来,为什么他们已经做好准备,并且愿意为我服务?再来看我之前的选择,我去买了一辆汽车,为的是能自己开车(而不是选择其他交通方式)去咖啡馆或超市。别人为什么能预计到我的需求,并且准备好车辆?

微观经济学研究的对象包括:数千万消费者购买什么样的商品和服务,以及他们如何做出选择;生产者如何做出决定以满足需求,以及双方如何互动。很多时候,交易相当顺利。这就是为什么微观经济学就像一条在夜里不会吠叫的狗,这也能够解释为什么非专业人士对于微观经济问题通常一无所知。但是,上述交易机制时不时会发生错误。举个小例子:有几天我到达咖啡馆的时间比平时要晚,然后我发现松饼卖完了(虽然我可以买烤饼或其他碳水化合物食品作为替代)。但有些时候,交易机制失灵的后果非常严重,比如20世纪70年代的汽油短缺,又比如21世纪初的房地产泡沫以及由此造成的经济危机。因此,所有的聪明读者都应该掌握微观经济学的要点:首先,交易在什么时候、以何种方式能够顺利进行;其次,交易在什么时候、以何种方式失灵;最后,当交易机制失灵或即将失灵时,我们可以采取什么措施。

信息与激励

在大多数社会中,消费者和生产者在市场中进行互动——不一定是传统的集市和市场,也可以是商店、餐馆和其他场所,比如谈判和拍卖会,还有越来越普及的互联网。在市场中,买家向卖家支付一定的价格来获取商品或服务。这个价格具有双重作用。首先,如果某些东西稀缺,其价格会上涨。因此,高价向外界传递有关稀缺性的**信息**。其次,当价格提高时,该商品或服务的供给者可以通过生产更多商品或服务来获利,而购买者将减少购买量,或者改为购买其他商品。因此,高价也为缓解稀缺性提供了必要的**激励**因素。微观经济学的主要研究对象,就是用于协调生产者和消费者达成交易的信息机制和激励机制,特别是价格能否实现双重作用,以及具体如何实现。

对信息和激励的关注也告诉我们,价格机制在什么时候、出于什么原因会失灵:它可能会传递不充分或错误的信息或激励,也有可能这些信号没有引起反应。当一个人的行为对他人产生溢出效应时,就会出现这种最常见的失灵现象。每个汽车司机都会造成空气污染,从而增加清洁空气的稀缺性。但是,清洁空气没有市场,也没有价格,因此没有人收到关于这类稀缺性的信号,也没有人会受到利润激励去缓解这种状况。

如果对于信号的反应受到抑制,价格机制也可能失灵。价格管控产生抑制作用。新的生产者进入市场时遇到的障碍同样如此,不管是自然环境造成的天然障碍,还是现有的生产者建立的战略障碍,抑或由政府造成的政策壁垒,都会产生抑制作用。此外,现有的生产者可以密谋合作,保持一定程度的稀缺性,从而推高价格,获取更多利润。在社会主义计划经济国家,由于生产和供给都掌握在国家手中,因此政府官员通过满足消费者需求所获得的个人收益非常有限。反之,忽略消费者需求所受到的惩罚也微不足道。在没有市场的情况下,政府官员甚至得不到关于稀缺性的足够信息。这就是此类社会体会造成物资长期短缺,并且质量很差的原因。

更微妙的是,传递稀缺性以外的其他信息也可能导致价格机制失灵。假设你知道一辆2010年生产的丰田凯美瑞二手车售价约为1.5万美元,但你不知道自己打算购买的这辆车的真实车况。可以推断,这辆车的实际价值不会超过1.5万美元。否则,之前有大量机会观察车况的车主不会以这个价格出售。但它的实际价值可能低于(甚至是远远低于)这个价格。这会降低你的购买意愿。如果所有的购买者都这样认为并放弃购买,那么需求低迷会导致价格回落,迫使更多的车主(卖家)退出市场。在最糟糕的情况下,整个市场可能崩溃。当然,如果卖家的车况良好,并且买家也想买到好车,传递可靠的质量信息可以帮助他们共同受益。他们之间用于沟通的信号也属于微观经济分析的对象。

道德或伦理层面会造成另一种市场失灵。如果潜在买家没有购买力来满足他们的愿望,那么价格机制的信号和激励就会失效。卖馅饼的人对天真的西蒙说:"让我看看,你有多少钱。"西蒙不得不说实话:"我没钱。"这是个小例子,但我们有理由认为,健康和教育等需求应该被视为宝贵的或基本的人权,不管这个人是否具备支付能力。制定和实施公共政策来满足这些需求是政治经济学的研究课题。

价格和支付不一定非要采取传统的货币形式。一物可以用来换取另一物,支付也可以延迟,变成贷款或欠下的人情。根据具体情况,一种"货币"形式可能比另一种更合适、更有效。在许多社交场合,金钱是粗鲁的、不恰当的,亲朋好友之间普遍存在互惠互助交换的非正式安排。为了医院和刚毕业的医生相互匹配，就会形成复杂的算法和组织。涉及多方的器官（例如肾脏）交换也是如此，因为大多数人都认为出售器官用于赚钱的做法令人憎恶。宽泛来说，如果把背景信息考虑在内，经济分析可以在这些多样化的互动和交易中取得巨大成功。

要说的内容太多，而可用的篇幅太少。所以，介绍性的闲聊和动力已经足够了。我们现在转入正题，开始分析经济活动的终端用户，也就是消费者。

第二章

消费者

替　代

消费者借助计算和本能来做出决定，同时还要考虑许多因素，价格只是其中之一。微观经济学也关注其他因素，但重点关注价格，以研究每个消费者与经济体其他部分的互动。消费者选择具有一个重要属性：当某种物品的价格上涨且其他条件保持不变时，消费者会减少该物品的购买量。由于这一属性几乎普遍适用，因此又被称为**需求定理**。

替代概念可以解释这种经验规律。在价格上涨的情况下，消费者的反应是减少这种商品的购买量。与此同时，他们会用其他相对便宜的商品来替代，从而满足自身的欲望，虽然效果比不上原来的商品。举个例子，假设窖藏啤酒的价格上涨而麦芽酒的价格保持不变。消费者在原来的价格会选择啤酒。在新的价格，增加的成本在一定程度上超过了对啤酒的偏好，因此消费者会选择减少啤酒的消费量，同时增加麦芽酒的消费量。也就是说，消费者会用麦芽酒替代啤酒。如果对啤酒的偏好并不强烈，或者价格涨幅很大，消费者可能会选择只喝麦芽酒。

在说明替代概念时，初级教材用的例子是某些商品大类，比如食品和衣服。读者可能想知道如何用衣服替代食品。在寒冷的日子里，如果食品价格上涨，难道消费者要穿更多的衣服以减少体热损失，从而弥补缺少的食物热量？实际上，消费者并不是在商品大类之间做出选择。相反，他们会在子类别之间做出选择，比如鸡肉和鱼肉，或者棉花和羊毛。类别越窄，替代的可能性越大。实际上，即使在大类之间也会产生些许替代效应，我们很快会在需求估算统计的例子中说到这一点。

替代性的强弱取决于时间。具有固定习惯的消费者需要时间来改变生活方式或适应替代商品。除非咖啡价格长时间上涨，否则喝咖啡上瘾的人不会用茶来替代。看到天然气价格下跌，用燃油炉加热取暖的人不会马上换成燃气炉，而是会一直坚持到旧炉子出现故障。如果预计价格上涨不会持久，消费者可能会选择熬过困难时期。事实上，当燃料价格上涨时，许多消费者依然使用耗油量巨大的汽车。

只有当物品价格稳定且可以估算或预测时，价格与需求量之间的关系才能用于经济分析。每个人的需求都受到许多特殊的偶然因素的影响。幸运的是，对于市场研究而言，我们只需知道消费者的全部反应，或者说总体反应。这使得市场需求更加稳定，更方便预测。

以加总的方式表示消费者需求会产生两点影响。首先，不管是出于心血来潮还是某些特殊的环境变化，个体消费者的决定具有随机性，但在大数定律作用下，随机性可以消除。其次，

6 某个消费者的替代可能会很突然，从购买一种类型的汽车转向另一种，或者从驾驶汽车转向骑自行车。但由于不同的消费者会在不同的价格做出改变，并且每个消费者仅仅占据市场很小的部分，个体的替代行为不会对总体造成重大影响。因此，相比个人，整体的市场需求表现得更连贯、更稳定。

　　市场需求的任何一种商品的数量不仅取决于其自身价格，还取决于其他因素。只要能估算和预测这些因素，问题就能解决。一些因素会影响整个市场，比如广告和季节交替。对于市场分析来说，最重要的因素是其他相关商品的价格。比如，一旦啤酒价格上涨，消费者就会用麦芽酒替代。因此，在麦芽酒价格给定的情况下，消费量会比以前增加许多。

互　补

　　但是，假设大多数消费者同时吃鱼和薯条，结果就会不一样。如果鱼的价格上涨（而薯条的价格保持不变），就会增加鱼和薯条组合的总价，于是消费者购买该组合的数量会减少。因此，对于任何给定的薯条价格，当鱼的价格上涨时，薯条的需求量会减少。消费者不会用薯条来替代鱼：这两种商品不是替代关系，而是**互补**关系。对于成对商品的市场组织来说，这一区别非常重要。在第五章，我们会分析公司之间的利润外部性，届时将继续讨论这个话题。

需求曲线

　　商品价格与需求量之间的关系最好以图形方式加以说明。如果有些读者不熟悉这样表示两者之间关系的方式，不妨先来看一个简要说明（见图1）。垂直和水平方向的这两条线被称为"轴"。在这个例子中，垂直方向的这条线是价格轴，水平方向的这条线是数量轴。在两轴包围的区域中，每个点都表示价格和数量共同构成的组合。在图1中，从任何点（比如点X）出发，看与轴平行的两条线：XP平行于价格轴，XQ平行于数量轴。这意味着，点X表示价格等于XP长度和数量等于XQ长度的组合。在图1中，根据设定，点X表示：价格=2（美元/每瓶啤酒），数量=3（百万瓶啤酒）。

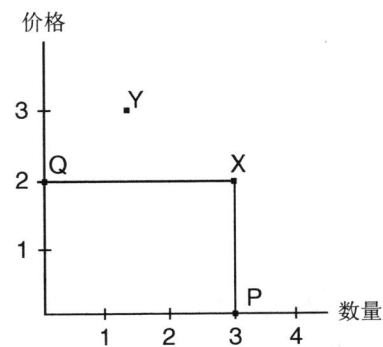

图1　用点表示组合关系

为加深理解，再来看点Y。同样画两条与轴平行的线，根据设定，点Y表示：价格=3（美元/每瓶啤酒），数量=1.5（百万瓶啤酒）。更多细节参见以下网址：

http：//www.mathopenref.com/tocs/coordpointstoc.html

借助上述方式，图2向我们展示了商品的价格如何影响总需求。这被称为（市场）**需求曲线**。切记，这条曲线代表着每个价格上许多不同的个体选择的总和。假设图中的商品是本章提到的啤酒。那么，左上角的这段曲线（价格高且数量少）来自那

8 些愿意支付最高价格的最喜欢啤酒的人。随着啤酒价格越来越低,需求量也越来越多。更重要的是,当麦芽酒爱好者和一部分葡萄酒爱好者改喝更便宜的啤酒时,后者的需求量会变得更多。最后,在非常低的价格,甚至一些原本喝茶的人也会尝试喝啤酒。

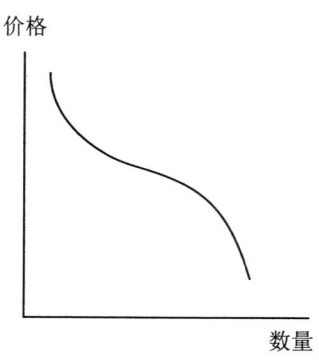

图 2　市场需求曲线

　　随着新的消费者在依次更低的价格陆续加入,增加的数量实际上就是图表中的水平线段,需求曲线就是由这些阶梯状的线段构成的。由于消费者人数可能有几千,甚至几百万,所以每一级阶梯的数量与整个市场的总量相比显得微不足道,因此图中的需求曲线看起来会平滑到一个充分精确的程度。

　　市场需求曲线显示了某物品的需求量与自身价格之间的关系。当其他因素(比如替代品或互补品的价格,或者消费者的收入)发生变化时,这种关系会随之变化。图3展示了这种转变。假设该图是咖啡的需求曲线。当茶叶(替代品)的价格上涨时,对于任何给定的咖啡价格,需求的咖啡数量都会增加。于是,咖啡的需求曲线就会向右移动。如果消费者的收入增加,也会发生类似的移动。换个例子,假设该图是鱼的需求曲线。当薯条(互补品)价格下跌时,鱼的需求曲线会向右移动。

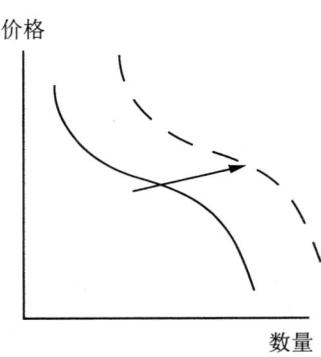

图3　需求曲线的变化

要弄明白税收或技术进步等因素产生的影响(之后我们会涉及这些话题),我们需要知道市场需求的价格反应。图4展示了两种可能性:左侧为高价格敏感度(经济学的专业术语称为**需求弹性大**),右侧为低价格敏感度(**需求弹性小**)。如果(1)

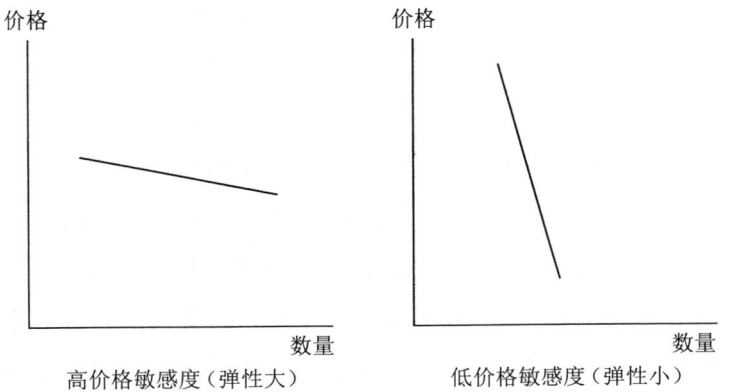

图4　高价格敏感度和低价格敏感度的市场需求曲线

有其他商品可以很好地替代相关商品,(2)并且时间跨度足以让消费者调整习惯或培养新口味,(3)或者消费者预计价格下降仅仅是短期行为,从而抓住时机购买商品,那么需求会呈现出更大的弹性。我将这些需求曲线绘制成直线,只是为了以最简单的方式来呈现敏感度——实际上,敏感度可以沿着需求曲线产生变化,如图2和图3所示。

消费者也是劳动者和储蓄者

除了少数靠遗产过日子的人,我们大多数人都是通过劳动来获取收入,并将部分收入用于消费。在一生中,我们的消费可分为几个阶段,比如在年轻时贷款用于教育或购房,在赚钱能力最强的阶段努力存钱,并在退休后逐步减少储蓄。这些决定可以用微观经济学进行分析,方法与之前对啤酒或咖啡需求的分析类似。工资的提高会增加工作的动力,减少休闲的时间。储蓄回报率的提高增加了储蓄的动力,减少了当前消费,转而支持未来的消费。

在这样的背景下,价格变化的另一个影响变得十分重要。如果你的工资从每小时20美元增加到每小时25美元,你可能愿意增加你的工作时间,比如从每周40小时增加到45小时(在你能做出调整的范围内)。但是,如果你的工资增加到每小时100万美元(你总是可以梦想),那么你就可以选择每年只工作几个小时:那么高的工资率上,你的潜在收入是如此之高,让你可以享受更多的休闲时间。这被称为劳动力价格变化的**收入效应**。同样,如果储蓄的回报率变得很高,那么你就变得更加富裕,可以将更多财富用于当前消费,减少储蓄。

任何价格变化都会产生收入效应,但对于你所购买的商品,通常只会加强替代效应。比如,在收入不变的情况下,肉价上涨会导致你的经济状况变得更糟,你就会减少肉制品(以及更大幅度地减少其他物品)的消费量来作为回应。只有所谓的劣质商品才会违背这一规律。当你的经济状况变得更糟时,你会购买更多的劣质商品,收入效应会抵消替代效应。经济学考试往往会涉及这些内容。

统计估计

许多统计学家和经济学家利用实际数据,研究了消费者需求与价格、收入和其他相关数据之间的关系。结果表明,宽泛的概念(比如,替代、互补和收入效应)与数据较为吻合,但更加精细的假设(尤其是认定消费者对其自身利益能够做出完美的理性计算的假设)并不能得到充分验证。接下来,我会援引伦敦大学学院的理查德·布伦戴尔关于消费者行为的一项有影响力的调查,对此进行简要说明。

基于1970年至1984年英国有子女家庭的年度支出调查,布伦戴尔估算了收入和价格对于某些商品大类需求的敏感程度。表1列举了收入增加1%(或者,左侧第1列的商品大类价格增加1%)对于商品大类需求(第2列至第7列)的影响。比如,当收入增加1%时,酒类产品消费增加2.014%;当燃料价格上涨1%时,交通需求量下降0.480%。

如果收入增加1%会使某商品的消费量增加1%以上,那么,富裕家庭相比贫困家庭会将更多收入用于购买该商品;换句话说,它被视为奢侈品。因此,酒类产品是奢侈品。(许多本科生都应该牢记这一点!)相反,在贫困家庭的支出中,食品和燃料占收入的比重较大,弹性系数分别为0.668和0.329。因此,这些商品是必需品。

表1 替代、互补和收入效应

1%的增长所带来的效应	对需求产生的影响					
	食物	酒类	燃料	服装	交通	服务
收入	0.668	2.014	0.329	1.269	1.212	1.654
价格						
食物	−0.246	0.032	0.110	0.066	0.021	−0.004
酒类	0.210	−1.869	1.043	0.080	0.999	0.218
燃料	0.464	0.671	−0.718	0.027	−0.480	0.223
服装	0.231	0.042	0.023	−0.716	0.163	0.045
交通	0.048	0.345	−0.257	0.106	−0.475	0.197
服务	−0.012	0.114	−0.181	0.034	0.298	−0.587

13 来源:布伦戴尔论文中的表2,1988年3月发表于《经济杂志》

商品价格上涨对自身需求量的影响均为负数。这验证了需求定理,即需求曲线向下倾斜。如果物品A的价格上涨增加了物品B的需求量,那么二者互为替代品(即单元格中的数据是正数)。在该研究中,许多商品大类之间都属于这种关系。需要注意的是,食物和衣服是替代品,虽然影响很小。交通和燃料是互补品,当其中一项价格上涨时,另一项的需求量就会下降(即单元格中的数据是负数)。

这类表格可以解释图2所示的需求曲线以及图3所示的变化。比如,食品需求曲线显示其数量和价格。每当价格增加1%,数量就会减少0.246%。收入增加、酒类产品(替代品)价增加,或者服务(互补品)价格下降,都会导致食品需求曲线向右移动。

生活成本指数

替代原则最重要的应用可能是生活成本指数。为了简要说明这一点,我们将选择范围限制在两种饮料:茶和咖啡。假设两种饮料每千克的价格都是10美元,你每月消费两种饮料各1 000克,那么你每月的饮料费用就是20美元。假设咖啡的价格翻一倍,按照新的价格,每种饮料各消费1 000克,总共需要30美元。但是,你可以用茶替代咖啡,从而获得更大的收益。按照旧的价格,你每种饮料各买1 000克。你原本可以买900克咖啡和1 100克茶,但你并没有那么做。按照新的价格,如果你放弃100克咖啡,你可以再买200克茶,这样就可以得到900克咖啡和1 200克茶。假设你喜欢这个新组合胜过原来每种饮料各1 000克的旧组合,也就是说,900克咖啡和1 200克茶的组合比每种饮料各1 000克的组合更适合你,而后者又比900克咖啡和1 100克茶的组合更好。那么,在这两个极端之间,一定有某个组合在你的偏好程度上等同于每种饮料各1 000克。假设这个组合是900克咖啡和1 150克茶,那么组合价格就是0.9×20美元$+ 1.15 \times 10$美元$= 29.5$美元。所以你只需要支付29.5美元,而不是30美元,就可以让你的饮料消费在新价格下获得和旧价格相同的满意度。

生活成本指数用于计算购买特定消费品组合的成本,通常是一组按原始价格选择的消费品。在这个例子中,饮料的成本指数从20上升到30,增幅达到50%。但你获得相同满意度的实际成本只增加了9.5美元,增幅为47.5%。这意味着,以传统方式计算的指数夸大了价格变化的影响。

指数夸大影响的原因在于,茶和咖啡的相对价格发生了变化。如果这两种商品价格都翻一倍,达到每千克20美元,那么你就可以像原来那样按照一比一的比例直接替代。如果之前没有选择替代,现在你同样不会这样做(尽管你可能选择从饮料转向其他价格没有上涨的物品)。

随着时间的推移,相对价格会发生巨大的变化。在过去的几十年里,医疗保健等商品的价格涨幅远远超过食品价格,而电子产品的价格急剧下降。许多工资合同和公共退休金方案与不考虑替代的生活成本指数挂钩。当相对价格变化时,这会过度补偿工人和退休人员,并且给公司和政府带来高昂的成本。解决方案是在成本计算时频繁进行数量调整,因为替代会改变选择。比如,2000年至2001年的生活成本指数增长,用2000年的数量进行计算。2001年至2002年的增长,用的是2001年的数量。依此类推。将连续十二年的增长量链接起来,就得到了2000年至2012年的指数增长。但是这样的解决方案在政治上难以实施,因为老年人拒绝将养老金支付与链式指数挂钩。他们喜欢现在的方案,因为根据固定权重指数他们可以获得过度补偿,而他们的投票对于政治家来说很重要。

许多旅游网站和商业网站会比较不同城市的生活成本,做法是用某一个城市(通常是纽约)的数字作为基准。这忽略了相对价格差异导致的替代行为。比如,这种做法没有考虑到在日本人们会放弃昂贵的牛肉,而转向优质廉价的鱼类。因此,相对于基准城市而言,所有其他城市测算出来的生活成本都高于实际成本。我相信你在旅行时已经注意到了这一点。

整个经济体的消费者价格指数可能不适合特定群体。比如,与总体人口相比,老年人在年龄和健康相关的项目上花费更多。因此,他们的生活成本应该根据某个基于此类费用的指数来调整,而不是基于总体人口。当然,在实际操作中,要做到这样的细微区分难度很大。

保姆效应

替代取决于相对价格,这一规律产生了**保姆效应**。假设一对没有孩子的夫妇要吃晚餐,他们要在20美元的匹萨和200美元的顶级餐厅之间做出选择——后者的价格是前者的十倍。有了孩子之后,他们不得不雇一个保姆。假设这要花费40美元。那么,去匹萨店的总费用变成了60美元,去餐厅的总费用变成了240美元,后者的价格降为前者的四倍。于是,这对夫妇可能会因为额外的保姆费用而减少外出用餐。但是,如果他们外出用餐,也有可能转向更高档的餐厅。

保姆效应在更大范围内同样存在。假设某个国家出口汽车,不管汽车的质量如何,运输成本几乎相等。因此,相对于出口目的国的高端车价格,它们提高了低端车的价格。买方将对此做出反应。结果就是,高端汽车在出口中所占比例将高于国内市场的比例。

时间及其他预算

在大多数人的预算决策中,价格是一个重要的参考因素。对于少数幸运儿来说,价格可能无关紧要,但每个人在做出选择时都面临着其他限制,尤其是时间。富人或许可以雇用其他人做家务，但他们不能雇用其他人来替代他们出席音乐会或体育赛事，也不能替代他们与家人共度美好时光。每个人都必须在有限时间内的竞争性需求之间做出选择，就像大多数人必须在有限收入内的竞争性需求之间做出选择一样。事实上，人们可以考虑用替代和互补的方式来分配时间，就像上述资金分配一样。比如，当洗衣机加快并简化家庭洗涤时，人们会比以往更频繁地洗衣服，但他们花在洗涤工作上的总时间仍然在减少。

机会成本

预算决策所涉及的思维过程可以用一个普遍原则来概括。当你决定把资金（或时间）花在某件商品或某项活动上时，你会把它与你可以用这笔资金（或时间）做的其他事情进行比较。由于收入有限，当你在当地的咖啡馆花4美元购买拿铁咖啡时，你就不能用那笔钱再去买啤酒或杂志等替代品。这种放弃做其他事情的机会是拿铁咖啡的真正成本。这就是为什么在经济学术语中它被称为**机会成本**。在做出任何决定时，需要考虑的问题是："这一行为所付出的机会成本是否值得？"这个问题不仅针对消费者，也涉及企业的决策行为；不仅关系到经济，也涉及社会、政治和其他方面。

经济学家总喜欢在多种替代方案之间进行比较，这种做法让他们成为好几个笑话的取笑对象。其中最古老的一则内容如下：两位经济学家很长一段时间后再次见面，很想了解对方的最新动态。其中一人问："你妻子怎么样？"对方回答："和谁相比？"

上述讨论包含另一个普遍经验：几乎所有的选择都必须在某些限制内做出，这些限制可能是金钱和时间，也可能是我们的网络和信息处理能力。在这样的限制条件下,努力做到最好是决策经济学的核心内容。

风　险

我们的决定充满了风险。如何在不同形式的资产(如股票、债券和外国证券)之间分配储蓄,如何购买房屋,如何选择教育、职业和配偶,这些是我们大多数人面临的最大的风险决策。许多商品的质量无法预知,因此许多购买行为也存在风险。此外,还有意外事故、疾病、盗窃等其他风险。

大多数情况下,人们不喜欢风险。没有多少人会接受一个简单的赌注,靠掷硬币来决定100美元的归属。为了诱使他们接受赌注,要么赢得的金额足够大,远大于他们可能损失的金额,要么获胜的概率远远超过50%。换句话说,人们的行为表现出风险规避的特征。**损失规避**很大程度上强化了风险规避:大多数人非常讨厌遭受损失,不管这种损失是相对于现状还是其他参照点。

稍后我将分析风险决策的其他一些特征,但现在我先从风险规避的一项重要结果说起。当面临风险时,人们愿意支付一笔保险费来获得保障。假设明年有5%的概率会产生1万美元的医疗费用,大多数人愿意支付超过500美元(在统计学意义上,这相当于他们可能遭受的平均损失)购买保险,用于支付这笔医疗费用。

假设A先生愿意支付550美元。假设B女士愿意承担A先生的风险,以换取525美元的保险费。这意味着A先生需要预付B女士525美元。到年底时,如果A先生有1万美元的账单,B女士会支付这笔费用,否则她不用支付。B女士有95%的可能在没有任何付出的情况下,得到525美元的保险费。但也有5%的可能她必须支付1万美元,因此将损失9 475美元。统计平均数表明,B女士的利润为:$0.95 \times 525 - 0.05 \times 9\,475 = 498.75 - 473.75 = 25$美元,当然这具有一定的风险。如果B女士对风险的厌恶程度低于A先生,她可能会喜欢这个方案,在盈利可能性和风险之间进行权衡。那么,A先生和B女士就有了互惠交易的基础。

实际上,将风险转移给最愿意承担风险的人,这可能是金融市场在经济体系中扮演的最有用的角色(尽管我必须承认,近年来它还扮演了对于社会贡献相对较小的其他角色)。之后我们会在其他章节讨论这个话题。

可能只是因为B女士比A先生更少厌恶风险,但实际上还有其他原因,可能促使她在承担风险时愿意接受的价格低于A先生回避风险而愿意支付的价格。最常见的原因是:B女士实际上代表着一家保险公司,为类似A先生这样的大量客户**汇集**风险,它们是相似但独立的。"独立"意味着不同个人面临的风险没有共同的影响源。因此,他们的账单不可能同时到期,甚至不会出现多人同时到期的情况。粗略地说,根据"大数定律",许多独立的随机结果加总后会消除原有的不确定性。在我们的例子中,当保险公司(B女士)有许多具有独立风险的投保客户(如A先生)时,大约5%的客户会产生高额医疗费用。此时,该公司几乎可以确定,从每位客户身上获得的利润接近25美元。

风险的独立性至关重要。如果存在某个连带影响所有投保风险的影响源,那么汇集风险将会产生灾难性的后果。2007年至2008年在美国和许多其他国家爆发的房地产信贷危机足以证明这一点。办理抵押贷款的业主可能因疾病、失业或家庭紧急情况而违约。如果业主的违约风险是独立的，他们可以通过汇集的方式获得保险。银行和其他抵押贷款机构会使用违约互换等金融工具为他们投保。但是，当大萧条降临，所有地区的房价都在下跌时，太多业主会同时违约，抵押贷款机构和它们的保险公司就会面临破产。严重衰退是破坏风险独立性的共同因素，这一点并未得到充分认识，也没有做好准备。

独立风险的潜在客户不必完全等同，也可以通过汇集的办法来降低整体风险，比如上一段提及的处境相似的大量房主。假设你有200万美元的储蓄。（你是个非常谨慎或非常幸运的家伙！）你可以将这笔资金用于投资蓝筹股。如果整体经济表现良好，蓝筹股将上涨60%；如果经济衰退，则下跌50%。假设这两种情况的概率相等，那么你将面临50%的风险失去100万美元。另外，你还可以将这笔资金投入一只生物科技风险投资基金，你的资金可能增加一倍，也可能减半，两种情况的概率相等。所以你同样有50%的风险损失100万美元。假设这两种风险（普遍的经济衰退和特定生物科技投资项目的成功）是独立的，那么你可以通过投资组合**多样化**来降低整体风险：换句话说，你可以将二者混合起来。假设你各投资100万美元。现在你只有在两个结果都很糟糕的情况下才会损失50%的资金，出现这个结果的概率只有25%，就像用两个正常的硬币同时掷出背面朝上的结果。表2显示了三种投资策略可能出现的四种结果。可以看到，财富降至100万美元的结果已经从两种可能性减少到一种，这样一来，概率就从50%降至25%。当然，现在你可能得到的好处也减少了：你永远不会得到400万美元。既然你要将所有的退休储蓄用于投资,那么你应该会厌恶风险(也许还厌恶损失),所以很可能你会接受这个投资组合。请注意,蓝筹股在你的投资组合中起作用,因为它们能实现多样化,即使在单独投资的时候它们看起来比生物科技基金更糟糕:二者具有相同的下行风险(损失50%),而蓝筹股的上涨幅度小于生物科技(前者60%,后者100%)。

最后,降低风险的一种办法是接受与前一个风险负相关的另一个风险。换句话说,当第一个风险结果良好时,第二个必然结果不好;反之亦然。二者的好坏部分相互抵消,使整体风险降低。这被称为**对冲**。举个小例子,下一届超级碗或世界杯决赛,你可以赌喜欢的球队赢球。如果失败,你至少可以从赌注中得到金钱的安慰。再举个更重要的例子,如果你的工作和收入取决于某个经济领域的成功,那么你的投资组合应该包括某些特殊资产,当该领域表现欠佳时,那些资产将会获得良好回报。如果你把养老金用于投资你本人工作的企业股票,这将导致你面临收入和财富的巨大风险,如果公司表现糟糕的话,你会损失惨重。要想实现多样化,你应该做相反的事情:卖空该公司的股票。换句话说,承诺在商定的未来日期以约定的价格出售部分股票,如果那时股票价格低于协议价格,你将从中获利。换成期权可以达到类似效果,只不过期权意味着你有权购买,而不是有义务出售。当然,拥有公司股票可能会抵消激励机制的积极影响,后者对高层管理人员来说很重要,但对于公司的普通员工甚至中层管理人员来说,没那么重要,因为他们都无法影响股价。我将在第三章的其中一节"企业组织"进一步讨论这个话题。

表2 通过多样化减少亏损风险

投资组合	二者都涨	蓝筹股涨，生物科技跌	生物科技涨，蓝筹股跌	二者都跌
蓝筹股	3.2	3.2	1.0	1.0
生物科技	4.0	1.0	4.0	1.0
混合	3.6	2.1	2.5	1.0

消费者是否理性？

传统的经济学理论假设消费者（以及经济活动的所有参与者，包括企业经理等）会理性做出决定。这意味着他们知道自己的偏好，并且在各种替代方案中做出选择，他们会计算出最佳方案，并且正确选择。心理学家和其他社会科学家始终认为，这一假设缺乏说服力。长期以来，标准的经济学观点认为，理性选择方法的确有效：在合理的时间跨度内，它对于消费者的总体市场行为给出了很好的解释，并且可以认为，消费者**似乎**真的是在理性行事。但是，有大量不同来源的证据表明，偏离传统理性（不管是实际的还是假设的）的情况越来越多。相关证据包括：实验室内进行的测试、现场观察，以及决策过程中大脑活动的影像分析。很多时候，这样的偏离会影响交易和市场运作的结果。因此，主流经济学已经接受并吸纳许多批评意见。新的观点通常被称为"行为经济学"，它补充了传统理论，并在某些情况下对其进行修订和替换。

最终共识尚未达成，但最受认可的是由心理学家丹尼尔·卡内曼提出并倡导的一套理论。鉴于他的卓越贡献，卡内曼和其他人分享了2002年诺贝尔经济学奖。他发现，大脑有两个用来做决定的系统,他分别称之为系统I和系统II,以避免偏见。系统I反应快速,依赖本能,并使用试探模式(基于试错的自动决策规则),而不是针对不同情况分别进行显性计算。系统II反应较慢,并且进行显性计算,更接近于传统经济学提出的设想。系统I有明显的优点。它在日常决策中节省了计算成本和时间;在紧急情况下同样如此,比如摆脱捕食者。因此,系统I可能是在人类进化过程中自然选择的结果。它也可能在冲动的决定中发挥作用。这些系统并非互不联系的独立存在:随着时间的推移,经验和计算对系统I的试探模式做了修改,并且在遇到重复情况时使用系统II,生成新的试探模式,然后将其变成系统I的一部分。

哪怕有人想要分析在系统II的有意识的计算框架中做出的决策,他或她也不可能得到完美的结果,因为计算需要用到大量信息,过程十分复杂。这对于穷人的决策尤其重要,因为他们有太多事情需要考虑,比如,尽量兼顾多个工作岗位,以及如何用有限的预算来支付每个项目的成本,等等。

卡内曼和其他人最重要的发现或许是,消费者不仅关心他们得到的最终结果,而且还关注它与某些**参照点**的比较。这些参照点取决于具体情况,可以是他们的收入现状或消费水平,可以是他们认为的群体正常水平,也可以是用于比较的其他标准。人们认为,低于参照点(假设为100美元)所产生的失落感,远超出高于参照点的同等收益,这就是所谓的**损失规避**。这可能是因为损失对于系统I的情绪所产生的影响更加严重,但它也同样体现在系统II的计算中,因为与现状或参照点的比较确实会影响偏好。

现状也会在**禀赋效应**中发挥作用,后者指的是人们会在所有权的影响下为他们所拥有的事物赋予额外价值。实验表明,人们为咖啡杯这样的小物件(在没有同类物品的情况下)付款的意愿,远远低于放弃它(哪怕二十分钟前刚拥有它)而换取现金的意愿。这可能是系统I的特征之一。经常交易的人对于交易物品的情感投入较少,他们往往不容易受到禀赋效应的干扰。

可以通过不同的方式来**框架**选项,从而创设并操纵参照点。最引人注目的例子是两场灾难,其中一场造成400人死亡,另一场危及600人生命,但有200人获救。人们会认为,这两场灾难有所不同。这可能是系统I的另一项特征。之后,速度较慢的逻辑思维将促使他们认识到,上述差异并非实质区别。

如果他们认为明显不公平,或者因为具体情形激起他们的愤怒(或其他情感),许多人会拒绝经济收益。这可能是系统II中冰冷计算后的结果,但是针对此类决策者所做的核磁共振成像研究显示,这类行为通常与系统I和深层情感相关的大脑部位有关。"最后通牒博弈"是一个很好的例子。在两个玩家A和B中,随机选择A,让他提出建议,把10美元分给二人。如果B接受A的提议,则实施分配。如果B拒绝,两个人都一无所获。冰冷的经济学逻辑暗示,B要么得到一定金额,要么一无所获,因此B应该接受A的任何报价,哪怕只得到一分钱。事实上,当很多人处于B的位置时,他们拒绝接受任何低于3美元的报价。并且,或者是出于预判,或者是受到公平信念的驱动,当很多人处于A的位置时,他们会提供高于3美元的报价,甚至经常出现对半分。如果提议者的角色不是随机分配,而是基于先前游戏中的分数,当许多人处于B的位置时,他们会愿意接受较小的份额——很可能是因为他们认为A之前的成功使他或她有权享受更大的份额!

在涉及时间的决策中,人们经常会前后不一。他们对当下的决策表现出很高的无耐心,却声称对今后的事务更有耐心。他们会在当下消费,却计划明年开始储蓄或减肥。当然,等到明年到来时,此刻的无耐心又会重复。这种表现并不奇怪,圣奥古斯丁就有过类似举动,他曾要求上帝:"赐予我贞洁和节制,但不是现在。"

最后,人们并非完全自私。他们的行为表现出共情,以及对公正和平等的关注。他们会做出利他的选择——首先当然是对亲朋好友,但也会帮助陌生人——为此他们要付出一定的代价。这种行为可能出于进化过程中群体生存的需要,或者是社会化和教育的结果,抑或是上述两种因素的共同作用。成长和生活的社会文化、亲密朋友的想法,以及其他因素都会影响人们的偏好。

篇幅有限,我必须就此打住。刚才我列举了一些特殊情形,它们偏离了经济学家所描述的完美的个人理性。接下来,我要讨论这种偏离所产生的后果。对于大多数日用品而言,新发现与市场总体行为的大致特征并不矛盾。出于本能的行为通常不会违背"需求定理",即当某物品价格上涨时,需求量会越少。但是,此类反应的幅度和时滞可能会受到影响。损失规避和风险决策的其他特征会以显著的方式影响金融市场。

当分析涉及两个人或更多人之间的交易时,理解各方行为变得更加重要。参与此类交易的人必须考虑合作伙伴或反对者可能采取的实际行动。并且，如果他们想要在这种情况下的决策博弈中表现良好，他们就不能用传统的理性假设来预判对方的反应。市场设计的一些问题（比如拍卖）同样涉及博弈理论，充分理解参与者的行为对于制定良好的市场设计至关重要。

政策制定者可以利用在框架、当下的无耐心和意志力有限等方面所取得的研究成果，"推动"大众采取符合自身系统Ⅱ的利益的行动。比如，选择健康的生活方式，制定谨慎的储蓄计划。比如，许多人发现，要评估多个储蓄计划并做出选择，需要完成大量的脑力计算。也可能会受到当下的无耐心影响，最终没能做出任何选择。不妨预先制定一些基本方案或默认选择（而不是没有任何计划），这有助于克服计算成本问题。让人们预先提交储蓄计划，留到将来需要时执行，这有助于克服他们当下的无耐心。实验表明，比起教育人们重视储蓄或者为储蓄行为提供补贴，上述措施更加有效。另外，框架和推动的做法在促使人们选择有利于环保的行为方面同样有效。如果环保行为成为默认选择，一些消费者会一直坚持下去。损失规避意味着，相对于某个参照点，损失造成的影响大于同等金额带来的收益，这同样会影响消费者的选择。相比其他选择，环保行为往往要付出更高的代价。如果默认选择是非环保行为，那么做出环保选择意味着接受损失，而消费者通常希望规避损失。如果默认选择是环保行为，尽管改成非环保行为将带来同等金额的收益，但是消费者不太可能接受这种改变。

因此，行为经济学能帮助政策制定者巧妙设计默认选项以改变消费者行为。这是一种温和的家长式统治：它帮助消费者克服短期诱惑（或者说，来自系统 I 的诱惑），从而符合他们经过计算的最佳长期利益（或者说，符合系统 II 的利益）。但是，我们必须认识到滥用的可能性——国家可能使用相同的方法侵犯个人自由，这一点十分危险。在涉及公共政策时，公民必须对政策制定者始终保持警惕。

第三章
生产者

成　本

　　通常来说,生产是一种将原材料和其他制成品,以及劳动力、土地和资本等要素投入转化为产出的活动。组织这项活动的任何人都必须注意这些投入的成本,包括投入的生产物资的价格,以及工资、租金和资本的成本(利息和贬值)。追求利润的生产者希望保持低成本;非营利性的生产者和公共部门的生产者追求成本效益,并且预算有限。是否生产,生产多少,以及投入的物资比例,这些决定都取决于成本。

　　大多数生产决策都涉及多个阶段。首先会建立一个组织(通常是一家企业),准备开展生产活动,这必然产生成本。在大多数发达国家,这一成本微不足道。但正如世界银行的一份报告(参见http://www.doingbusiness.org/rankings)所显示的,在许多欠发达国家,这需要大量的金钱和时间。其次是购置土地、办公空间、机器设备等的成本。根据生产活动的性质,成本差异很大。石油化工厂需要大量的资金投入，而小型服装厂只需要一个房间和几台缝纫机。然后，有些企业在开始生产前需要支出大笔费用。比如，用于操作系统、浏览器、应用程序和游戏的软件，必须在销售之前进行开发和测试。这样的成本被称为初版成本。最后，实际生产过程中还包括劳动力和材料等的成本，接下来还有市场营销；对于服装业来说，这部分成本比重很高，但对于软件业来说，这部分成本比重很低。

每个阶段做出的决定，比如是否开展这项业务、进入的规模等，都必须着眼于收回成本或实现盈利。每个阶段，都有一些成本是必须承担的，或者说是**沉没的**。这意味着，如果前面出了问题而导致后续阶段必须中止，那么之前的成本得不到补偿。因此，剩余阶段的决定只应考虑尚未沉没的成本是否能够收回。

比如，服装零售店必须租用经营场所，保持库存，并雇用员工。如果它没能实现销售，就无法补偿这些成本（除非它有特权，可以退货给厂家）。因此，在这个阶段，上述成本都属于沉没成本，实际销售一件衣服的行动的额外成本几乎为零。那么，如果你出价1美元，店主是否愿意把这件衣服卖给你？当然不会，因为愿意支付更多钱的顾客可能明天就会上门。每一个行动都必须与所有的潜在备选方案进行比较，只有当它比剩余选择都要好时，才会付诸行动。因此，今天出售这件衣服的真正成本是机会成本，即放弃在明天或以后出售这件衣服的机会所隐含的成本。具体数字并不确定。因此，如果你试图与业主讨价还价以获得更好的价格，业主需要对这些机会和风险进行复杂的估算才能做出决定。这就是为什么商店以固定价格出售商品，并且很少给低级别员工与客户讨价还价的权力。服装店可能会在换季时大幅打折,就像农贸市场上卖家会在当天结束时低价卖掉易腐烂的水果或蔬菜,因为到了那个时段,放弃未来销售的机会成本非常低。

上述简要讨论足以表明,成本计算不仅仅是在明细账或空白表格中进行数据汇总,而是需要对不确定的前景做出判断。

企业在进行决策时如何考虑成本,这取决于市场的性质。接下来,让我们来分析各种可能性。

小企业:供给曲线

一些市场中的生产者规模太小,无法单独影响价格。真正决定价格的是整个市场的供需关系。大多数农产品市场中的农民,以及大多数采矿企业和石油生产企业,都属于这种情况。这样的企业只需做一个基本决策:在现行价格下,究竟应该生产多少数量。

对于寻求利润的企业来说,他们的决策遵循一个普遍原则:只要数量增加所产生的额外收益超过供给成本(经济学专业术语称为**边际成本**),那就继续扩大经营。但是,边际成本的正确解释取决于具体背景。换句话说,取决于做出决定那一刻的精确"边际"。到了最后阶段,投入的全部成本都变为沉没成本,此时边际成本可能为零或非常小。当火车或飞机带着一部分空座位准备出发时,额外搭载一名乘客的边际成本实际为零。但在初始阶段,当决定是安排火车还是航班时,边际成本包括所有的机组人员和燃料成本,以及为此目的(而不是为其他路线)使用该设备需要付出的任何机会成本。最后,同样在初始阶段,在考虑是否设立一家铁路公司或航空公司,或者考虑是否扩大现有的铁路或航业务时,边际成本包括为此目的(而不是其他目的,比如设立一家制药企业)投入资本而需要付出的机会成本。

很多情况下，边际成本随着数量增加而增加。比如，采矿作业首先从最容易开采或储量最丰富的矿藏开始，然后转向更难开采因而成本更高的矿藏。农民首先耕种最好的土地，然后逐渐转向生产效率较低的土地来扩大产量。在任何给定的价格下，这个扩张的过程会自然结束。最终，边际成本赶上了价格，使得进一步扩张无利可图。这决定了企业在该价格对于数量（其供给）的选择。接下来，我们可以展示价格与市场总供给量之间的关系。换句话说，画一条（市场）供给曲线，就像我们之前根据消费者选择画的市场需求曲线。

其他情况下，边际成本随着数量增加而减少（或至少不增加）。因此，在给定的价格下，进一步扩张带来的利润更大。比如，一旦软件开发的初版成本变成了沉没成本，后期制作光盘并邮寄的边际成本其实很低，而网络下载的边际成本几乎为零。石油化工厂建造成本的增长幅度小于产能增长。因此，当产能逐步扩大时，边际成本会下降。这种情况下，一家或几家公司会发展到一定规模，在市场中占据相当大份额，并且每家公司都能对价格产生影响。下一节的策略分析会涉及这个话题。现在，让我们继续讨论现有情形，即每家公司在给定价格下的产量只占到市场很小的部分，没有影响价格的实力。

市场供给曲线的结构只是前一章中提到的市场需求曲线的镜像。图5提供了一个例子。供给曲线向上倾斜，因为在更高的价位，会有更多公司发现有利可图，于是它们会进入市场，扩大产能，增加轮班，或者加大营销力度。这取决于上述安排需要的时间，以及所在行业生产和销售的具体情况。在非常低的价格，只有少数企业能够供给，因为它们拥有卓越的专利技术、土地或其他资源。因此,供给曲线的左下角表现出较低的价格敏感度。在更高价格,许多采用标准通用技术的公司进入了这一领域,因此价格敏感度变得更高,曲线更平。最后,在右侧曲线,行业遇到了产能瓶颈,价格敏感度再次下降。

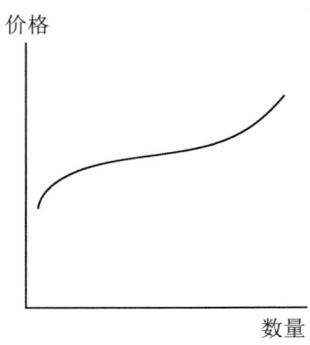

图5　市场供给曲线

正如市场需求曲线会随着某些背景变量(比如消费者收入、替代品或互补品的价格)的变化而变化,供给曲线也可能随着投入成本或技术进步的变化而变化。图6的例子可以说明供给曲线的变化。曲线右侧的变动幅度比左侧更大,因为曲线左端对

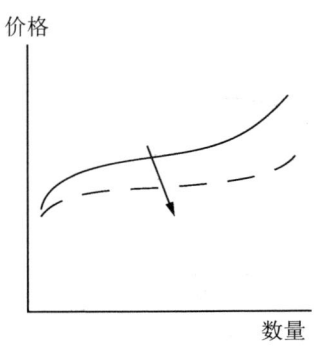

图6　供给曲线的变化

应的是那些已经处于技术前沿、从后续进步中获益不多的企业，而其他企业则通过追赶前者在后续进步中获益良多，因此它们的成本降低得更多。

我们还可以进一步分析供给曲线的变化规律。分析曲线在什么情况下会变得平坦，或者说，就像图7左图示意的高价格敏感度（弹性大）；曲线在什么情况下会变得陡峭，或者说，就像图7右图示意的低价格敏感度（弹性小）。以下例子中会出现高价格敏感度：（i）如果时间跨度较长，更多企业可以进入或退出市场，现有企业可以在生产计划中进行更多调整；（ii）在所有企业都能轻松获得标准技术的行业中，围绕单位成本的普遍水平出现小幅度的价格上涨就会产生一个很大数量的反应；（iii）如果采掘业的价格上涨被认为是暂时现象，企业希望通过当下生产更多产品来获利，并对价格上涨迅速做出反应。在相反的前提条件下，或者遇到其他情况，就会出现低价格敏感度。比如，当整个行业遇到产能限制（受到可用土地或运输瓶颈的局限）时，价格激励就无法带

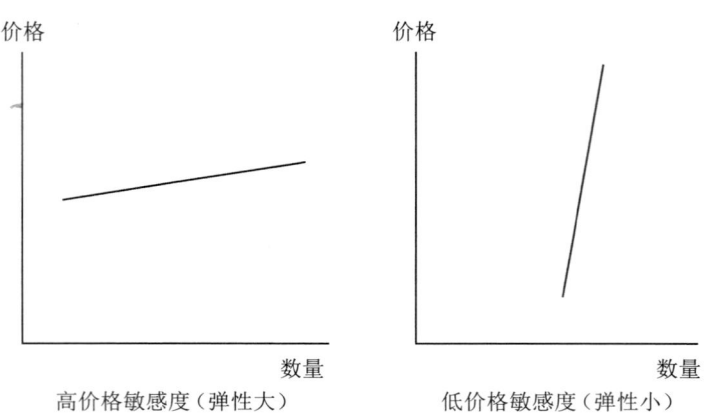

图7 高价格敏感度和低价格敏感度的市场供给曲线

来更多的供给。

上述例子并不是最典型的,也不是仅有的例子。列举这些,只是为了激发你对于经历过或观察到的情况进行思考。在第四章中,我会把需求曲线和供给曲线结合起来,帮助你理解市场的运作机制。

在第二章中,我用消费总需求的统计估算作为例子来解释若干概念。在微观经济学中,类似的涵盖整个经济体的供给曲线意义不大。关于特定行业的、利用统计数据进行估算的成本曲线确实存在,但它们也不可能展示每家企业的角色。因此,接下来我将用一个实例来分析成本曲线和供给曲线,但我不会用到统计数据。

不妨来看原油的短期供给曲线。在这个阶段,不需要考虑新油田的勘探和已探明储量的开采,这些属于沉没成本。边际生产成本指的是现有油井及相关设备的维护和运营成本,以便将石油从地下采到地表(在行业术语中,这被称为**采油成本**)。与此同时,石油供给受到现有油井产能的限制。一些国家的成本和产能数据是可得的,如表3所示。

表3　原油采油成本及产能,2009年

国家或地区	采油成本(每桶)	产能(百万桶/日)	该成本下的总产能
中美洲和南美洲	6.21	10.28	10.28
中东	9.89	24.27	34.55
非洲	10.31	9.36	43.91
美国	12.18	8.62	52.53
加拿大	12.69	3.40	55.93

来源:成本数据来自 http://www.eia.gov/tools/faqs/faq.cfm?id=367&t=6,产能数据来自 http://www.eia.gov/forecasts/steo/data.cfm?type=tables,表3b和3c

图8在供给曲线中显示了同样的信息,即当价格超过边际成本时,每个国家或地区都愿意提升产量至最大产能。

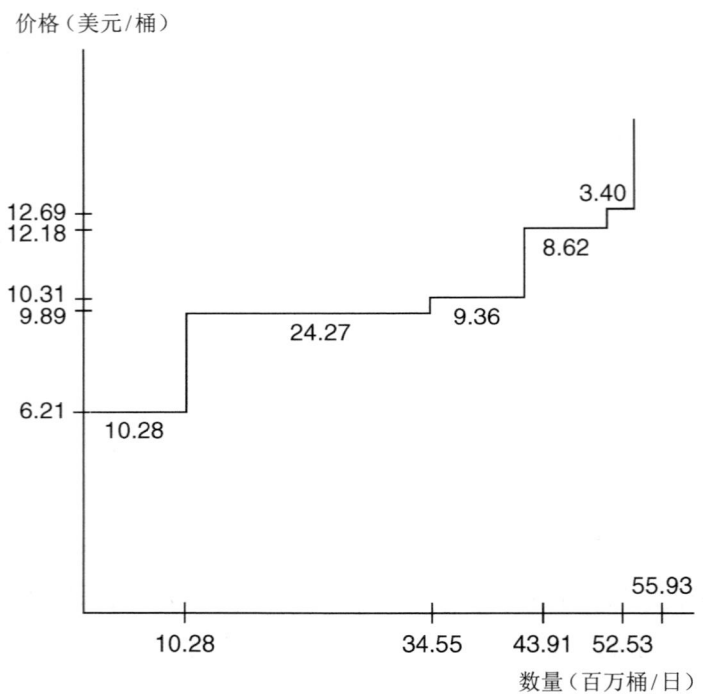

图8 原油短期供给曲线

虽然这个例子清楚说明了供给曲线的概念,但它只是图示而已。首先,并非所有国家的相关数据都能获得。比如,俄罗斯和中国因缺少成本数据而被省略。其次,国家或地区并不适合作为分析单位。理想情况下,我们应该拥有每一口油井的采油成本和产能数据。即便在同一个国家内部,这些数据也有着巨大差异;它们可生成一条光滑的供给曲线,而不是之前显示的巨大阶梯状。最重要的是,采油成本并不适合作为短期边际成本。

如果石油公司相信未来价格会上涨,他们可以选择将石油留在地下,以低于满负荷的产量生产。换句话说,机会成本才是正确的衡量标准。但这些都是基于公司内部的预期和计算,在公开的数据中见不到。因此,这个例子可以用来帮助大家理解相关概念,但不应等同于现实。

就许多方面而言,决定生产或供给的数量是一件微妙和复杂的事。除了按订单生产外,这一决定必须是在确切需求未知的情况下做出。如果你生产太多,就有卖不完的风险;如果生产太少,就有让一部分客户失望和疏远的风险。除非公司能收回成本,否则它们不愿意生产更多产品。在富裕的市场经济体中,消费者愿意支付更高的价格以获得有保障的产品供给,有竞争力的公司则通过为他们提供服务而获得收益。这有助于解释,为什么我常去的咖啡馆几乎从不断货。在计划经济体中,生产者不会因为让顾客失望而受到惩罚。相反,它们享有某种权力,因为它们能将稀缺商品分配给关系好的顾客。这有助于解释为什么这些经济体总是物资短缺。

定价策略

当一家企业能够影响其所在市场的价格时,它必须制定定价策略,因为它与客户和竞争对手是相互影响的。我将关注以盈利为主要目标的私营企业。非营利性企业或公共企业的分析与此相关,但有所不同。

任何一家企业的客户从其产品中获得的满意程度,都不同于他们可能会花钱购买的其他物品,因此他们对其产品的支付意愿也有所不同。一家追求利润的企业会为任何支付金额超过其边际成本的客户提供服务,并从中受益。但是,该企业却并不打算给愿意支付更多的其他客户提供同样的交易。企业试图从每个客户那里获取对方愿意支付的最高金额,可以解释我们观察到的许多定价策略。

最著名的例子是航空公司。商务旅客愿意支付比普通旅客或探亲旅客更高的价格。航空公司希望能以低票价吸引后者,同时向商务旅客提供更高价位的机票。明目张胆的价格歧视不仅非法,而且不切实际。消费者可以轻易掩盖商务旅行的明显迹象(比如由公司的差旅部门预订机票、穿西装,等等)。因此,航空公司会利用这两类旅客之间的其他差异。商务旅客需要灵活性,而普通旅客和探亲旅客愿意提前购买机票,并遵守行程安排。此外,商务旅客(实际上是他们的公司)更愿意购买商务舱或头等舱,以便在长途旅行中更加舒适。因此,航空公司提供不同类型的机票:经济舱机票便宜,需要预购,不可退款;商务舱或头等舱机票昂贵,不受限制。当价格以正确的方式计算并设定后,不同类型的旅客会选择航空公司意图为其提供的机票和服务类型。

以不同的价格提供不同版本的产品,并让消费者进行选择,这种策略被称为**通过自我选择筛选**,从而区分或"筛选"愿意支付不同价格的买家。一旦你了解这种用价格进行区分的方法,你会发现它无处不在。以下是几个例子。

计算机软件通常分为专业版或商务版和精简版或学生版。后者价格较低,功能较少。企业通常购买专业版:它们认为员工需要全部功能;或者说,员工应该拥有这些功能,以备不时之需。价格对它们来说不那么重要。对于自己掏钱的临时用户来说,他们通常只需要基本功能。供应商可以将这两类用户分开,并在制定价格时,向每类用户收取更接近对方支付意愿的价格。如何制作精简版?通常是在完整版的基础上,禁用高级功能!因此,价格差异与高级功能编程的额外成本无关,唯一目的就是通过筛选实现更大的利润。

咖啡馆有两类顾客:常客和临时顾客。常客对镇上不同咖啡馆的价格差异很敏感,会很快做出反应,这样他们全年节省的钱相当可观。临时顾客很可能是随机在街上找一家咖啡馆,而不是花时间寻找更低的价格。为了将两类顾客区分开,这家咖啡馆定价很高,并提供"买10杯,送1杯"的忠诚卡促销。通常来说,数量折扣也能达到类似的目的。

保险公司希望对风险较高的投保人收取更高的保险费。它们可以评估不同类型的风险,并收取相应费用。比如,吸烟的人、洪水易发地区的房主等,需要支付更高的保险费。其他风险可以通过自我选择进行筛选。人们对自己的风险通常比保险公司了解更多,而风险较高的人不愿意自己承担风险。因此,不同版本的保险单可以将这些人区分开来。风险较低的人预期不会经常需要保险赔偿,因此他们更愿意购买高免赔额或共同保险、费用较低的保险单。风险较高的人更渴望避免更多支付或经常自掏腰包,因此他们更喜欢范围较广的保险单,哪怕保费更高。保险公司可以将这两类投保人分开,为他们各自设计合适的方案(包括保险费和分摊费用),从而获得更高的利润。

信用卡发行机构有三类潜在的客户。从它们的角度来看,可能违约的人是最糟糕的客户,但是每月付清全部账款的人几乎同样糟糕。只有使用循环余额并支付大量利息的人才是最好的客户。发行机构采用了一个聪明的策略以有选择地吸引这些有利可图的客户：在最初的几个月里，客户可以从另一张信用卡转移余额，只需支付非常低的利息。很显然，这对于那些已经在其他地方用完余额并正在支付更高利息的人很有吸引力。

这种策略具有局限性。它们并不能从每一个买家那里获取充分的支付意愿。原因很简单，卖家通常没有这些信息。策略必须更加粗放，就像之前提到的航空公司制定票价时采取的双票价策略。在每一类消费者群体中，存在不同的支付意愿。例如，商务旅客（或他们的公司）愿意为灵活性和舒适性付费的意愿并不一致，在高层和中层管理者之间，以及在不同企业之间都会有所不同。双票价策略并没有利用这些细节，但对于航空公司来说，这个策略足够有效，可以增加利润（或减少损失）。现在，互联网上的商家从以往的购买记录和其他数据库中可以得到个人买家的大量信息，从而可以通过定价策略来实现完美的客户区分：当你登录它们的网站时，它们会立即估算你的支付意愿，并给出单独定制的价格来获取全部支付。汽车保险公司可以在车内使用来自"远程信息处理"设备的数据（参见http://en.wikipedia.org/wiki/Telematics）来详细监控驾驶员的行为，并根据其技能和关注给出精确定制的保险费。

还有更多的限制。第一，如果买家可以轻易转售商品或服务，那么就无法通过价格来区分客户。因为任何人都可以假装成支付意愿较低的客户，从而降低公司想要向他们收取的价格，然后在买到商品或服务后，再转售给其他人。第二，基于消费者之间可观察到的某些差异（如年龄或性别）来区分客户，这可能违法，也可能无法被社会接受。第三，通过自我选择进行筛选，这种方法具有局限性：愿意支付更高价格的买家说不定就会选择更便宜的版本。比如，商务舱和经济舱之间的票价差异不能超过商务旅客赋予额外舒适性的额外价值。因此，公司可能无法充分获取他们的支付意愿。但以盈利为目的某些区分策略是可行的，而且经常被使用。

一些定价策略用到了行为经济学的研究成果。卡内曼发现，人们通常使用本能的系统I来做决定。在购买决定中，他们只关注产品最明显的主要信息项，不会花时间和精力去调查次要的其他问题。因此，卖家故意给出一个优惠的价格，却隐藏了其他费用，等到顾客发现时已经来不及反悔。航空公司宣传低票价，却隐瞒行李费、飞机上的食品饮料费等。一家航空公司甚至计划向乘客收取在飞机上使用卫生间的费用，这一做法引起了太多的负面宣传，航空公司不得不放弃。许多酒店都在宣传诱人的低房价。只有当客人安顿下来后，他们才发现自己必须为网络和健身房等服务支付额外费用。

企业对通货膨胀的反应利用了消费者行为的重要特征，即价格比产品的其他属性更引人注目。价格上涨可能使一些消费者望而却步，哪怕这是合理的决定，因为成本在上涨。相反，如果可能的话，企业会保持价格和包装外观不变，但会悄悄地逐渐减少产品分量。比如，在包装内放入更少或更小的饼干。当这样做日渐引起顾客注意时，他们会重新增加产品的分量（实际上只是回到原来的水平！），并以此作为理由，大幅度提高价格。

大企业间的竞争

除非一家企业占据的市场份额很小，以至于它能做的唯一决定就是现行价格下的产量,否则它必须了解竞争对手,并制定应对策略,有时还要和对方联合行动。这种策略思维的第一步就是要认识到,竞争对手同时也在制定类似的应对策略。

让我们先来了解一些术语,你在经济学书籍和商业报刊中会经常遇到这些术语。一个市场如果只有一家企业,这被称为**垄断**。这个词源自古希腊语 *monos*(单独)和 *poleein*(出售)。(与之相对应的是一个市场只有一个购买者,这被称为买方垄断。)政府通过专利在一定期限内将垄断权授予发明人,通过版权将垄断权授予艺术品和软件的创作者;但政府有时也会将垄断权授予有关系的企业,或用来交换政治捐款或贿赂。一个市场如果只有少数企业(通常少于10家),这被称为**寡头垄断**,这个词源自古希腊语 *oligos*(很少)。如果寡头垄断者串通一气,保持高价,把新的竞争对手排除在市场之外,它们就组成了一个**卡特尔**。在大多数国家,这种做法是非法的(至少不能公开进行),反垄断政策会努力保持市场竞争。要定义什么是"一个市场"并不容易,因为大多数事物都有替代品,而且说到底,在消费者的预算范围内,一切事物都在竞争。但是,出于经济分析和反垄断政策的需要,可以划出大致的而非绝对的界限。

博弈论可以用来分析寡头垄断中的策略互动。这类企业之间的竞争通常是一种**囚徒困境**。在典型案例中,警方逮捕了两名可能被判轻罪的人,但怀疑他们犯有更严重的罪行。警方分别审问这两人,并让他们承认对方也牵连其中。如果一方供认不讳,而另一方坚持不说,则认罪的一方会得到宽大处理,但未认罪的一方会受到特别严厉的判决。因此,无论他或她认为对方会做什么,每一个人都会为了自己的利益而认罪。但当二人都认罪的时候，他们会被判处更重的罪行。相比之下，如果二人都不认罪，他们会被判较轻的罪行。也就是说，二人都认罪反倒更糟糕。

在寡头垄断中，每家企业都试图通过提供更低的价格、更好的产品、更多的售后服务和广告等手段，牺牲其他企业的利益来为自己赢得客户。如果其他企业没有采用这样的竞争策略，那么采取竞争策略的企业将获得巨大的优势。如果其他企业采用这种策略，那么没有竞争策略的企业将被甩在身后。但当所有企业都加入竞争时，它们的行动就会互相干扰。它们成了进退两难的囚徒：最终它们采取的策略都是更低的价格或更高的成本，这也就意味着更低的利润。当然，消费者从价格竞争中受益，正如我们将在第四章看到的那样，竞争提高了社会的整体效率。但这些企业确实输了。为了解决它们的困境，它们必须想办法减少竞争的激烈程度。相反，如果反垄断政策以社会整体利益为目标，那就应该预见并防止企业串通。

企业需要与已经**进入**相关市场的其他企业展开竞争。它们为了**争夺**这个市场，竞争会很激烈（或者说，更加激烈）。当一个利润丰厚市场中的支配地位岌岌可危时，比如，某个大城市准备出售用于移动通信的无线电波频谱，竞争对手就会为这一权利展开激烈的竞标，从而耗散掉它们所能获得的利润。这样的困境也可能损害社会的整体利益。假设两家企业都在研发用于治疗高胆固醇或勃起功能障碍的药物。其中一家企业以一天之差击败对手，从而获得这种大众市场药品的发明权和专利权。这带给社会的好处很小，因为可获得的治疗只提前了一天。但对于获得专利权的企业来说，好处相当大，因为它可以得到整整二十年的垄断利润。因此，这种研发竞争往往表现过度。为了抢占利润丰厚的非法市场（比如，毒品交易或赌博），真的会出现你死我活的局面。

企业能避免囚徒困境吗？要想实现这个目标，最基本的要求是保持持续而稳定的互动。假设某个行业中的所有企业已经达成了维持高价的协议。在法律上，这些协议大多无法执行。事实上，根据大多数国家的反垄断法，这样的明确共谋是非法行为。因此，任何隐含的协议都只能依靠自觉来维系。每家企业都会受到诱惑，它可以降低商定的价格，以牺牲其他企业的利益来增加自己的利润。但这样做会引发其他企业以牙还牙报复性降价的风险，最终导致协议崩溃，包括自身在内的所有企业的利润都会受到严重影响。因此，每家企业必须在当前利益和未来损失之间进行权衡。如果它期望持续而稳定的互动，它就会更加看重长远利益，从而更有可能避免破坏协议的做法。但是，如果该行业正在衰退，或者因为技术变革而过时，或者原本不属于该行业的新企业扰乱市场均衡，那么这家企业就会通过降价来获得短期优势。当然，当所有的企业都这样做的时候，就会出现囚徒困境。

有的企业确实会违反反垄断法，尝试明确共谋。近期最著名的例子是赖氨酸市场，这是一种广泛用于动物饲料的化学品。库尔特·艾兴瓦尔德在《告密者》中生动地描述了这个案例。龙头企业美国的阿切尔·丹尼尔斯·米德兰公司和日本的味之素公司的高层管理人员在会面后经过协商，决定维持高价，瓜分市场。当然，客户遭受了损失。这些阴谋家在私底下提出口号："竞争对手是我们的朋友，客户是我们的敌人。"

为了私下达成共谋,企业也会想出一些巧妙的办法。比如,在一轮涉及多个区号的美国移动电话频谱拍卖中,竞拍者会将特定区号的最后三位数加到报价中,以此表达它们对特定区域的兴趣。比如,如果某家企业给出 10 000 415 美元的报价,这相当于告诉其他竞标者,我想要旧金山(区号为415),所以你们最好别介入。其他企业则可能想要其他区域。这些信息使它们能瓜分整个市场,避免单个区域内的竞争。

根基深厚的垄断企业或寡头垄断企业希望阻止新企业加入市场,因为后者会削弱它们的市场力量。它们可能会威胁要开展一场价格战,这会导致新企业无利可图。如果只是嘴上说说,可能会被当作空洞的威胁,所以必须让新企业相信它们的话。一种做法是将价格调低,低于现有市场力量所能接受的价格,目的是让潜在的加入者相信,市场内现有企业的成本非常低,因此加入后的竞争会十分激烈。此外,现有企业也可以保持高产能。一旦有新企业加入,它们可以轻松扩大产量,并开始价格战。这种策略可以控制成本:通过高产能的投入,换句话说,就是把产能成本变为沉没成本,从而降低了未来扩张的边际成本。

创建并长期维持卡特尔的成功记录并不多。石油输出国组织欧佩克(OPEC)在20世纪70年代取得了巨大的成功。但是,由于受到一些较小的成员国欺骗,加上非成员国的石油产量猛增,以及买家设法减轻石油依赖,欧佩克的市场力量在十年后大幅削弱。其他商品和采矿业试图模仿石油输出国组织,但没能成功,或者只维持了很短的时间。近年来,中国试图加强稀土元素的出口管理,这些元素对于包括计算机、智能手机和武器在内的尖端科技至关重要。但是,其他国家的稀土供给正在迅速提高，技术进步也在减少这些设备中所需元素的数量，同时回收利用也降低了对新供给的需要；这些因素共同削弱了对中国稀土出口的依赖。戴比尔斯公司领导的钻石卡特尔可能是唯一延续并蓬勃发展近一个世纪的钻石垄断组织。这需要永远保持警惕，吸收一些新的生产者并阻止其他企业加入，通过富有想象力的广告来创造和维系市场，还要避免二手钻石销售者的竞争。要做到最后一点，需要引导钻石所有者的心态，让他们不要转售钻石，更不要低价抛售。

供应链

有时买家并非最终消费者。大多数商品的生产涉及多个阶段，需要组装不同部件。前一个阶段的产品被卖给另一家企业，后者对其进行加工，与投入的其他原料一起形成新的产品。与此同时，企业也会购买其他企业制造的零部件。集装箱和航空运输降低了运输成本，同时国际贸易体制变得更加自由，因此在20世纪90年代和21世纪初，供应链已经拓展到全球范围，虽然有些公司近年来放弃了彻底外包的做法。企业之间的交易已经成为整体市场经济的重要部分，就像针对终端消费者的销售环节一样。供应链管理几乎与企业组织自身的生产活动一样重要。

如果一家企业卖给另一家企业的是标准化商品，比如燃料或内存芯片，那么这笔交易就属于标准化的供需分析。这种情况下，需求曲线的数据源自企业，而不是消费者。但替代原则依然适用，需求定理依然成立。不过，更多时候交易的物品并非标准化商品；购买的企业有特定要求（比如用于特定的机器设备或定制软件），并且要专门设计交易物品以满足需求。交易需要两家企业之间订立合同,其条款需要双方协商。成交的价格受到相对议价能力的影响,这反过来又取决于它们的选择机会:准备购买的企业可能有其他的潜在货源,而准备销售的企业可能会签订其他的潜在合同。合同一旦订立,这两家企业在某种程度上相互依存。没有任何合同能够预见并涵盖所有的突发事件。因此,每家企业都有一定的灵活应对的空间,这使它可以抓住机会,牺牲合作伙伴的利益,巩固自己的优势。相比简单的供需关系,上述因素使得企业之间的交易操作变得更加复杂,也让相关分析变得更有难度。在本书中,我无法详尽论述,但接下来我要说到一个重要意涵。

企业组织

企业所使用的生产原料,一部分来自其他企业,另一部分则是自己生产。选择权在它们手里,需要考虑的是由此引出的一些有趣的基本问题。

通过价格体系,市场可以提供良好的信息和激励。我在第一章已经提到过这一点,并且在第四章还将详尽分析。那么,为什么不把一切都留给市场呢?为什么不让各个企业分别生产供应链的每个细小环节,然后将产品通过市场卖给另一家企业,由后者来完成下一个环节?或者,为什么不采取相反的措施,即在一家企业内部生产全部产品?将这一想法推到逻辑极限,为什么整个国家的经济不能简化为一家超大型企业,名字就叫"国内生产有限公司"?

罗纳德·科斯给出了解答,奥利弗·威廉姆森丰富并发展了科斯的思想,他们因为各自的贡献都获得了诺贝尔经济学奖。

核心观点是，使用市场需要大量成本。对于公司之间的交易来说，大多数商品都必须根据买方的要求量身定制。因此，买方必须找到合适的供应商，并洽谈合同。合同无法详细规定所有事项。因此，每一方都可以抱着侥幸心理采取行动，比如削减成本，略微降低质量，或者当另一方无法找到新的合作伙伴时，要求改变合同条款，为自己争取更多利益。因此，必须监督合同的履行，争议必须通过协商或最终在法庭上解决，等等。所有这些都需要付出昂贵的代价。在一些国家，司法体系可能行动迟缓，效率低下，并且存在偏见或腐败。另外，合同的自动履行必须基于长期保持的声誉和关系，建立和维护这些基础同样要付出昂贵的代价。所有这些成本（专业术语称为**交易成本**）的重要性不亚于普通的生产成本。

企业内部的生产也涉及交易成本，只不过类别不同。市场价格中包含的信息和激励必须在内部复制。企业整体的盈利方式是对更高的价格做出反应：扩大生产，并以成本有效的方式实现这一目标。要将这种激励转移给个体管理者，就必须在他们的薪酬中加入利润分享。对于企业的最终所有者（股东）来说，这也是成本。另外，必须监督工人的表现。随着管理层级的规模化和复杂化，公司治理的内部交易成本迅速上升。激励管理者；监督工人；监督监管者；防止低层级的工人和管理者相互勾结，违抗上级管理者让他们工作更努力、更灵活的要求——所有这些操作都变得更加困难，需要更高的成本，这限制了企业的控制幅度。把整个经济体当作一家企业来运营，这几乎不可能做到，而且会适得其反。在计划经济中，中央计划的失败就是这方面的确凿证据。

除了内部生产的普通成本以及从另一家公司购买的价格之外，企业在决定内部制造或外部购买时，还必须考虑两种模式的交易成本，并选择总体成本较低的模式。根据具体情况，结果将有所不同。因此，我们看到一些高度整合的企业几乎可以在内部完成全部生产环节。另一些企业只负责设计产品并进行最终组装，几乎所有的制造环节都外包。还有很多企业介于这两个极端之间。许多石油公司体现出整合性。由输油管连接的油田和炼油厂紧密联系在一起，如果其中一方选择与另一家企业重新建立关系，代价将非常高昂。因此，投机行为具有很大风险。相比之下，将这两项业务整合后由同一家企业完成，这是缓解问题的最省力的方式。一些台式电脑制造商以及许多服装企业和制鞋企业具有相反的极端表现：它们都属于"空心"企业，自身几乎没有任何制造能力。具体而言：它们采用标准化组件；供应商提供的材料质量相对容易监控；它们可以相对轻松地换成其他供应商（如有必要，甚至换成其他国家的供应商）。因此，它们的交易成本很低，可以将制造环节外包给工资最低的外部企业。

在决定内部制造还是外部购买时，企业有时会决策失误。许多企业已经将制造环节转移到工资较低的国家，却发现那里的低劳动力成本优势被其他因素抵消，比如：质量存在问题，将产品运回国内市场需要成本和时间，供应中断的风险增大，存在违约风险，而且研发、设计、生产和业务处理等环节失去了协同效应。与此同时，中国等国家的劳动力成本优势也在下降，因为它们的工资增长速度超过美国。

交易成本有助于解释我们在欠发达国家时常见到的大型企

业集团。这些企业集团通常归家族所有,并且经营的品种五花八门,比如纺织品、化学品、汽车、饮料、酒店、信息技术服务等。在这些国家有缺陷的司法体系中,可以找到合理解释。正式的合同执行是不可靠的,商业交易是通过声誉和关系来治理。如果你的企业已经积累了一定的利润,但是最好的投资机会属于其他经济领域,你不可能将资金借给一家没有关联的企业,并指望如实得到投资回报。相反,你会将这项业务纳入你自己的家族企业之下,那里的关系最可靠。这样的企业集团不必在生产中创造任何协同效应,或者传统意义上的效率;但它降低了治理成本。

第四章

市　场

供给与需求

据说，托马斯·卡莱尔曾经说过，"教一只鹦鹉学会说供给与需求，你就有了一个经济学家"。正如很多类似的滑稽说法一样，它恰恰抓住了一整套复杂而美好机制的起点，但这是一个很不错的起点。尽管经济学已经变得更依赖数学，但是供给曲线和需求曲线的简明图示仍然是大多数经济学家进行思考的基本工具。这一做法可以追溯到一个世纪前，很大程度上要归功于英国经济学家阿尔弗雷德·马歇尔。

在第二章和第三章中，我们已经见过需求曲线和供给曲线。现在我把一些商品（比如咖啡）的需求曲线和供给曲线整合到同一个图中，如图9所示。两条曲线的交点为E，对应于价格P和数量Q。如果市场价格保持在P的水平，消费者需求的数量等于生产者供给的数量，也就是Q。此时供给等于需求，这意味着市场出清，我们得到了均衡状态。

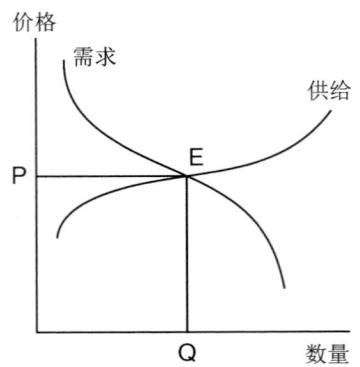

图9 供需均衡

什么样的过程或机制能产生这个价格？答案很简单。如果价格高于P，那么在该价格上，生产者愿意提供的数量将沿着上升的供给曲线而超过Q，而消费者需求的数量将沿着向下倾斜的需求曲线而小于Q。因此，在这样的高价格，供给超过了需求。于是，生产者将接受更低的价格，而消费者将对此做出反应。如果价格低于P，一系列事件将反向展开。因此，从任何方向开始，价格都将朝着P移动。

然而，这个答案存在问题，因为供需曲线意味着每个消费者和生产者都会对"现行价格"做出反应，并且都没有能力控制这个价格。那么，究竟是谁将价格调整到均衡位置？

一些金融市场和商品市场确实存在公开的做市商，由他们来制定价格。做市商会将某些资产或商品的库存保持在一定水平，然后将一部分库存卖给买家，并且将卖家销售的产品加入库存。如果发现库存在减少，他们会提高价格；如果发现库存在增加，他们会降低价格。因此，价格调整使得库存流入和流出的数量相等，从而保持供需相等。促使做市商这样做的原因是买入和卖出价格之间的差价,但是在一个"厚的"(也就是说,交易量非常大)市场中,差价很小,结果就会出现类似于供需曲线交叉的故事。

大多数市场缺乏做市商,此时匹配买卖双方和设定价格的过程就更加复杂,情况也各不相同。是否可以用这种方式来描述和研究结果,**仿佛**它就出现在供需曲线的交叉位置,这一点目前还不清楚,只能根据经验来判断。在第六章中,我们将讨论其他机制的一些例子,但是现在我将重点分析供给与需求,因为这是最简单的解释,同时也是关于市场的大多数常见看法的来源,这些看法有些是对的,有些则是错的。

效 率

图10展示了供需关系。图中每条曲线都被改为直线,这纯粹是为了视觉上的简化。设想一下,从零开始连续增加数量,从而在价格P和数量Q的交叉位置实现均衡。购买第一个单位商品的人愿意支付的价格等于高度A,但实际只需支付P。因此,买方获得的额外收益(经济学的专业术语称为**消费者剩余**)为高度AP。第一个单位商品生产时的边际成本为B,但生产者得到的价格为P。因此,生产者获得额外的收益(**生产者剩余**)等于高度BP。加上这两部分之后,第一个单位商品为整个经济(**社会剩余**)提供的额外收益等于高度AB。

随着数量的增加,支付意愿下降,边际成本上升。当数量达到X时,买方愿意支付的价格为C,并获得消费者剩余CY。生产者的边际成本为D,并获得生产者剩余YD。此时所产生的社会剩余为:CY+YD=CD。最后,当数量达到Q时,买方支付他或她愿意支付的价格,并且生产者收回他或她的边际成本,此时每个人获得的盈余都为零。

对于任何高于Q的数量,买方的支付意愿(沿着下降的需求曲线衡量)将低于生产者的边际成本(沿着上升的供给曲线衡量)。此时,每增加一个数量单位都会造成负的社会盈余,因此继续生产并不划算。

换句话说,供需机制只会生产社会剩余为正时的数量,不会生产更多。这个结果最大化了社会总剩余,它在经济上是有效率的。

市场效率的这种特性可以在更广泛的背景下得到验证,并构成经济学的基本"定理"。当然,任何定理的结论只有在其基本假设成立的前提下才能成立,关于这一点,之后我会详尽分析。首先,我要澄清效率的概念。

最重要的是,这个概念没有说明最大化的社会剩余如何在参与经济运作的个体之间进行分配。在图10中,消费者剩余总量是由AP和CY这样的高度构成的区域,即三角形APE的面

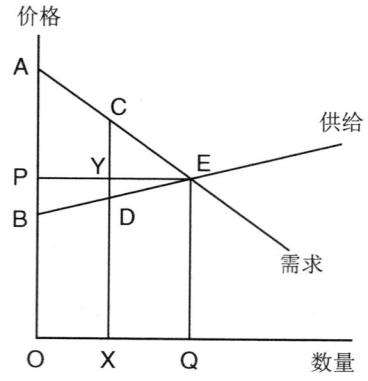

图10 供需均衡的效率

积。同理，生产者剩余总量是三角形BPE的面积。它们的相对量取决于需求和供给曲线的偶然形状，并且不能说明这种分配的价值或正义。生产者剩余是企业利润的重要来源，并作为股息或资本收益流向企业所有者。这种做法的道德价值尚不清楚。或许你会认为，企业所有者都是不择手段的有钱人，但实际上他们也可能是普通股东，就像你的祖父母或父母那样从养老基金中获得一定的退休收入。

某个结果具有经济效率，仅仅意味着能够使其中一个人受益的任何改变都会伤害到其他人。它并不涉及分配正义或道德价值。这个概念被称为**帕累托效率**，以纪念提出这个概念的意大利人维尔弗雷多·帕累托，19世纪后半叶和20世纪初的工程师、社会学家和经济学家。举个极端的例子，如果某个结果的任何改变能给纽约街头的无家可归者带来好处，同时会给沃伦·巴菲特带来伤害，那么这个结果就被认为具有帕累托效率。

经济学家有时会过分强调帕累托效率，显得缺乏同情心，他们因此遭到辛辣的嘲讽。我最喜欢的一则笑话是这样说的：一个商人、一个牧师和一个经济学家组成了高尔夫三人组。行动迟缓的另一个小组阻挡了他们前进的道路。在长时间诅咒对方之后，他们发现那些球员都是盲人。商人感到羞愧，并承诺向盲人基金会捐款一万美元。牧师发誓要为他们祈祷，帮他们恢复视力。经济学家却说："如果他们到晚上再出来打球，是不是有助于提高帕累托效率？那样对我们更有利，对他们来说反正没有差别。"

在我看来，效率不应该是判断经济结果的唯一标准；或者说，在某些情况下，甚至不应该作为首要标准。如果能在社会或道德标准的其他方面取得足够的改善，那么就应该牺牲一部分效率。我相信沃伦·巴菲特会同意我的观点，尽管自由派或极右翼的一些政客不会同意。我说的是"应该牺牲"，至于这种情况在现实中能否实现，取决于政治制度和实际流程。

且慢，还有更坏的消息。即使在有限的帕累托意义上，市场结果也可能无效。当买方或卖方行为通过市场以外的渠道影响他人时（比如，污染和拥堵会产生不利影响，而接种疫苗会产生积极影响），市场结果并没有实现帕累托效率。要想纠正这些低效行为，经济学家纸上谈兵很容易，但在现实的政治世界中却很难实施。我将在下一章讨论这些问题。现在让我告诉你一个常见的陷阱。"均衡"这个词会误导人们以为，一切都是为了取得所有可能世界的最好中的最好。事实并非如此，也没有必要这样做：这个词的意思仅仅是，特定的价格出清了市场，此时供给等于需求。任何其他属性，即使是像帕累托效率这样的有限属性，或许能成立，但必须单独进行论证。

现在让我们来关注好消息。许多善意的政治活动家使用"为人民提供食物，而不是为利润"这样的口号来谴责市场。我们对市场机制的研究表明，人民和利润并非必然发生冲突。当市场运作良好时（可能需要提高警惕，加强监督和监管），生产者追求利润的私人目的同时也能满足消费者对于食品和其他物品的需求。高价格释放出需求信号，利润提供了满足需求的动力。事实上，这是经济学最早的洞见之一。亚当·斯密在《国富论》（这本书可以说是经济学的奠基之作）中对此做了精彩的分析："我们预期的晚餐并非来自屠夫、酿酒师或面包师的仁慈，而是来自他们自利的考虑。"

均衡的变化

如果需求和供给的基本条件发生变化，市场均衡将从旧的交叉点转移到新的交叉点。价格和数量的增加或减少取决于需求和供给的变化类型。如图11所示，这些变化有四种基本类型。当你观察到这些变化并且弄明白其中的道理，那么你就能解释许多日常市场中观察到的价格和数量的变化。

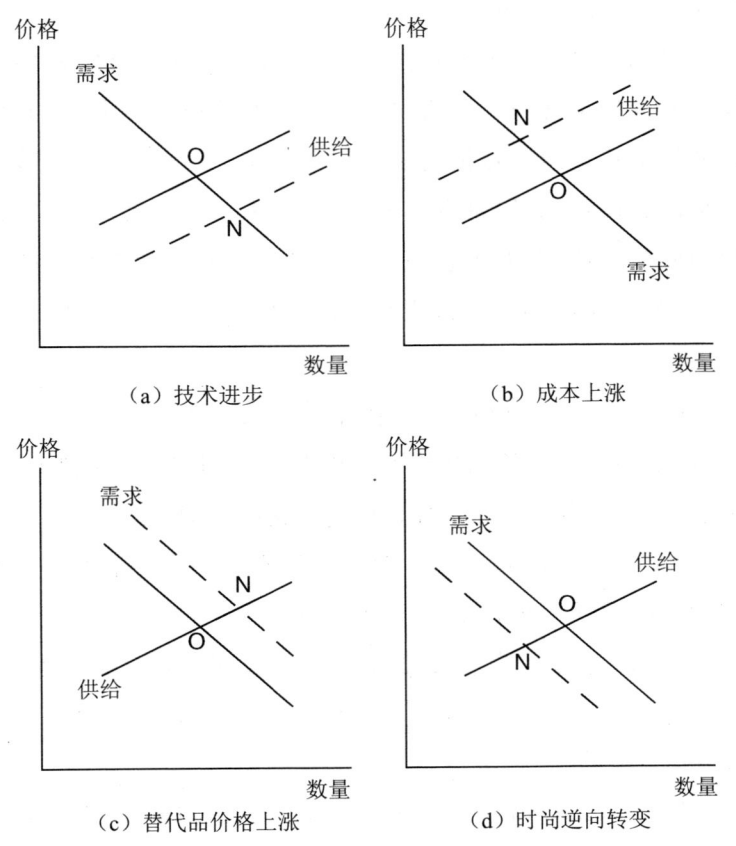

图11　均衡变化示例

上面共有四幅图，分别用英文字母（a）—（d）标记。在每幅图中，初始状态的供给曲线和需求曲线显示为实线，其中有一条曲线将会发生变化，移至虚线所示的新位置。（再次提醒，原本应该是曲线，图中显示为直线，纯粹是为了视觉上的简化。）旧的均衡点标记为O，新的均衡点标记为N。

如图（a）所示，技术进步降低了生产成本，使供给曲线向下移动。新的均衡点价格低于旧的均衡点。这类变化近期最引人关注的例子是平面电视。

图（b）显示了成本上涨产生的影响，比如1973年和1979年的原油价格猛涨。这增加了生产汽油的边际成本，因此供给曲线上移。结果是价格上涨和数量减少，因为人们会减少开车，或者转向更省油的汽车。当然这种反应需要时间，因此我们应该预计，最初的影响主要取决于价格。随着数量的变化，价格会小幅回落。这正是原油价格两次出现震荡时发生的事情。

在图（c）中，推动转变的因素是替代品价格上涨。假设图中的需求曲线和供给曲线代表窖藏啤酒，并且麦芽酒价格上涨。于是，不管窖藏啤酒处于什么样的价格，它的销售量都超过以往，因此需求曲线向右移动。结果就是销量更高，并且价格也更高，因为生产更多窖藏啤酒的边际成本上升了。

图（d）显示了需求的逆向转变，比如某种服装不再流行。这样的变化将导致数量减少和价格下降，因为沿着供给曲线边际成本下降了。

我们继续来分析时尚转变的案例。从短期来看，生产运行已经开始，商店有了一定数量的库存。因此，供给的价格敏感度较低(弹性小或曲线陡峭),而且随着商店清仓销售,这种转变将对价格产生直接影响。之后,厂家逐步将生产线转移,用于生产其他的时尚服饰,供给曲线对于价格变得更加敏感(弹性大或曲线扁平)。结果就是,那些不再流行的服装产量将会减少。图12显示了这些变化:新的均衡点在左图中标记为S,在右图中标记为L。

因此,价格和数量可能小幅上升或下降,也可能出现巨大变化,具体取决于实际情况。可能你已经于不同时间在不同市场看到了所有的可能组合,并且想知道为什么价格和数量在某些时候会一起移动,而其他时间却并非如此,同时你也想知道为什么价格在某些时候会发生巨大的变化,而另一些时候却是数量发生变化。现在,你可以思考究竟是什么原因导致供给曲线向上或向下移动,或者导致需求曲线向右或向左移动,以及均衡调整的时间长度。当你弄明白背后的原因,你就能理解所有的变化。

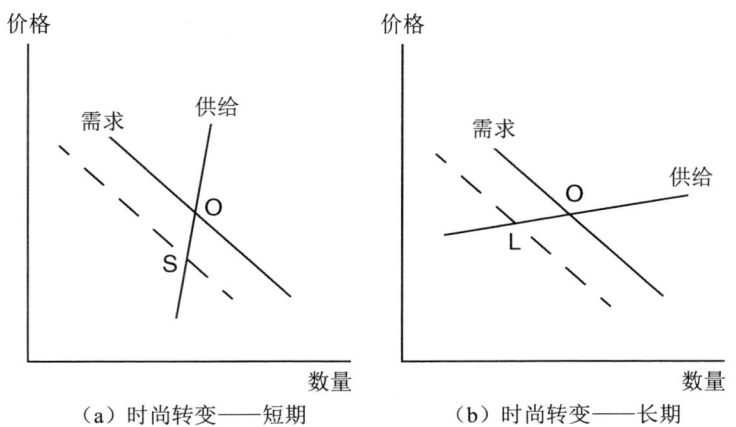

(a)时尚转变——短期　　(b)时尚转变——长期

图12　时尚转变产生的短期影响和长期影响

税　收

值得注意的是，征税也会造成均衡变化。举个最简单的例子，每单位数量征收定额税。假设卖方需要保存记录，并向政府缴纳税款。这样一来，卖方的税后边际成本上升，增加的金额等于税收，供给曲线垂直上移。结果如图13所示。新的均衡点为N，买方支付的价格为B。其中，政府获得的税款为BS，相当于供给曲线的变化高度。卖方得到的价格为S。在征税之前，买方支付的费用等于卖方收到的钱，即点P。税收将买方支付的价格从P提高到B，并且将卖方得到的钱从P降低到S。可以说，在总税收BS中，买方支付的金额为BP，卖方支付的金额为PS。这些影响被称为税收**归宿**。

即使卖家会将税款交给政府，买家也需要支付更高的价格，相当于支付部分税款。事实上，谁最初支付税款无关紧要。随

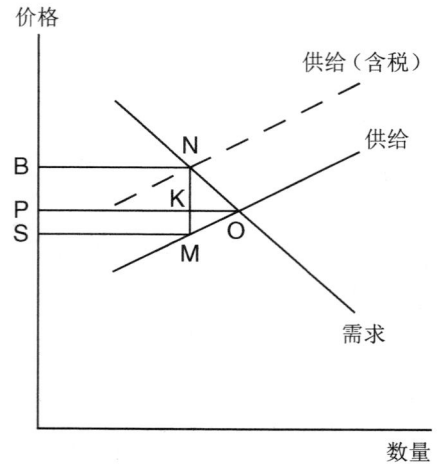

59　图13　税收的影响

着税收对市场均衡产生影响，最终的归宿是相同的。在市场形成新的均衡之前，可能只会出现短暂的差异。

人们通常不理解这一点。不妨想一想美国的社会保障税。表面看来，雇主支付其中的一部分，工人支付其余部分。但这笔费用最终会在劳动力市场上发挥作用，它对于工资产生的影响，和一方支付全部税款的做法完全一样。我们经常看到一些政策辩论，质疑由工人支付部分税款是否公平，或者由雇主交税是否会对就业不利。其实这些辩论大多无关紧要。

税收减少了市场交易量，新均衡点N的数量小于旧均衡点O。N和O之间的数量原本可以加入交易，从而提升买卖双方的共同利益：如果没有税收，买方愿意支付的价格高于卖方的边际成本。税收造成效率低下：总体剩余等于三角形NMO的面积，其中，消费者剩余为NKO，生产者剩余为KMO。但是，这些效率损失不应简单归罪于税收：如果它所筹集的收入有利于整个社会，那么收益就超过了表面的损失。

补贴会产生类似的归宿效应。美国和许多其他国家的住房按揭贷款利息可以抵扣，这本质上是一种补贴。通常认为，该政策的目的是让大众得以拥有住房。图14显示了住房市场中不同供给条件下该政策产生的影响。在这两幅图中，补贴导致住房的需求曲线上移：任何之前愿意支付x的人现在都愿意支付x加上补贴，因为政府提供了补贴，个人只需和以前一样支付x。市场均衡从旧的O点移到新的M点。这一转变的性质在很大程度上取决于供给条件。在左图中，供给对价格不敏感（几无弹性）。不仅短期内如此，如果当地政府限制新住房的建设，那么即使从长期来看也是一样。从O点到M点的价格上涨几乎等于补贴，数量的增加幅度很小。这意味着,现有住房的价格上涨几乎耗尽了全部补贴,而自置住房几乎没有增加。现有的房主是主要受益人,所以这种做法在政治上备受欢迎。愿意支付更高价格的新买家大多是富人,帮助他们拥有住房并不是政策的本意。在右图中,供给对于价格非常敏感(弹性很大)。当数量增加时,价格出现小幅上涨,这更符合政策意图。但要想实现这一点,政府不能通过划分特定区域或其他规定来限制新住房的建设。

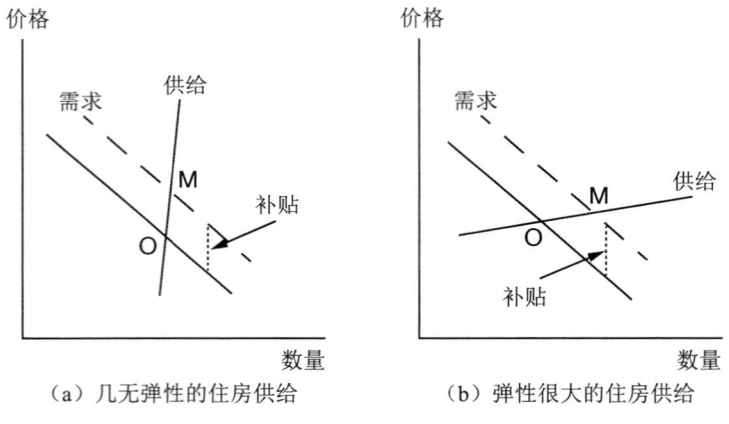

(a) 几无弹性的住房供给　　(b) 弹性很大的住房供给

图14　住房按揭贷款利息抵扣产生的归宿效应

美国和其他国家政府的预算赤字和债务积累促使它们考虑修订所得税法,取消或限制住房按揭贷款利息抵扣的做法。回推上述分析,你会发现这样的改革将会伤害现有房主的利益,至少短期内如此。这足以解释为何这些提案会遭到强烈反对。

繁荣与萧条周期

我之前已经提到,大多数市场并没有做市商来确保需求等于供给,并使市场一直保持均衡。现在我再次强调这一点。当然，市场的确有朝着均衡发展的趋势。比如，当价格过高，供给过剩时，一些生产商就无法出售产品。它们最终将采取清仓销售来吸引买家，价格会因此下跌。但是，这可能是一个缓慢的过程。而在其他情况下，调整则可能过快，导致价格循环总是高于或低于均衡水平。下面来看几个例子。

在某些市场，比如住房和采掘业，供给在短期内是固定的，但对于价格的反应会滞后。首先确定价格，使需求等于可得的固定供给。在图15中，左图显示了可能发生的情况。假设最初制定的价格过低，供给方会做出反应，调整市场到点1。需求压力抬高了价格，将市场推向点2。经过一段时间的滞后，供给方对这个更高的价格做出反应，把我们带到点3。为了吸收过剩的供给，价格必须下降，从而产生点4。依此类推。图中需求曲线和供给曲线的变化意味着，这个过程实际上并不稳定。如果曲线呈现其他形状，周期可能逐渐减弱，但不均衡状态可能会持续很长时间。

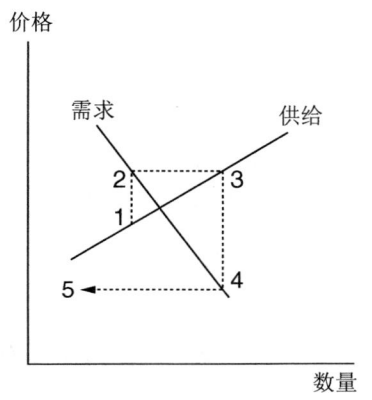

（a）供给繁荣与萧条　　（b）需求狂热与恐慌

图15　价格波动

有人会认为，随着时间的推移，生产者会理解价格波动的本质，从而可以更好地预判未来，而不是对最后观察到的价格做出反应。然而，这似乎并没有发生，我们确实观察到住房和采掘业的这种波动，甚至不稳定。

图15的右图表明，当需求随趋势变化时，许多金融市场会出现价格波动。如果没有投资者的趋势行为，均衡将稳定在N点（正常情况下）。但是，假设由于某些意外原因，价格略高于N。投资者认为这将是未来的趋势，他们预计价格会涨得更高，如果现在购买，他们将从中获利。需求向上移动，价格可能上涨到H点。这会产生更大的需求压力——你可以称之为贪婪或狂热。最终，新买家缺乏，价格上涨缓慢，甚至下跌。这就形成了相反的反应——你可以称之为恐惧或恐慌。这会使需求向下移动，价格可能下降到L点。下一次，如果投资者能弄明白整个过程，他们可能不会做出如此极端的反应，但个人和作为整体的市场很容易忘记之前的教训。于是，每隔几年我们就会看到繁荣和萧条交替发生。

最高限价和最低限价

有时，政府会对价格施加限制，从而使市场远离均衡。这样做的动机可能是为了政治上照顾特殊群体的利益而牺牲他人，或者可能是为了在社会层面上解决更为重要或更为紧迫的需要。（或者，它可能是出于第一种动机，却伪装成第二种！）在这两种情况下，限价政策都有副作用，并且往往是有害的影响，有时甚至会伤害到预期的受益者。

欧盟共同农业政策旨在"确保农民得到公正的生活水平，

并以可承受的价格为消费者提供稳定和安全的食品供应"。近五十年来,欧盟通过规定各种农产品的最低价格来实现这些崇高的目标。在图16中,左图显示了政策的结果。在价格P,生产者希望提供数量B,而消费者仅需要数量A。供应商可能受到限制,但欧盟通常允许并出资购买额外的供给量AB。媒体给这些剩余部分起了丰富多彩的名字,比如"黄油山"和"葡萄酒湖"。一些剩余以极低的价格出售给欧盟以外的国家,欧盟的纳税人承担了向农民支付高价并以低价转售的损失。农业人口众多的国家是净受益者,而工业化程度较高的成员国是净损失者。这个政策在欧盟造成了很多政治冲突。最近,政策进行了改革,直接为农民提供与其生产无关的收入支持。这消除了剩余,但各国间的利益和成本分配差异所造成的冲突仍然存在。

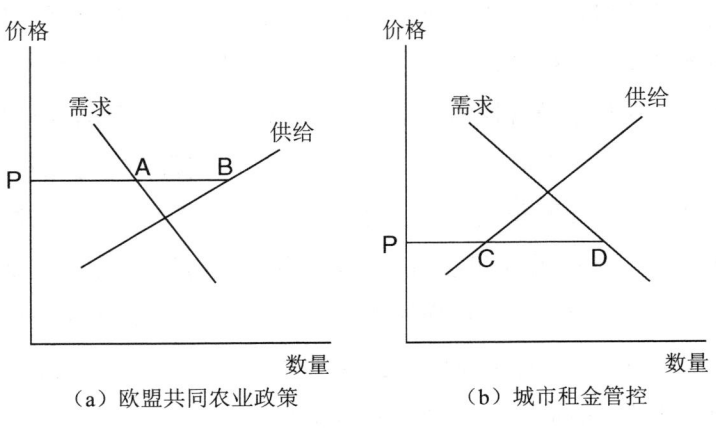

(a)欧盟共同农业政策　　(b)城市租金管控

图16　价格的上限和下限

从20世纪30年代到80年代,美国有类似的乳制品价格支持政策。其结果是:一座废弃的矿山里堆满了发霉的奶酪,代价是每年40亿美元,每天花费100万美元。

随着城市的发展，需求压力导致租金上涨。现任租户不愿意支付更多费用。一些城市的政府部门通过管控租金来应对这个问题。第二次世界大战后的纽约是一个典型的例子，但其他城市也是如此。你可能生活在一个类似的城市，并且已经感受到影响。在图16中，右图显示了这个政策的直接影响。由于价格不允许超过P，需求为D，供给为C，产生的需求超过DC。这引发了一系列事件，其中大多数事件效率低下，甚至产生负面影响。房东或中介在租房时会偏袒或歧视某些群体，或者向潜在的房客索取"看房费"等额外费用。租户转租房间（经常通过非法手段），造成过度拥挤。房东提供的服务很差，而且疏于维修，因此管控租金最终导致租户得到的住房质量低下。建筑商发现在租金受管控时建造新房子将无利可图。随着时间的推移，这会加剧住房短缺。作为应对策略，政府可以去除对新建住房的租金管控，但这阻碍了有效的空间分配。比如，一对老年夫妇原本居住在租金受管控的大型公寓里，现在想搬进规模较小的新公寓，但他们却做不到，因为那里的租金要高得多。与此同时，年轻家庭需要面积更大的公寓，却找不到合适的住处。在极端情况下，这些副作用可能会损害最初住户的利益，哪怕他们是政策的预期受益者。但这样的政策仍然在延续，因为政客们担心废除政策带来的直接影响：受管控的公寓租金将上涨，这将会造成媒体的负面报道，损害他们的政治利益。

刚才我们举例说明，某些带有良好意愿的政策（比如，确保农民获得体面的收入，为城市居民提供负担得起的住房），最终产生了代价高昂的副作用，从长远来看，甚至会伤害到预期的受益者。在下一章中，我们将看到更多市场失灵和政策失灵的例子，由此我将得出结论：不可能做到完美；在经济问题的各种解决方案中，我们必须接受负面影响最小的一种方案，那就是将基于市场的解决方案和政府的解决方案结合起来，用混合模式来应对每一个问题。

第四章 市　场

第五章

市场失灵与政策失灵

垄断与寡头垄断

需求曲线和供给曲线的交叉点要想产生有效结果,就必须要求价格不受任何生产者的控制。如果一家公司的规模足以影响市场价格,它就可以减少供给,沿着需求曲线抬高价格,从中获得更多利益。一些公司可能会串通一气,达到同样的结果。确切地说,供给量的减少幅度取决于实际情况。本书只是通识读本,我们要做的并不是具体分析,而是关注这样做产生的影响。

图17是图10的修订版。假设垄断或寡头垄断导致数量减少到小于Q的某个点,比如X,那么X和Q之间的数量差所产生的社会剩余(即愿意支付的价格超过这些数量的边际成本的部分,等于CDE的面积)就会失去。这种方法可以用来衡量垄断或寡头垄断导致的效率低下(经济学的术语称为**无谓损失**)。

如果数量X的所有买家都支付相同的价格,即需求曲线上的点C,那么总金额就等于矩形MCYP。在完全竞争的情况下,这将是消费者剩余的一部分，现在则成了公司利润的一部分。任何成功的价格歧视都能从消费者身上榨取更多的剩余。这就增加了一种可能性，即企业可能会花费资源来获得垄断权，具体包括：阻止竞争对手进入市场，支付政治捐款，甚至贿赂以获得并维系垄断权，有时还会以"全国冠军"的名义掩饰自己的垄断行为。同样，这些资源支出对于整体的社会福利没有帮助，只能算作效率低下。

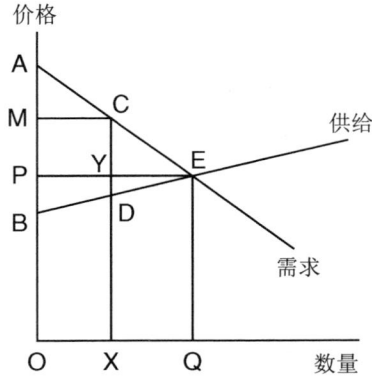

图17　垄断造成的效率低下

垄断的影响有多大？美国的医疗服务就是一个极端的例子。患者在他们的区域没有或几乎没有竞争性的选择，他们对于医疗价格和具有成本效益的治疗方案所知甚少，他们既没有时间也没有能力在紧急情况下做出合理的选择。如果某些患者购买了合适的医疗保险，并且具有合理的计算能力，他们也不会在乎高价。因此，供应商可以收取10倍乃至更多的费用。比如，一家脊柱刺激器的制造商以大约1.9万美元的价格把设备卖给一家医院，后者向病人收取了49 237美元的费用！（这还不包括医生和医院收取的安装费,一天门诊手术的总费用是86 951美元。)作为普遍规律,需求的价格敏感度越低,价格高于成本的潜在幅度就越大。

垄断和寡头垄断给整个经济体造成多少效率损失?研究者估算的数据相差很大,有人认为效率损失只占美国国内生产总值的0.1%,也有人认为比例高达7%。在反垄断法实施不那么严格的国家,这一比例可能更高。就算是1%的国内生产总值也已经相当可观:在美国,这一数字约等于每年1 500亿美元,即每个美国公民要承担500美元。从另一个角度看,国内生产总值下降2%,这大致等于1947年至2006年间经济衰退的平均水平,2007年至2009年的大衰退导致美国的国内生产总值下降了大约5%。但是,垄断造成的损失每年都会发生,而衰退则有所不同,每隔四五年才会出现一两年的衰退。因此,垄断造成的效率低下是一个严重问题,其规模不亚于宏观经济衰退。有效的反垄断政策也同样重要,但正如之前所言,政治进程可能会被现有的和未来的垄断者所控制。

创新和增长是否需要一些垄断力量?在这一点上,理论分析和实证研究都没有明确的结论。新的创意或产品所带来的暂时性垄断利润的前景,无论是受专利保护,还是仅仅因为其他公司需要时间来模仿和生产竞争对手的产品,都可能激励研发。以往的垄断权所产生的利润,也可能为这些活动提供内部融资。但是,牢固的垄断可能会削弱创新动力,企业可能会犹豫,是否开发足以蚕食其现有产品市场的新产品。在我看来,最重要的是保持进入市场的自由。这样,拥有新想法和新产品的企业家可以试探消费者的接受度,现有企业也将继续创新,以免输给新加入的企业。

正负外部性

消费者或公司的许多行为都有副作用,可能给他人带来好处,也可能造成伤害。当你开车的时候,你污染了空气,损害了别人的健康,而且你让道路变得更加拥挤,这增加了别人的驾驶时间。当你接种疫苗时,你不仅可以降低自己感染这种疾病的风险,还可以降低把它传染给他人的风险。如果你让自家院子保持美观,你会增加邻居和路人的乐趣。矿业公司和发电厂的有毒排放物和释放的温室气体会损害人们的健康,并可能危及人类的未来。

类似的情况下,个人和企业在做出选择时缺少让他们考虑副作用的激励。我们中的大多数人在计算得失时没有充分考虑到不自觉地给他人带来的伤害或利益。当我们忽视自己对他人造成的伤害时,我们的行动就会超过总体社会效率的最优水平。当我们忽视他人的利益时,我们就会做得太少。这就是为什么我们在路上总是会看到交通拥堵,为什么疫苗接种的人口覆盖率有时极低。经济学家将这种影响称为**外部性**。如果有益于他人,就称为正外部性;如果损害他人利益,就称为负外部性。

必须强调的是,并非每个行动造成的影响都属于外部性。当你买了某个物品,你就占用了制造该物品的人力、物力和其他资源,留给别人的物品更少。但是,在一个运作良好的竞争性市场中,你在购买时所支付的价格等于产品的边际成本。因此,你在行动时面对的是正确的稀缺性价格,并有正确的激励去节约利用社会的稀缺资源。只有当你没有面对正确的稀缺性价格,比如涉及清洁空气和道路，你的行动才会产生外部性。因此，什么是外部性取决于市场是否为该行动设置了正确的价格。不幸的是，市场往往缺失或者运作不当，因此外部性无处不在。

外部性的社会总成本是多少？有太多不同的情况都会产生外部性，很难计算可靠的总数字，但是有一个重要的实例有助于说明问题的严重性。1994年，《美国科学家》杂志刊登了理查德·阿诺特和肯尼斯·斯莫尔合作撰写的论文。他们的计算结果表明，美国的交通拥堵程度为60亿辆车/小时。假设每辆车的平均载客人数为1.5人，并且人均时间成本为每小时12美元（当年的平均工资），那么交通拥堵的总成本就是1 080亿美元。从那以后，这个数字肯定上升了。其他情况可能代价更高。如果全球气候变化的影响被证明像某些人担心的那样糟糕，碳排放的外部性成本可能十分巨大。

如何改善效率低下的问题？有两种方法：一种基于市场，另一种基于政府。每种方法都有各自的优缺点，哪种更有效取决于实际情况。两种方法都不够完美，但分别或组合起来，它们产生的显著改善总比什么都不做要好。

我们已经看到价格如何激励人们生产出消费者愿意花钱购买的商品和服务，同时减少对高价商品和服务的消费。基于市场的方法可以将这些洞见应用到包括清洁空气或有毒废物在内的特殊商品，否则这些就不可能有市场或价格。

一个市场要想正常运行，交易的物品必须明确界定，并且某人必须对它拥有"可转让"的权利，也就是可以把它出售给他人的权利。假设社会授予所有公民转让清洁空气的权利。如果某家企业的经营活动污染空气，该企业就必须从他们那里购买权利。它愿意支付一定的价格,最高不超过经营获得的额外利润。在某个价格,如果公民判断他们得到的钱比他们即将遭受的污染所造成的损害更值钱,他们可能愿意出售权利。如果公司愿意支付的价格超过了公民需求的总数,双方就能开展交易。交易使双方都过得更好(根据各自的判断),从而提高了帕累托效率。

或者,公司可以被赋予污染的权利,并允许与公民签订可强制执行的合同,承诺在对方支付一定价格后,就不会造成污染。这也提高了效率(为强化理解,我建议你们围绕这个案例自行推理)。两种情况下,效率收益的分配有所不同:任何一方在拥有权利时总是比另一方得到更多好处。

如果这样的市场能够建立起来并且运作良好,那么价格就会存在,并且会以平常的方式有效地传递信息和激励。比如,如果清洁空气非常稀缺,公民将索要高价来许可污染。如果企业必须为此付出代价来污染,它们就有强激励使用或开发污染较少的技术。这就是碳排放交易市场背后的激励因素,比如欧洲和美国加利福尼亚州已经在进行这样的操作。

不幸的是,很难创造和维护这种运作良好的市场。也许排放市场最大的困难在于,清洁空气是一种公共产品,而不是每一个人都会购买并消费的私人产品(比如面包)。同样的空气影响到同一地区的每个人,碳排放可能影响到地球上的每个人。市场必须找出每个受影响的人愿意接受的允许排放量增加的价格,并且计算总价。人们会把这个体系变成博弈。每个人都认为,如果他或她夸大价格,对结果的影响很小。然而,当他们都这样做时,总价会变得如此之高,以至于公司不愿支付,最终市场崩溃。更糟糕的是，如果长期存在的污染和排放可能造成永久性伤害，比如全球变暖，而将受到不利影响的未来世代的人却无法参与如今的市场。在其他情况下，还会出现其他困难。大体上，罗纳德·科斯提出的市场具有交易成本的洞见在这个例子中是正确的，正如讨论企业在做制造还是购买的决策时他的洞见有效一样，我在第三章已经讨论过这个问题。

事实上，科斯对于如何用市场方法来应对外部性影响做出了开创性分析。他认为，**如果**没有交易成本，市场将产生有效的解决方案，不需要政府的干预（只需扮演通常的角色，即界定和执行产权，并且强制执行自愿签订的私人合同）。这个观点后来常常遭到误解：人们经常忘记科斯在提出观点时强调的**如果**，同时，一个重要的隐含条件——有效的市场——被很多人错误地认为是一个普遍规则。

在小规模的稳定群体中，借助长期关系和声誉，行动易于监控和执行。哪怕没有自上而下的治理结构，也可以维持科斯的有效结果。事实上，内部人可获得的本地信息使自下而上的集体行动更具优势。试想一下，房东如果保持房屋和花园的美观，可以给邻居带来好处。公寓管委会可以制定日常规范和制裁措施，很好地处理这一问题。即使只有非正式的社会压力要求个人遵守社区规范，也能产生正确的效果。政府官员会发现，很难弄清楚某个群体对这些问题的真实看法，并制定和执行适当的法律条文。

在原始案例研究和关于其他研究的分析中，埃莉诺·奥斯特罗姆展示了自下而上的集体行动所具有的潜力和局限性，她也因此荣获诺贝尔经济学奖。渔业是一个很好的例子。每个人的捕鱼量都会减少其他人潜在的捕捞数量。这种负外部性可能导致过度捕捞,甚至种群灭绝,从而损害所有人的利益。渔民们全都意识到这个问题,但他们每个人对灭绝风险的影响微乎其微,而且增加捕鱼量对他们都有好处。因此,他们陷入了囚徒困境。小规模的稳定群体,比如在湖泊捕鱼的人,可以规定鱼的大小和分配方式,并且使用包括社会排斥在内的惩罚威胁来执行这些规定。但是,海洋渔业要想做到这一点,难度更大,因为鱼类迁移得很远,而且渔民来自许多国家和地区。过度捕捞已经导致大西洋鳕鱼、智利黑鲈、蓝鳍金枪鱼和其他海洋鱼类濒临灭绝。

有时,科斯提出的解决方法不只是适用于小规模的关系密切的社会群体。养蜂人提供授粉服务,使果园主受益。这是经济学著作中最早提到的正外部性的例子之一。实际上,私人安排很好地解决了这个问题:养蜂人通过租借的方式,向果园主提供他们的服务。这超出了地方交易的范围,养蜂人把移动蜂箱安放在卡车上,随着开花季节的变化,从南到北途经不同的地区。

接下来,考虑基于政府的解决办法。其中包括与价格类似的激励措施,即税收或补贴。这类政策被称为"庇古税",因为20世纪英国经济学家阿瑟·庇古率先提出这类分析。碳排放税促使企业采用清洁技术;对太阳能或风能发电提供补贴,同样会促使电力公司采用这些方法。

一项行动的税收或补贴应等于该行动附带产生的对于他人的损害或利益。为了快速理解这一点,不妨想一想,汽车驾驶人违反交通法规的行为,要比行人违反道路交通法规的行为受到

74 更仔细的监控和更严厉的处罚。这样做很有道理，因为汽车驾驶人的错误会比行人造成更大的负外部性。

外部性的成本很难评估。客观的衡量往往做不到。如果询问当事人，他们可能不会给出诚实的回答。如果政府决定赔偿公众和企业，弥补别人的污染给他们造成的损失，他们或许会夸大其词。如果政府决定向公众和企业征税或罚款，对他们排放有毒物质进行惩戒，他们或许会转移到危害更大的排放口，从而避交税款。如果所需的信息是纯粹的统计信息，只与人口的总数有关，而不关乎个人或特定的企业，那么更有希望把外部性计算清楚，因为可以通过匿名抽样调查获得数据，前提是人们相信他们的匿名性会受到尊重！

现代技术使得某些情况下更容易收集所需信息。比如，许多城市现在对进入拥挤的市中心的汽车征收通行费。管理者使用安置在中心区域外围的摄像头拍摄汽车牌照，并向车主发送账单，或者使用更先进的安装在汽车上的应答设备。这些费用的金额会根据一天中的时间变化而变化，甚至可以根据实际拥堵程度进行调整，市中心有许多地点安装了摄像头，持续进行监控。

政府也可以尝试数量管控，比如限制或禁止排放，规定汽车的最低燃油效率，等等。但是，这些政策需要大量信息，而那些发布和实施管控的政府机构通常无法直接得到信息，而且企业又缺少如实汇报的激励。比如，假设该国已经限定了总排放量，但仍需在各个企业之间进行分配。一家没有许可证的企业必须找到其他办法来减少或消除排放，这需要付出昂贵的代价。因

75 此，将排放配额分给减排成本最高的企业，是一种有效的办法。

但这样一来,为了获得更多的许可证,每家公司都想夸大成本。最好还是用一种类似市场的解决方案,让企业采取实际行动:拍卖配额。这样一来,那些最难做到减少排放的企业就会为配额出价最多。

总配额的确定也很困难,而且常常变得政治化。事实上,欧盟的碳排放交易市场正受到这些问题的困扰。颁发的许可证太多,导致价格暴跌,这项计划因此偏离了原先的意图。

综上所述,无论是科斯式的基于市场的方法还是庇古式的基于政府的方法,都有各自的问题。幸运的是,两类问题各不相同。科斯式的方法在小规模的关系稳定的群体中效果更好。如果可以使用匿名统计信息,庇古式的方法在大规模群体中效果更好。即便如此,如果政府的政策具有市场化的特点,比如拍卖排放配额,而不是通过官僚程序直接授予,那么这些政策的效果可能会更好。在某些情况下,两种方法混合之后,或许能达到最佳效果。比如,规定拍卖配额,但同时可以在二级市场交易。情况会随着时间的推移发生变化,改变这些市场的均衡以保持效率。即使这两种方法联合起来也不能完美地解决所有的外部性,但没有东西是完美的,我们必须接受缺点最少的解决方案。

有一个例子能让你记住这两种方法的相对优势。这个例子用在这里可能不太妥当,我要为此道歉,但正因为如此,它才令人印象深刻。如果你提高自己的性爱技巧,你的伴侣会得到更多乐趣。如何处理这种外部性?在一夫一妻制社会中,夫妻可以通过私人协议实现科斯的最优解。但是在某些性行为混乱的社会中,政府可以为"婚姻技艺"教育提供类似庇古税的专项补贴,从而实现更好的结果。

信息不对称

市场要想运作良好,需要一个重要的、时常被忽视的前提条件:交易各方应该清楚知道他们在买卖什么。但在许多情况下,一方比另一方更了解内幕:卖方比买方更了解产品质量,购买保单的个人比发行保单的保险公司更了解自己的风险。解释、发掘、隐藏或揭示信息的各种策略,在这类互动中起着关键作用,并且影响市场结果。

诺贝尔经济学奖得主乔治·阿克洛夫对"柠檬"(代指有严重缺陷的汽车)市场的分析向经济学家发出了警告,提醒他们注意此类影响,包括市场彻底崩溃的可能性。我在第一章中提到了这一点,接下来让我们来看更完整的分析。

考虑下面的例子。每辆车的状况是个未知数,如果它的质量可以得到可靠的保证,那就是价值1.5万美元的完美选择。但也有可能质量糟糕,毫无价值。在全部汽车中,优质车占三分之二,劣质车占三分之一。每个卖家都知道自己的汽车类型,但潜在买家不知道任何一辆车的质量。买家愿意支付他们认为的市场上汽车的平均价值。

市场价格是不是 $2/3 \times 15\,000 + 1/3 \times 0 = 10\,000$ 美元?是的,前提条件是,市场上的汽车是总体的代表性样本。但事实并非如此。卖家在知道汽车质量可靠的情况下,不愿意以10 000美元的价格卖掉它。有些人可能会因为搬家、财务困难或其他原因出售。为便于计算,假设优质车的卖家中有一半的人愿意以10 000美元的价格出售。劣质车的卖家当然很高兴能卖出这个价格。因此,市场上的汽车组合包括:占车辆总数三分之一的劣质车，加上三分之二的二分之一的优质车。因此，整个市场是不同质量汽车的混合体，两种车的数量相等，汽车的平均价值为：$1/2 \times 15\,000 + 1/2 \times 0 = 7\,500$ 美元。

但这并不是故事的结局。在这样的低价格下，更多的优质卖家退出了市场：搬家的人可能决定自己开车，或者那些陷入经济困境的人说服他们的亲戚帮忙。假设只剩下四分之一的优质车，此时市场上的组合是：占车辆总数三分之一的劣质车，加上三分之二的四分之一的优质车。劣质车和优质车的比例是二比一：在市场上的二手车中，有三分之一是优质车，三分之二是劣质车。所以平均价值下降为：$1/3 \times 15\,000 + 2/3 \times 0 = 5\,000$ 美元。

这一过程可能一直持续，直到所有的优质车都退出，只有劣质车留在二手车市场。但是，即使没有如此彻底的市场崩溃，二手车市场也已经成为汽车总体不具有代表性的样本。劣质车比重过高，优质车十分罕见。

虽然富有戏剧性，但现实中是否真的会出现市场崩溃？任何买过二手车的人都知道这一过程充满了不确定性，买家对质量充满了担忧。但二手车市场总是存在，买家能够买到优质二手车。这些优质车主有办法向买家提供可靠的保证。

声誉是一种重要的手段。在私人市场中，如果卖家是朋友，或者是朋友的朋友，甚至是关系链上隔了好几层的朋友，那么卖家会希望保持整个友谊网络的良好关系，并且很可能会坦诚告诉对方，车子有哪些已知的缺陷。保修是一种很好的手段，但买家不确定在需要时是否能找到卖家，并且后者是否会履行承诺，这最终还是取决于卖家的声誉。

那么，专业经销商可靠吗？二手车经销商可能会欺骗一些客户，从而迅速获利，但它们的不良声誉会传播开来，这样它们在这一行很快就干不下去了。但你如何知道正在和你谈判的经销商是准备长期经营还是打算捞一票？你在寻找证据，观察对方是否稳定经营。经销商是否同时销售知名品牌的新车？经销商在那个地方待了一段时间了吗？这家店是给人一种持久经营的感觉，还是一切看起来都可以拆除，店面在几天之内就能变成一家餐馆？稳定经营的迹象需要付出昂贵的成本，没有铺设路面的停车场和一间临时充当办公室的小屋，要比豪华的店面和保养良好的停车场便宜得多。正是这种经营成本让人信赖。想长期从事这项业务的商人可以分期偿还多年成本，因此他能负担这些，而只想捞一票的人却做不到。同样的原则也有助于解释，为什么银行拥有令人印象深刻的宽敞经营场所。他们宣称：“我们一直在这里经营，所以你把钱存放在我们银行很安全。”

迈克尔·斯彭斯因发展了工作中高成本信号的思想，而与乔治·阿克洛夫及约瑟夫·斯蒂格利茨共同获得了诺贝尔经济学奖。他们三人开创了不对称信息经济学。斯彭斯的理论在劳动力市场上得到了最好的解释。想象一下你正在面试一份工作。谈话内容如下：

雇主：这项工作需要优秀的量化分析技能和可靠的职业道德。

你：没问题，这两样我都有。

雇主：我为什么要相信你？任何人都可以这么说。

你：看我的大学成绩单。我选修了高难度的数学、统计学和经济学课程,然后拿到了优秀的成绩。这不仅需要一流的量化分析技能,而且需要毅力,每天晚上完成所有的习题集作业。

雇主:难道不是每个人都会做同样的事来争取这份高薪工作吗?

你:不,一个没有掌握量化分析的学生不可能胜任这项工作,一个缺乏真正奉献精神的学生会屈服于校园社交生活的诱惑。

好话谁都会说;雇主希望你"拿出证据来"。你提供了你的教育成就作为**信号**,证明你拥有雇主想要的品质。信号的成本是昂贵的:你必须花费时间和努力,抵制诱惑,才能得到信号。但更重要的是:一些人缺乏你的信号所展示的品质,对他们来说,信号的成本非常昂贵,因为需要付出大量的时间和努力,还要放弃各种校园聚会。这种**成本差异**意味着,当你拥有了雇主需要的品质,你可以负担信号的成本,而缺少这些品质的人却不能。正是这样的差异把你和任何想要模仿或伪装的人区分开来,并且使雇主相信你对自身品质的断言。

因此,信号可以解决信息不对称的问题,但要付出成本。谁付出这个成本取决于具体情况。在教育的例子中,那些缺少定量分析技能和职业道德的人想要得到高薪工作(至少一年左右,直到他们被发现并淘汰),他们就得模仿真正的专业人士的行为,除非某些行为实在难以模仿。其中的障碍通常必须超过真正有助于提高工作效率的教育水平。因此,天生技术娴熟和敬业的人必须花费一些时间和努力来获得教育,就生产力而言,这样的教育其实是种浪费，仅仅是为了传递信号。只要有傻瓜和懒汉存在，那些更好的学生就必须证明他们不是傻瓜或懒汉，这同样是一种成本！

我们可以把这个例子与前一节中关于外部性的讨论联系起来。这些傻瓜和懒汉，只要他们存在，就把负外部性强加于那些拥有技能和敬业精神的人，后者必须在教育中投入超额成本，以证明他们不是傻瓜或懒汉。事实上，外部性可以用来分析信息不对称的许多影响，而外部性引起的市场失灵可以通过科斯式的方法或庇古式的方法（视情况而定）加以补救。我将在本章的结尾部分讨论和说明这种方法。

与信号恰好相反的是我们在第三章中遇到的价格歧视的筛选做法。在筛选时，企业成了互动关系中缺少信息的一方，它们需要选择定价策略，来挑选和吸引那些能够带给它们最大利润的买家，同时排斥其他类型的买家。拥有足够信息的一方发出信号，但在许多情况下，可以由缺少信息的一方实施筛选。比如在教育的例子中，雇主可以（并且经常这样）规定足够严苛的资格，只有真正拥有技能和敬业精神的工人才能达到。然后他们开始筛选，而不是向他们发出信号的申请人。

一旦你理解了这个概念，你就会发现信号和筛选无处不在，不仅在市场上，而且在各种社会互动中都能看到。下面是一个小例子。

黑手党有入会仪式，要求新招募的人员执行特定的犯罪行为，通常是谋杀。这些措施用来确保新手具备必要的强硬和残忍，但它们同时也是筛选警方卧底或调查记者的有效手段：如果测试只需要表现出强硬，准备卧底或调查的人可能会遵守，但如果需要犯罪,他们就做不到。

进化生物学中的性选择理论认为,雌性选择配偶时特别注意遗传优势,因为它们的繁殖机会有限,必须设法使每个后代的适应性最大化。雄鹿的大鹿角,或者孔雀和天堂鸟浓密而精致的羽毛,都是一种携带和防御的障碍。因此,它们是遗传质量的可靠信号:只有极为强壮的雄性动物才能拥有足够资源来生长和维持这些特征。

最后是日常生活中的一个例子。假设你第一次和你觉得有魅力的人约会。你知道你要留下良好的第一印象,因为不会有第二次机会。但你也知道,你的约会对象会提防虚假的第一印象。换句话说,你发出信号,你约会的对象在筛选。如果对方发现你很有吸引力,那么在其他方面也会有交流。在这种情况下,什么是好的信号?什么是好的筛选方法?二者都可能取决于特定的环境,所以我把问题留给你,想想看,在你所处的环境中,什么样的做法能够产生效果。我只强调仔细思考的重要性。如果你不知道正在进行的信号游戏,那么你很可能会失去一辈子的幸福:没有给出可靠的信号,或者没有做出有效的筛选。

道德风险与逆向选择

用保险市场作为例子,可以说明两种重要的信息不对称类型。人们可以通过饮食和锻炼来减少健康风险。保险合同可以规定投保人必须这样做,但保险公司对于投保人执行情况的监控很不完善。人们会逃避锻炼,或者吃高热量的甜点。某种程度上,在拥有医疗保险的情况下,他们更容易受到诱惑。保险公司当然认为这种行为不道德。保险业为此创造了**"道德风险"**

一词。它现在已成为标准的经济用法,指在特定的交易环境中,一方的行为对于另一方来说无法观察,或者对于可能被要求执行合同的第三方来说无法证明。

与保险公司相比,投保人更了解自己的固有风险。那么,任何给定的保险合同对风险最大的人都极具吸引力,保险公司有选择地吸引了这些人购买它的产品。这叫作**逆向选择**。同样,该术语更为常见的用法,指的是当交易的一方比另一方更了解某些属性时做出的选择。阿克洛夫研究的劣质车市场就是一个很好的例子。二手车的车主比潜在买家更了解汽车的质量。因此,无论在何种价格,市场吸引的总是汽车质量相对较低的卖家。

我们已经分析过,二手车市场为什么有可能会失灵。医疗保健也会出现类似问题。美国颁布的《平价医疗法》(所谓的"奥巴马医改")规定,所有申请人都可以按规定的价格投保。老年人和健康程度较差的人更希望得到医保。年轻人和健康程度较好的人可能选择不参加保险,即使他们必须支付法律为此规定的小额罚款。于是,保险池逆向选择了最坏的健康风险;如果政策要求财务上自给自足,那么保险费必须足够高,以支付它们的成本。

在交易中处于信息劣势的当事人可以用各种办法来应对他们的劣势。我们在上一节中讨论的筛选是应对逆向选择的方法。通过设定免赔金额和共付金额而提供部分保险,可以降低保险业中的道德风险。这迫使投保人面临一定的风险,并给予他们一定的激励,以降低风险。通过将员工的报酬与其行为的可观察后果挂钩,可以减少工作场所的道德风险。比如,假设雇主可以观察到产出或利润,并且员工工作的质量或数量在一定程度上对于产出或利润产生影响,那么基于产出的薪资或利润分享将会减轻道德风险。但是,这些方式都不可能达到理论上所假设的具有完全和对称信息可能性的效率结果。仍然存在的低效率类似于一种外部性,在本章的后面部分,我会用近期的金融危机作为案例来进行分析。

企业间的利润外部性

一家企业的行为会影响其产品的替代品和互补品的需求,从而影响销售这些产品的企业的利润。这种相互作用对市场结构有影响,因此对这些产品的消费者也会产生经济影响。

假设咖啡和茶(互为替代品)由不同的企业生产和销售,每家企业都有一定的市场影响力。我们不妨将这两家企业称为爪哇和阿萨姆。如果爪哇提高了咖啡的价格,需求就转向茶(参见第二章的图3和相应的分析)。随着茶叶需求的增加,阿萨姆可以提高价格,获得更多利润。这就好像爪哇将正外部性赋予阿萨姆。但是,爪哇并不关心阿萨姆的利润,它忽略了外部性。因此,它不会将价格提升到两家公司的综合利益所能达到的最大值。阿萨姆的定价决定也有同样的问题。这两家公司最好合并成一家,我们不妨称之为咖啡因,这样一来,两家公司的产品价格都会上涨,利润也会超过各自公司的利润总和。当然,更高的价格伤害了消费者。由此可见,互为替代品的制造商有合并的动机,反垄断政策应该警惕由此导致的价格上涨,以免损害消费者的利益。

接下来考虑互补品。假设计算机硬件和软件分别由两家企业制造和销售，我们不妨将它们称为芯片和代码。如果芯片提高了硬件的价格，对软件的需求就会下降，这将减少代码的利润。这是一种负外部性。在任何像污染这样具有负外部性的活动中，私人选择都会导致过度。在这个例子中，芯片推动其价格上涨的幅度超过了两家公司的共同利益。代码也是如此。如果这两家企业合并，它将会降低两种价格来增加总利润：每种产品的较低价格足以刺激对另一种产品的需求。更低的价格也有利于消费者。这是一种罕见的双赢局面，合并有利于两家企业和消费者。反垄断政策不应该禁止互补企业合并。相反，应该鼓励它们！

艰难的权衡

许多产品的初版成本很高，并且这些成本产生之后，供给每个单位的边际成本很小。最好的例子来自科技行业。为操作系统、浏览器和大型应用程序创建和调试软件需要许多程序员花费数月时间，并且要花费数百万美元。然而，这些程序一旦准备就绪，就可以在网络上快速传播，几乎没有新的成本。制药行业的情况类似。研究、开发和测试每种新的特效药需要花费巨额成本，特别是因为每种成功的药物背后都需要进行许多次失败的试验。然而，一旦药物获得批准，生产和交付的成本很低。

这些产品应该如何定价？试试考虑这些产品上市后的情况。此时要做到有效率，就必须扩大供给，直到下一个单位产品的支付意愿等于其边际成本。这意味着软件的价格非常低，几乎为零。事实上，许多理想主义者提出了这样的倡议。他们说信息可以免费（或几乎免费）传播给每个人，所以不应该收费。他们认为，一种救命药的价格如果高于低廉的生产成本，在道义上就应该受到谴责。

但是，如果定价过低，这些产品的制造商将无法收回高昂的初版成本。如果真的出现这样的案例，以低价销售现有产品，使制造商承担初版成本，这将会打击未来的药物研究人员和软件开发商的热情，也将伤害未来的消费者。这个观点很有道理，不过有时企业会故意宣扬这样的观点，以证明垄断价格超出初版成本和必要激励的合理比例的正当性。

因此，社会政策面临着不可避免的两难困境（或者说权衡），一方面要促进新的研究和开发，另一方面要以低廉的边际成本传播成果。解决办法是采取折中方案：开发或生产此类产品的公司或个人在有限的时间内被授予垄断权，用于销售相关产品：对于药品和其他创新产品来说，这种权利被称为专利权；对于软件和书籍来说，这种权利被称为版权。

为什么不用一般税收收入来支付初版成本，让生产者只收取较低（可能接近零）的边际成本呢？因为这样的制度会产生负面的激励作用。没有人预先知道一种新药是否有效，或者一本新书是否值得阅读，或者一个软件是否值得使用。江湖骗子和有内部关系的人会通过游说政府来获取丰厚报酬，其实他们只是在虚张声势，直到最后承认失败。稀缺的药物或高度专业化的计算机程序只有极少数的潜在消费者，他们会鼓动造势，以获得纳税人对他们特殊需求的支持。专利和版权制度让开发者和消费者用他们的钱而不是他们的嘴来降低这类风险。这并不是完美的制度，但再强调一次，任何事物都不是完美的。

集体产品

当市场运作良好的时候,它能以经济有效的方式满足个人的需求。下一章中,我们将会讨论其他制度,在市场效率低下的某些环境中,这些制度也能做到这一点。但许多商品和服务本质上具有集体属性。让个人来决定是否付钱享受这些商品和服务,这往往行不通。因为每个人通常都会尽量减少用于商品或服务的支出,希望能从别人的付出中得到搭便车的机会。如果尝试这样做的人太多,那么付款总额不够成本,商品或服务也就无法提供。这是囚徒博弈最糟糕的均衡状态:不管其他人做什么,对于每个人来说最好的策略都是不付钱,但是当他们都这样做时,结果对他们所有人来说都很糟糕。

教育人们认识这种困境并要求他们减少自私行为还不够。是的,如果人们充分考虑到他人的利益,他们就不会去搭便车。不过,尽管行为经济学发现人们并非完全自私,但在涉及数百万人的经济体中,能够观察到的利他主义的程度普遍过低,以致无法在纯粹自愿的基础上充分提供大多数的集体产品和服务。还记得《第二十二条军规》中的约塞连上尉吗?在几乎获胜的战争中,他不想成为最后死去的人。上级军官试图劝说他:"如果每个人都这么想,会发生什么?"他回答说:"既然大家都这么想,如果我的想法和别人不一样,那我肯定是个傻子,不是吗?"

解决此类困境的集体行动是原因之一,正如1776年《美国独立宣言》所言,"人们在他们中间建立政府,而政府的正当权力,源自被统治者的同意"。政府可以通过征税或其他收费来为集体产品和服务提供资金。

我特意强调"可以"这个词,因为对于许多集体产品的供给来说,政府利用征税来提供或许并不是唯一的甚至最好的办法。我们必须区分这种商品的两个不同方面。一个方面是它的集体属性:它可以同时被几个人消费或使用。这和面包不一样:如果一个人吃了面包,其他人就没法再吃。集体产品的另一个方面是,不可能排除那些没有付款的人,不让他们消费或受益于集体产品或服务。国防可能是最极端的例子:当一个国家受到攻击时,军队会保卫所有公民,不可能把那些不缴税的人挑选出来提供给敌人,任由他们被俘虏或杀害。集体消费的产品和服务以及无法排除他人的商品和服务被称为**纯公共产品**。

实际上,集体消费和排除他人都是程度问题。一条道路可以容纳许多车辆,但会变得拥堵。因此,如果有太多的司机同时到达,道路状况就会很糟糕。排除他人可以在一定程度上允许私人为许多集体产品提供资金。就连看似供路过船只免费使用的灯塔,也可以通过向经过附近港口的船只收取费用的办法来获得资金。收费公路已经有几个世纪的历史。设有门岗的社区雇用私人警卫来保护居民。涉及广泛公共利益的服务,比如教育、医疗保健和垃圾收集,可以由私人来提供(哪怕是用税收来支付),而且通常比公共服务更有效。有了这些限定性条件,政府能够在提供接近于纯公共产品概念范畴的产品和服务方面发挥重要作用。

政策的政治经济学

我们已经分析了几个原因,用来解释市场为何没能展现其最狂热信徒所期盼的魔力。市场失灵的主要类型有垄断势力、外部性、集体产品和不对称信息成本。在每一种情况下,政府都可以制定并实施政策来改善市场结果,有时甚至可以完全取代市场。事实上,市场狂热信徒的反对群体期望政府能创造奇迹。在我看来,事情更加微妙和复杂。政府也会遭遇失灵,但这种失灵不同于市场失灵。明智的选择是让每个机构在其能够提供更好结果的领域中运作,但缺乏可靠的机制来确保这种选择。在实践中,整个社会只能混沌前行,接受一些效率低下的现象,同时希望在问题变得过于严重之前发现并纠正它们。

为什么许多人相信市场的魔力?通常是因为他们错误地认为结果总是(帕累托)有效的,但他们没有考虑到我强调的那些条件和限制。为什么另一边的极端主义者相信政府的魔力?通常是因为他们把自己想象成仁慈的计划制定者,他们可以根据自己的诸如效率、平等、公正、可持续性等标准,对经济中的每一件事都进行最好的排序——这样的场景与制定和实施经济政策过程的现实相去甚远。实际的过程在许多方面都不符合理想。在这里,我只想指出一些突出的问题。

即使在最好的环境中,也就是每个人的选票都同等重要的民主国家,政治学告诉我们,政策结果将代表中间选民的偏好,即在相关维度(例如从左派到右派,或者从富到穷)的政治光谱中恰好排在第五十个百分位的选民。这也许能或不能反映每个人的福祉之和,更不用说担心像公正或可持续性这样的问题。

事实上,这个过程不同于理想化的代议制民主。与立法者和官员接近的渠道、媒体和公共论坛的发言权、游说能力和政治献金,以及在某些情况下的直接贿赂,这些都是制定和实施政策过程中至关重要的部分,并且这些都会造成不平等。富人有明显的优势,有组织的群体同样如此。对于有共同利益的群体来说,组织政治参与是一种集体行动。贡献金钱、时间和努力都涉及搭便车现象,每个人都希望其他人去做这些事,自己则坐享其成。不同的群体在不同程度上成功地解决了集体行动问题。简单来说,如果群体规模相对较小,并且每个成员涉及的利益较多,他们就比利益分散的大规模群体组织得更好。美国的食糖进口和价格支持政策就是一个引人注目的例子。这些政策使美国的糖价居高不下,有利于国内糖料作物种植者和替代品(比如高果糖浆)生产商。据估计,在20世纪80年代中期,消费者的损失约为39亿美元,生产者的收益为28亿美元,因此美国经济的净损失为11亿美元。但美国当时有约2.5亿人口,每个消费者的损失仅为15美元,就不值得去鼓动或组织。作为对比,甜菜种植户平均每人可以获得5万美元,甘蔗种植户平均每人获得50万美元!因此,他们自发组织起来,游说政府支持限制性政策。

具有特权渠道进入政治舞台的个人、企业或团体会为政策进行游说,以牺牲全体公民的利益为代价,争取对他们有利的政策。企业和行业通过限制竞争而受益,因此它们可以保持较高的价格,享受垄断或寡头垄断带来的利润。它们想要监管和许可,以阻止国内的新企业加入市场;以及关税、配额或其他壁垒,来应对进口产品的竞争。对于后者,它们得到了劳工组织的支持。它们通常声称这些政策是亲企业的,但实际上这通常意味着有利于现有企业。它们歧视那些会带来新想法、新产品和新方法的新企业,担心后者带来竞争,影响到现有企业的利益。真正有利于整个国家的不是**亲企业**的政策,而是**亲市场**的政策。这意味着促进竞争,从而节约成本,促进产品创新,并提高市场效率。

任何稀缺性都会创造一种收益,这被称为**经济租**。图18显示了某个市场的状况,在价格N,供给曲线上的点D对应的数量为X。如果政策限制供给的数量,需求和供给相等的点变成了C,此时价格为M,高于原来的N。因此,高度MN是从O到X每一单位数量所获得的额外收益。图中阴影所表示的矩形MNDC的面积,是从稀缺性中获得的总收益或经济租。这种商品的生产者将会因为创造这样的稀缺性并获取租金而受益。如果它们不能协调一致在本行业形成垄断或寡头垄断,它们就可以利用某种借口游说政府制定相应政策,创造出对自己有利的稀缺性。这种寻租的政治活动很普遍,可以说无处不在,而且尽管它们声称出于公益的动机才寻求政策支持,但事实上这些政策通常会像私人垄断一样损害整个经济的利益。进口壁垒就是如此。还有一些政策,比如限制进入某个职业的认证要求,限制在一座城市中运营的出租车数量,或者限制在用餐时能够售卖酒精饮料的餐馆数量。现有的专业人士、出租车司机和餐馆老板从中获利,损害的是潜在的加入者和公众的利益。

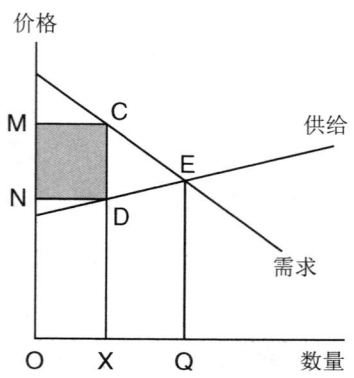

图18　经济租

糟糕政策的影响可能因它们创造了特殊利益群体而变得更加复杂,后者会为了延续政策而战。比如,美国设立了食糖的进口限制,这使得像高果糖浆这样的替代品有利可图。玉米农场主和高果糖浆的生产企业随后成为维持进口限制的有力游说者,这不仅损害了美国消费者的经济利益,甚至不利于他们的健康,如果有关高果糖浆有损健康的说法属实的话。执行政策的官僚体系和办事机构同样有利益牵涉,它们也会强力抵制政策改革。

在西方分权制民主国家,游说和寻租活动最为明显。这可能会让一些读者认为,集权体制能够更好地提高经济效率。这种想法也符合一种倾向,即认为集权更有利于经济发展,因为它们更容易做出决断。比如,许多评论者注意到,印度的分权式民主进程减缓了基础设施建设的速度,而中国凭借其高效的征地制度实现了快速发展。但一些国家的集权体制也有其自身的内部政治和只惠及一些特殊群体的低效政策,通常是掌权者和他们的亲属,或者他们的民族同胞或地区民众。这是一个很容易理解的问题。假设你确信迅速做出决断是好事,并希望你的国家能拥有一个集权体制,那就需要确保他或她最终会成为下一个李光耀(新加坡前总理,带领该国走向繁荣),而不是下一个蒙博托·塞塞·塞科(刚果前总统,导致该国陷入贫困)。

金融危机

金融危机始于2007—2008年,当时美国和其他许多国家房价下跌,导致住房抵押贷款违约,持有这些抵押贷款或抵押担保证券的金融企业受到牵连,有些甚至破产。这场危机导致了所谓的"大衰退"。虽然到了2013年一些国家的经济状况有所复苏，但这场危机的负面影响仍然在持续。

这或许不是微观经济学的研究内容。金融危机的主要表现形式，即许多国家出现高失业率和国内生产总值大幅下降，实际上属于宏观经济。但这些现象背后的驱动因素——多重市场失灵以及本章讨论的政策失灵——依然属于微观经济学。2010年，美国金融危机调查委员会召开会议，委员会主席菲尔·安吉利迪斯将这次危机比作阿加莎·克里斯蒂的小说《东方快车谋杀案》。这种说法很贴切，因为在此次事件中，"每个人都犯错"——银行家极度贪婪，房主容易受骗，决策者迎合特殊利益群体，等等。篇幅有限，我只能分析几个方面，我特意选择那些能够说明市场失灵和政策失灵的例子。

大多数金融公司都是**中介机构**：它们在储蓄盈余或利润盈余的人（称他们为"存款人"）和因支出或投资需要而出现赤字的人（称他们为"借款人"）之间提供资金往来的渠道。如果借款人承诺他们将来给出的回报高于存款人提供资金时提出的要求，中介机构就可以进行一项惠及所有人的交易。它为双方当事人提供回报，同时为自己赚取利润。当然，这些活动会带来多种形式的风险。

首先，借款人可能无法兑现承诺的回报。如果他们最终破产，可能什么也不会返还，包括本金。价格波动、自然灾害和政治变动等随机因素可能会摧毁企业的价值。但借款人如果出现能力不足、疏忽大意或直接欺诈等问题，也可能会影响还款。中介机构应当有能力判断借款人的资质，并对借款人的行为进行尽职调查。事实上，这是中介机构存在的理由之一。中介机构还可以贷款给彼此风险没有关联的不同借款人，以此来降低存款人的风险。当然,这些做法都不能完全消除风险。

其次,许多金融中介机构进行**期限转换**。这使得存款人能够在临时通知或没有任何通知的情况下,收回他们的资金,因为借款的个人往往无法归还或不愿归还这笔钱。每一家中介机构都与许多储户打交道,只有一小部分储户可能会在同一时间提出取款要求,除非有什么事情使存款人惊慌失措。因此,中介机构能够将存款中相对较小的一部分作为流动资产或资本储备,以长期贷款的形式借出其余部分,以换取更高的回报。然而,这当中仍然存在**流动性风险**,即中介机构无法满足存款人当场取款的要求,虽然说最终它能够提供足够高的回报——换句话说,它仍然**具有偿付能力**。

另一个复杂的情况是,存款人对流动性或偿付能力的看法取决于他们的信念,而他们的信念可能受到其他因素的影响,不仅限于借款人或中介机构这样的客观因素。最好的例子来自文学作品。在小说《欢乐满人间》中,两个孩子简和迈克尔的父亲在一家银行工作。孩子们去银行找他,迈克尔拿着两便士,准备去买鸟食,因为他们过会儿要去特拉法加广场。父亲的主管建议迈克尔先把钱存到银行里,这样还能拿到利息。他从迈克尔手里抢走了两个便士,迈克尔喊道:"把钱还给我!"在柜台办理业务的一位女士听到他的喊声,以为银行没钱了。她要求取走她的全部存款。别的客户听到之后,也提出同样的要求,于是银行遭到挤兑。

这个故事展示了流动性风险如何在银行业中创造两种均衡。首先,人们相信银行的安全性。因此,他们愿意把钱留在那里,要求立即取款的呼声很低,银行确实很安全。另一方面,人们又怀疑银行的安全性,每个人都试图在形势恶化之前把钱取出来，因此银行遭遇挤兑，无法正常营业。因为意外和错误所造成的恐惧，结果可能会从前者突然转到后者，就像《欢乐满人间》中的这段小插曲。但也有可能面临真正的恐惧，比如房价下跌时，公众得知某家银行拥有大量的抵押贷款组合——在恐慌蔓延的过程中，真正的恐惧会被放大。

不良贷款不仅会给银行带来流动性风险，还可能会带来偿付能力风险。借款人任何粗心大意、疏忽或欺诈行为，都会给银行和存款人带来风险。银行放贷时的任何疏忽大意都会增加这种风险。如果当事各方充分了解借款人或银行的资质和行为，他们就可以签订带有适当附加条款的合同。比如，存款人可以规定银行在选择借款人时应保持高度警惕。但这显然不现实，因为信息严重不对称。在这种情况下，如果银行在选择或监控借款人时粗心大意，就会给存款人带来代价高昂的风险，而借款人如果缺乏能力或疏忽大意，也会给银行和存款人带来代价高昂的风险。这些都是由信息不对称引起的溢出效应或外部性。有句名言叫"了解你的合作方"，这句话提醒每个人提高警惕，有助于减轻外部性。但影响很有限。此外，违约风险可能会产生连锁反应。如果A未能支付他欠B的款项，那么B可能无法支付他欠C的款项，依此类推。因此，刚才那句话必须扩展为："了解你的合作方的合作方；了解你的合作方的合作方的合作方；无限类推。"这当然不切实际。因此，一家银行的行为可能会给其他银行及其存款人带来代价高昂的风险：信息不对称会扩散，并造成大面积的溢出效应。金融危机提供了许多例子。

给收入不足的人发放住房抵押贷款，可能是这次金融危机的起点和驱动力。贷款决策由银行官员和抵押贷款经纪人做出，如果他们的贷款出现问题，他们不希望受到任何惩罚：他们认为数年内不会出现这种情况，甚至永远不会发生——如果大众普遍持有的看法是正确的，即房价永远不会下跌。房价的上涨足以支付抵押贷款未来的高额利息。因此，贷款人并不关心逆向选择，即借款人的低资质（低收入人群，同时背负其他债务）。许多业主乐于接受这些贷款，因为他们相信房价将永远上涨。许多人把自己的房子当作摇钱树，贷款购买豪华汽车、等离子电视和其他消费品。如果他们没能按时支付抵押贷款，这些商品将被银行收回，但是对银行来说，这些商品价值很低。政府希望让低收入公民也能拥有住房。因此，监管者忽视甚至鼓励这些高风险的"次级"贷款。抵押贷款在打包后，变成了证券组合，并且被信用评级机构打了高分。这些机构的打分动机很可疑，因为他们的收入来自接受评估的企业。

中介机构缺乏尽职调查的动力，很难做到挑选优质证券并对其进行监督。单个存款人没有能力让中介机构为缺乏勤勉负责。存款人必须集体行动，但这很有难度。在银行存款得到政府公开或隐性保障的情况下，存款人没有理由担心，他们相信银行会利用他们的资金谨慎投资。事实上，当银行承担重大风险时，它们会做得更好：如果风险得到回报，它们会得到很高的收益；如果风险恶化，存款保障机制就会启动，纳税人会承担损失（只要政府的支持率和信用不受怀疑）。银行高管也更喜欢风险：如果他们的贷款进展顺利，他们会做得很好；如果进展糟糕，他们会得到政府的救助。因此，整个资产持有和转换的关系链充满了道德风险和逆向选择，并且在缺乏激励的情况下控制得很糟糕，而政府的决策使其雪上加霜。

当零售银行或商业银行也大量从事投资银行业务时,金融中介固有的风险就会被放大。所有类型的中介机构都在为自己的利益进行操作,通常利用债务来杠杆化投资。如果你用自己投入的1美元股本加上借来的9美元进行价值10美元的投资,那么只要投资价值下降10%,你就会资不抵债。而一些银行和其他中介机构(如对冲基金)的债务/股权比高达50%。

这些风险遍布整个关系链。一次失败动摇了公众的信念,他们就会怀疑其他机构是否还能正常营业。因此,不仅破产会直接产生外部性,一旦公众对所有相关的金融机构失去普遍信任,同样会产生外部性。比如,2008年3月,美国政府出面援助投资银行贝尔斯登公司,但是金融市场针对雷曼兄弟公司的投机操作在增加。到了2008年9月,雷曼兄弟公司宣告破产,美林证券也受到质疑。

小范围的金融危机迅速蔓延成大规模的经济危机。银行面临流动性或偿付能力的风险,于是它们削减了贷款。无法得到贷款甚至无法获得信贷额度的企业难以扩大经营,甚至难以维持就业。收入损失导致经济需求下降,进而导致生产和就业下降。宽松的货币政策和财政激励必须以前所未有的规模来支撑需求,防止整个经济因缺乏金融资本的润滑而陷入停顿。因此,金融业的微观经济缺陷(糟糕的激励和外部性)是宏观经济陷入困境(产出损失和高失业率)的根本原因。

金融机构声称,监管不仅没有必要,而且会造成伤害。这可能只是对市场魔力的盲目崇拜和错误信仰。简单来说,这种观点认为,金融机构可以自行管理,借助科斯定理来应对外部性。艾伦·格林斯潘担任美国联邦储备委员会主席时,这类观点得到了他的大力支持，并被历任总统所接受。金融危机之后，其他行业的人很少再坚持这种看法。大众普遍认为，需要有某种形式的监管，尽管最佳的监管形式依然有待讨论，不同的国家采取了不同的方法。大多数国家都开始限制零售银行所承担的债务和风险。20世纪30年代经济危机爆发后，美国颁布的《格拉斯—斯蒂格尔法》一度将零售银行业务和投资银行业务完全分离。现在很少有人再支持这种做法，但是包括英国银行业独立委员会在内的一些管理机构会建议采取某些特定的隔离措施，比如安装"防火墙"或"隔离"风险更大的投资银行业务。其他建议还包括"宏观审慎监管"，主要包括采取类似庇古税的措施，控制一家中介机构过度冒险给其他机构带来的外部性影响。具体措施包括：要求银行的资本或流动准备金不低于设定的最低比率，或者采取其他形式对债务和杠杆征税。监管机构还可以明确破产程序，有序解决由于投资固有风险而必然发生的破产问题。这可以最大限度地降低市场失灵的风险在关系链上蔓延。几乎没有人主张政府发挥更大的作用，因为这可能导致贷款被用于政治优先事项，而不是创造经济价值，从而在消灭问题的同时扼杀积极的创新举措。

金融机构的大多数内部人士都反对加强政府监管，原因或许是，他们相信保持现状对他们更加有利：他们知道当风险恶化时，政府会来拯救他们，从而确保高风险利润的安全，最终纳税人将会承担损失。我认为他们的观点是错误的，他们不应该抵制所有监管。受到有效监管是一种承诺和信号，表明他们资质良好，并将谨慎行事。这将增强公众的信心，减少恐慌心理，降低流动性危机的风险，从而更有利于所有银行的长期利益。

第六章

制度与组织

　　几千年前,人类就不再满足于自给自足。依据比较优势的专业化(无论是基于资源禀赋还是技术差异),以大批量、长周期的方式组织生产,再加上生产设备的不断积累,这些因素都使生产力有了巨大的提高。与此同时,运输成本的降低使得生产者有可能将商品和服务通过贸易输送到世界各地,从而让全球消费者受益。

　　上述发展过程中的每一步,都意味着增加专业化个人和企业之间交易的数量和复杂性。这些交易反过来又要求一个制度和组织所构成的基础结构。在这些制度中,最常见、最著名的就是市场,这就是为什么它们一直是微观经济学研究的重点,同时也是本书分析的重点。但其他的交易安排确实存在,在某些方面可能比市场做得更好。在第三章中我们讨论过,企业如何利用内部组织来节省交易成本,从而有效利用市场。在其他情况下,家庭、社会群体和网络、行业协会和政府则运作得更好。对这些制度的研究丰富了微观经济学,并且将微观经济学与其他的从不同角度研究这些制度的社会科学分支联系起来。

产权与合同执行

专业化和交易要想取得成功,有两个基本前提:财产保障和合同保障。如果财产不安全,人们就不会改造土地,开展研发,积累资本,也不会做任何有利于提高经济生产潜力的事情,因为他们担心劳动成果和储蓄会被偷走。如果合同不安全,就会破坏所有的交易,除了一些无足轻重的买卖活动,即用质量可靠的某种商品或服务交换另一种同样可靠的商品或服务,或者换取现金。除了最原始的经济体以外,所有经济体都需要制度来保护财产并执行合同。

虽然财产和合同的安全性很重要,但我必须再次强调:不可能做到绝对安全。根据法律规定的"征用权"原则,民主国家出于公共目的,可以征用私人财产。这应该是极为罕见的做法,相关的法律和程序应该明文规定,并对外公开,业主应该得到公平的补偿。同样,合同并非总是神圣不可侵犯。在合同双方无法控制的特殊情况下,比如发生战争、暴乱、飓风和地震,合同的其中一方或双方可以免于承担原有的义务和责任。如果其中一方破产,签订的合同也将宣告无效。发生业务往来的其他各方必须申请索赔,并依次排队,力争得到任何可以变现的资产。当然,征用权有时会被滥用,或者没有给予充分补偿。一些公司利用破产作为借口,威胁它们的工人,要求对方在签订工资合同时做出让步。但大多数现代经济体都有足够的财产保障和合同保障,能够支持高水平的经济活动和交易。

国家与非国家治理制度

大多数现代经济体依靠国家法律和执行法律的组织（警察和法院）提供必要的财产保障和合同保障。但是，当代有许多国家受到效率问题的困扰，或者说，所有国家在各自的历史上都曾有过这样的低效时期。这些国家的制度和组织现在或过去因太过薄弱、迟缓、低效、片面和腐败而让人难以信赖。这些社会发展出替代制度，以提供必要的经济治理。即使在现代的发达经济体中，非国家制度也会成为国家制度的补充，并在某些方面更具优势。

所有自愿的经济交易都会给双方带来收益，否则当事方会当场拒绝交易。但是，任何一方或双方都有可能违反合同条款，通过牺牲另一方利益的投机行为来获利。这是一种囚徒困境，合同执行制度可以提供解决困境的办法。迭戈·甘贝塔在他关于西西里黑手党的著作中研究了此类非国家制度。他引用一位当地养牛人的话："当屠夫来找我买一头牲畜时，他知道我会骗他（给他一头劣质的牲畜），而我也知道他会骗我（否认原定价格）。所以我们需要佩佩（黑手党），这样我们才能达成一致。我们都按交易金额的1%支付中介费用给佩佩。"我会在后面的章节中分析佩佩如何保障合同的执行，现在请允许我先卖个关子。

当家庭成员和亲密朋友之间发生多次交易时，他们对于法律或黑手党的需求最低。在互惠模式中，他们可以自行解决囚徒困境，因为他们都很看重彼此关系的延续，不会为了短期利益去投机。如果关系良好，双方甚至不会准确计算究竟谁欠谁更多，而是随着时间的推移自动达到平衡。如果一方试图准确计算得失，可能会导致亲密关系的结束。要求对方付钱或付钱给对方，都是完全不可接受的做法。小说《教父》提供了另类"家庭"背景下让人印象深刻的例子。殡仪承办人博纳塞拉不熟悉黑手党的规矩。他问黑手党头目维托·柯里昂需要支付多少钱，才能帮他为遭到强暴的女儿报仇。人称"教父"的柯里昂回答道："我的朋友，将来某一天或许我也会请你帮个忙，但愿那天永远不会到来。在此之前，请接受这次援助，就当是我送你的礼物。"

某些情况下，一个人不是与另一个人进行足够频繁的多次互动，而是与规模相对较小社群的**某个人**打交道。比如，在某个小城市的商人中，A可能很少与B打交道，但他必须与其他人打交道，不管他们是C或D，还是其他人。这些群体可以制定规范、沟通规则和多边制裁约定，以维持成员间的合同诚信。规范包括两个部分。第一部分禁止其成员做出投机行为，欺骗其他成员。如果有人违反规范，群体的通信网络会通知所有成员。制裁意味着，任何成员将来都不会与违反规范的人进行交易。因此，如果A欺骗了B，包括C和D在内的其他人未来都不会与A打交道，从而迫使他或她退出经营。如果A惧怕这种多边惩罚，那么他或她就会保持诚信。但是，包括C和D在内的其他人会不会被盈利商机所吸引，从而与A合作呢？因此，制裁还有第二部分：拒绝参加对A的处罚本身就是一种违反规范的行为，同样会遭受其他人的排斥。包括C和D在内的其他人惧怕这种惩罚，所以他们会遵守规范。

这类似于几所大学的荣誉守则。学生在学习和考试中必须遵守规定的学业操守标准。如果一个学生看到另一个学生违反校规，他或她必须向荣誉委员会报告。如果没有报告，就意味着第一个学生也违反了守则,将会受到类似于对欺诈或剽窃等重大违规行为的惩罚。

和往常一样,这样的体制不可能做到完美,或者说,不可能在任何时候都做到完美。但是在许多地方和许多时候,它都能运作得足够好而得以存在。以下是两个来源不同的例子。

阿夫纳·格雷夫描述并分析了公元11世纪在马格里布地区(历史上对北非地中海沿岸平原国家的统称)经营的一个犹太商人群体。他们把货物送到数百英里以外的其他市场,由那里的代理商出售货物并汇出收益。他们的代理商在许多方面善于投机,比如为了获得工作,他们声称自己拥有相应的商业技能,但实际上并不具备;他们声称货物送达时已损坏;他们不会费力寻找最有利的价格;他们捏造信息,声称货物必须低价出售,实际上利用差价获利。类似的行为还有很多。商人们会通过信件,就各种商业事务交流看法,他们在信件中对代理商的不良行为表示不满。如果有足够的证据,他们就会联合起来,将那些无赖逐出市场。

丽莎·伯恩斯坦研究了纽约钻石商人如何通过仲裁庭来解决他们之间可能产生的合同纠纷。担任仲裁员的是经验丰富的钻石商人,他们了解现行的惯例和规范,并且比缺乏专业知识的法庭更善于评估证据。因此,他们的仲裁工作更快、更便宜、更准确。如果被判定有过错的一方违反仲裁委员会的裁决(通常是赔偿或罚款),那么违规人员的姓名和画像将展示在钻石商人俱乐部的公告牌上,警告其他会员不要与他或她打交道。这种惩罚意味着被逐出行业,基本上等于失去生计,这远比法院可以征收的罚款严厉得多,因此是对投机行为更有效的威慑。另外,还有其他的一些仲裁法庭,他们的裁决受到国家法院的尊重和执行。

在这些例子中,贸易共同体的成员通过自身来提供合同治理的机制。其他情况下,他们会雇用外部的服务。甘贝塔笔下的佩佩(黑手党)就是一个例子。他提供两种服务。首先,他收集并保存交易人员此前行为的相关信息。如果A发现了一个可盈利的商业机会,为此他必须与B合作,那么他可以支付一笔费用给佩佩,要求后者披露B是否在过去与他人的交易中有过作弊行为。(当然,佩佩可能与B共谋,提供虚假的担保。因此,付给佩佩的费用必须足够多,这样他就不会为了与B勾结获得一次性的利益而破坏他作为诚信中介的声誉。)如果此前保持诚信的B在本次交易中欺骗A,那么在这种模式下,佩佩能做的就是把B的名字列入作弊名单,供日后参考,而B面临的唯一惩罚是日后的业务损失。在另一种模式中,佩佩并不关心过去的行为。如果A是他的客户,而B欺骗了A,佩佩会对B施以某种适当的伤害作为惩罚,比如击碎膝盖骨,甚至更加严重。毫不奇怪,在第二种模式下,需要支付佩佩的费用要高于搜寻并提供过去行为信息的费用。

佩佩使用的信息模式可以追溯到中世纪欧洲的大型集市。各国商人从遥远的本国来到集市。有专门的法律用于治理他们之间的合同,这被称为**商人习惯法**。作为一项由惯例和实践构成的制度,商人习惯法经过演变发展,最终成为许多国家的正式合同法的基础。私人法官负责法律事务。他们拥有一定的商业背景,从中获得专业知识,声誉良好,立场公正,能迅速有效地提供服务。他们收取费用,提供专业服务,包括提供当事人过去行为的信息，裁决争议，并且将新的作弊者和不遵守裁决者的姓名加入黑名单，从而更新信息，以备将来使用。这项制度与钻石商人俱乐部的仲裁做法有相似之处。

这些用于保障合同执行的私人制度可以运作良好，因为它们为特定的共同体服务，而共同体成员都受益于成功治理带来的交易安全。用于保障财产权利的私人制度则较难维系，因为它们必须阻止成员之外的其他人加入，如果这种机构失败，后者将从中受益。尽管如此，当牵涉足够大的利益时，类似的制度仍然可以发挥作用。比如，加利福尼亚的淘金热始于1849年，当时该地区尚未成为一个州，也没有设立正式的执法机制，但探险者自发组织，建立并维护采矿权的保障体制。相比之下，19世纪末在美国西部的边远地区，当地人试图将联邦林业产品和牧场土地产品归入私人产权的范围，但他们的做法并没有完全取得成功，因为涉及的人数更多，而且他们的利益更加多样化。

经济治理的私人制度在规模相对较小、关系较为稳定的共同体内运作良好。但这些共同体内的交易机会可能并不多。专业化的收益、大规模生产的经济，以及种类繁多的商品消费，这些因素需要在地理、社会和经济层面与相隔很远的其他人打交道。远距离与陌生人进行交易需要更有效的、客观的治理制度。建立了市场或类似市场平台的中介机构则可以提供帮助。下面就让我们来看看这类制度。

市场设计

通过创建特殊的市场或类似市场的平台，供交易双方见面，可以最好地满足某些专业化交易的需求。其中一些市场甚至为交易提供了特定用途的资金。保姆俱乐部是一个为人熟知的例子，但它们只限于朋友，或者至少是熟人，并且限于狭小的地理区域。互联网极大地扩展了这类市场的范围，并创造出所谓的"共享经济"或"点对点经济"。

爱彼迎公司创建了一个私人市场，用于房间、公寓或房屋出租，并匹配主人和客人。各方都有充分理由担心与陌生人进行交易。主人担心客人可能很脏，很吵，或者很讨厌，甚至可能偷东西，客人则担心住宿质量。平台所有者会执行背景检查，他们还邀请用户在使用后对服务进行评级。此前没有任何记录的主人必须接受低租金，随着良好评级的积累，他们就可以提高价格。当然，这个系统并不完美。比如，你可以让你的朋友帮忙刷好评。但整体上，对于爱彼迎公司来说，这个系统看起来运行良好。类似的网站还有很多，比如私家车、自助工具和设备出租等。

其他网站，如eBay、克雷格信息分类列表、亚马逊的入驻商家等，则提供了范围更广的商品和服务。要想取得成功，所有的市场或交易平台都需要注意几个问题。它们必须方便检索交易对象，从而让每个使用网站的个人都能完成匹配。它们还必须方便检索价格，帮助卖家寻找他们能够获得的最高价格，帮助买家寻找他们必须支付的最低价格（这需要对商品质量和交货时间等因素进行适当调整）。它们必须确保合同履行，并且解决争议。传统的市场通常包括城镇的中心广场、中世纪的集市、现代的购物中心、证券交易所等，这些市场将潜在的交易者吸引到一个物理场所，从而实现检索和匹配功能。在互联网上，场所是在地理上分散的百万台计算机或其他设备，但这些设备以电子方式彼此连接。智能手机甚至使跨市场的价格检索变得更加便捷。比如，印度西南海岸的渔民可以获得沿海地区不同城镇的价格信息，并决定在哪里出售他们捕到的鱼获。所有这些发展都提高了经济效率，因为它们使市场更具竞争力，也更容易实现供需均衡。（在传统的实体经济中，商品交易需要征税，而网络交易通常都能避税。必须承认，某些情况下这是它们存在的理由。）通过多种制度可以保障合同履行和争议解决，包括：国家的法律机器、行业仲裁、基于同行评审和评级的商业信誉等。

匹配市场

许多交易需要匹配人员或物品，并且需要平台和制度来促进此类交易。最明显的例子是寻找婚姻伴侣，这需要非正式或正式的婚介制度，但也有许多其他的例子，比如，申请者和大学、学生和宿舍、刚毕业的医生和医院、器官捐赠者和需要器官移植的患者等。在某些情况下，匹配必须满足限制条件，比如，器官和接受者必须具有兼容的血型。在其他情况下，其中一方的每个项目可以与另一方的任何一个项目相匹配，但是某一方或双方对于备选方案有所偏好，比如，大学生对宿舍有偏好，而宿舍无所谓哪个学生入住；又比如，大学和申请者都对匹配结果有所偏好，就像准备结婚的准新娘和新郎一样。重要的是，要检查现有平台或制度是否实现了某种意义上的良好匹配，以及是否可以设计出更好的平台或制度。

传统市场在处理许多匹配需求时存在问题。首先，项目不可分割，各有不同，而且每一方的项目数量可能很少。市场可能会变为成对的协商过程，每对的每个成员都拥有巨大的市场势力。其次，并非所有的交易都用到金钱，特别是在某些情况下

（比如器官移植），金钱交易可能令人厌恶。有时交易会变相使用金钱，比如，大学争相提供更好的经济资助，以吸引它们想要的学生；又比如，许多文化中都存在嫁妆或彩礼。但是，如果限制或禁止使用金钱，就会使匹配交易变得更复杂，超出了市场上的常规交易。

戴维·盖尔和劳埃德·沙普利等人率先提出匹配市场理论。随后，这一理论被拓展到几个重要的应用领域，包括医院和医生之间的匹配。埃尔文·罗斯和其他人将其应用于器官捐赠的分析。沙普利和罗斯因其贡献获得2012年诺贝尔经济学奖（盖尔已于2008年去世）。接下来，我将简要介绍这项研究。

匹配过程的理想属性是什么？首先当然是经济学家的最爱：帕累托效率。换句话说，不可能再设计另一种匹配方案，让所有参与者都会过得更好（这意味着，新的匹配方案在他们的偏好排序中位次更高）。与此有关的另一项属性是稳定性。用大写字母标注参与者并将其放在一侧，另一侧用小写字母标注。假设某种机制将A与a匹配，B与b匹配，但实际上A更愿意与b匹配，B更愿意与a匹配。在没有强制的情况下，A和b能够自行匹配，比起原有的机制，这样的结果更好，因此原先的结果并不稳定。如果不能自行选择，那么原先的结果就是稳定的。当参与者的偏好不为他人所知时（通常都是如此），第三个重要属性是不可操纵性：任何参与者都不能通过故意透露虚假的偏好来获得更好的结果。

如果市场中只有一方对匹配选项有所偏好（比如大学生和宿舍的例子），一个被称为"首位交易循环"的简易程序可以满足这些需求。让我们从任何指定的匹配结果开始：这可能是现状或初始所有权模式。每个学生都说出自己最喜欢的房间。如果最初的配对不稳定，那么一组学生可以相互交换，获得他们心仪的房间。让他们这样做，然后把他们从市场上撤走。对剩余的学生重复这个过程，让他们在剩余的房间中选出最喜欢的房间。继续这个过程，直到分配完所有房间。已经证明，该方法具有三个重要属性：稳定性、帕累托效率和不可操纵性。当然，和其他类型的帕累托效率一样，这个操作的最终结果取决于最初的分配模式，整个过程并不需要做到平等或公正。如果你没有足够幸运地进入交易循环的最初几轮，那么在轮到你之前，你最想要的房间可能已经被人挑走了。

如果双方都对自己的选项有所偏好，事情会变得更加复杂。比如，假设四个学生a、b、c、d要申请四所大学A、B、C、D。表4显示了他们的偏好，用＞表示在偏好排序中的更高位次。比如，大学B最喜欢的是学生d，其次是学生a，再次是学生c，最后是学生b。

盖尔和沙普利设计的匹配程序被称为"延迟接受算法"，其工作原理如下。假设其中一方（比如大学）发出要约。每所大学都向偏好排序最高的学生提供一份录取通知书。在这个例子中，大学A发给学生a，大学B和D发给学生d，大学C发给学生b。每个学生都坚持选择自己最喜欢的大学，拒绝其他学校。在这个例子中，学生d有两份录取通知书，分别来自大学B和D，她更喜欢B，所以拒绝D。在其他人中，a和b各有一份录取通知书，并愿意接受。c没有收到通知书，将等待第二轮机会。重要的是，此时接受行为没有约束力，因此被称为"延迟接受"。在第二轮中，D（在第一轮中被学生d拒绝）向次优选择（学生c）

发出录取通知书。现在C有了一份通知书,并愿意接受。此时每个学生都已收到录取通知书,程序停止。最终匹配结果为:A—a、B—d、C—b、D—c,该结果具有约束力。

表4 双方偏好的匹配示例

	大学的偏好		学生的偏好
A	$a>b>d>c$	a	$D>B>A>C$
B	$d>a>c>b$	b	$D>A>B>C$
C	$b>a>d>c$	c	$D>B>C>A$
D	$d>c>b>a$	d	$A>C>B>D$

如果改由学生来提出要约呢？在第一轮中,学生a、b、c均向大学D提出申请,学生d向大学A提出申请。现在,大学D收到三份申请,并决定接受学生c(在偏好排序中位次最高),拒绝a和b。在第二轮中,学生a向大学B提出申请,学生b向大学A提出申请。现在,A收到两份申请,第一轮的申请人是d,第二轮是b。它拒绝了偏好排序较低的那个学生,也就是d(记住,直到整个程序结束,接受行为才具有约束力)。在第三轮中,学生d向他的次优选择大学C提出申请。现在我们得到了最终的匹配结果：a—B、b—A、c—D、d—C。匹配完成,程序结束。

可以证明,这个程序最终产生了稳定的结果,对于提出要约的一方来说,具有帕累托效率。然而,结果可以操纵：收到要约的一方通常可以通过故意展示虚假偏好来获得更好的结果。在上例中,当大学提出要约时,按照真正的偏好来匹配,结果是学生d匹配大学B,后者在她的偏好序列中排名第三。如果她假装偏好为$A>C>D>B$,她可以申请到大学C,后者在她的真实偏好序列中排名第二！整个推理过程很长，需要经过六轮选择。如果有些读者感到疑惑，或者勤于思考，不妨自行推导，当作有益的思维训练。

医院与医学院毕业生的匹配方案经历了若干次变化，我们可以从中学到许多。在20世纪上半叶，这是一个极为分散的市场。20世纪40年代，美国各家医院展开激烈竞争，提前向医学院学生提供实习机会，希望借此引入最佳人选。这种做法并不能很好地解决问题，因为在学生的专业素养或他们对特定专业的兴趣变得清晰之前，匹配就被固定了。如果发出的要约被拒绝，那么再向另一位候选人提出新的要约就太晚了。到了20世纪50年代，全国居民匹配计划开始实施，这就像是之前分析的延迟接受算法，由医院来提出要约。此后，这项计划继续实施，并且有了一些变化，尤其是改由申请人发起要约，而不是医院。另外，还为准备到同一所医院工作的已婚医生夫妇提供住房。

整个程序可以概括为，某些匹配结果比不进行匹配更糟糕，因此其中一方无法接受这样的结果。它也可以推广到类似的情况，即一方的每一项结果与另一方的数项结果进行匹配，就像之前讨论的大学与学生匹配的例子。

另一个重要的平台是匹配肾脏捐赠者和接受者。这些匹配通常成对出现，其中一个人愿意将肾脏捐赠给需要肾脏的亲属或爱人，但他们的血型不相容。可能出现的情况是，A愿意捐赠给a，B愿意捐赠给b，但自愿的配对并不兼容，而A与b兼容，B与a兼容。这需要一整套协调操作，其中A和B同时捐赠，器官分别移植到b和a身上。由众多捐赠者和接受者组成的更为复杂的关系链，需要通过集中的清算机构来协调。

拍　卖

许多交易以拍卖方式进行，而不是以公布的价格或协商的价格进行销售。拍卖会将指定商品（或商品组合）的所有潜在买家召集起来，在他们之间制造出某种形式的竞争。事实上，这就是许多卖家使用拍卖的原因。和拍卖会正好相反的是供给或建设合同的投标竞争，后者由买家将潜在的、彼此竞争的卖家召集起来。

拍卖有多种不同的形式。在密封投标拍卖中，每个竞拍者在不知道其他人行为的情况下提交标书。卖方同时查看所有的标书。出价最高的人得到标的物，并支付报价。如果卖方在一个非常高的价位启动"价格时钟"，并逐步降低价格，也能取得类似的结果。在任何时候，任何竞拍者都可以停止计时，并支付相应价格，从而获得物品。与之相反，卖方也可以在较低的价格水平启动"价格时钟"，并逐步提高价格。竞拍者可以随时退出（但不能重新进入）。当只剩最后一个出价者时，他或她按照时钟指示的价格获得标的物，这实际上就是倒数第二名出价者退出时的价位。在熟悉的升序模式或"公开喊价"模式中，拍卖人要求竞拍者比前一次出价"再增加一点"，或者由拍卖人逐步提高出价，竞拍者可以选择留下或退出。在这种模式中，愿意支付最高价格的人会一直坚持到最后，但他或她支付的金额仅略高于第二名的支付意愿。（我之所以说"略高于"，是因为竞拍可能会以这种形式离散跳跃。假设 A 出价最高，愿意支付 120 美元；其次是 B，愿意支付 112 美元。拍卖人每次增加 5 美元，以这种方式来竞标。在 110 美元的价位，两人都愿意支付。接下来，

B会在115美元的价位宣布退出。A愿意支付120美元,但实际上只需要支付115美元,比112美元多一点。如果改用不断上升的"时钟"模式,B会在时钟超过112美元时退出,A可能会支付112.01美元并赢得竞拍。)这在**次价竞拍**模式中非常明显,因为规则规定,出价最高者获胜,但只需支付次高报价。相比之下,如果出价最高者获胜并需支付自己的报价,就被称为**首价竞拍**。

此外还有"全支付"拍卖,即出价最高的竞拍者得到标的物,但所有竞拍者无论输赢,都要支付各自的报价。你可能觉得奇怪,但这或许是日常生活中最常见的形式。在美国总统选举的四年周期中,有许多政客花费了大量的时间、精力和金钱,这些支出就像是在竞标。每四年只有一次成功,输家的报价不会得到任何退款。同样的道理也适用于运动员(他们为了在奥运会上赢得奖牌进行着大量训练)和竞争丰厚合同的人,还有其他类似的人群。

竞拍者各自制定竞拍策略。由卖方来决定拍卖的形式,也许是最低价格或"底价"。这使得拍卖变成了策略博弈。信息不对称使其变得更加复杂。卖方可能掌握标的物的有关信息,而竞拍者却不知情。每个竞拍者都会将一定的附加价值赋予标的物。这可能是个人偏好或感情用事的结果(比如,奥黛丽·赫本在《蒂凡尼的早餐》中穿过的黑色小礼服),也可能是出于商业价值考虑(比如,拍卖的土地中需要估算的原油储量)。每个竞拍者都无法直接获知其他竞拍者心中的附加价值,但在竞拍过程中一些信息可能会被披露。比如,在逐步提价的公开喊价拍卖中,其他竞拍者的退出速度。卖方不知道竞拍者的估价。如果知道,他或她会直接去找估价最高的人,在略低于该价位的价格出售标的物。拍卖的最终结果是,这场信息不对称的博弈达到均衡,因而具有广泛的实际用途。在经济理论和博弈论领域,这一课题的研究取得了蓬勃发展。接下来,我要谈到几个主要的话题。

在首价竞拍模式中,如果你的出价等于你对该物品的估价,那么你即使赢了,也不会得到任何利润或盈余。如果出价低于你的估价,会降低你获胜的概率,但如果真的赢了,你会得到更多的利润。你的竞拍策略应该综合考虑这两个因素,这意味着,你的出价应该略低于估价。在次价竞拍模式中,如果你真的赢了,你要支付的是别人的出价,这是你无法控制的因素。因此,最好的策略就是争取获胜概率的最大化,也就是让你的出价等于你的全部估价。现在再从卖方的角度来看这些策略。如果卖方使用首价竞拍模式,那么竞拍者的出价低于他们的估价。如果使用次价竞拍模式,那么他们的出价等于估价,但是卖方只能得到次高的价值。哪种模式能给卖方带来更高的收入?在任何一种情况下,竞拍者对估价和出价的配置可以朝着任何一个方向进行。但卖方事先并不知道这些。在所有配置中应用适当的概率平均值,结果表明,在非常宽泛的条件下,这两种效应(首价竞拍模式中的降低出价和次价竞拍模式中的次高价值)完全抵消:这两种模式给卖方带来的收益相等!事实上,在这些条件下,所有拍卖形式都是收益等价的,这是拍卖理论早期带给我们的非凡观点。

接下来考虑一种特殊的拍卖,标的物具有客观价值或商业价值,但不同的竞拍者给出的估价有所不同。如果他们的估价过程是公正的,并且有许多竞拍者参加(比如100人),那么根据大数定律（群众的智慧），估价平均值接近真实值。但是，平均出价并不能赢得拍卖，只有出价最高的人才是获胜者。最终结果将取决于最高估价，并且很可能会高于真实值。一个真正具有策略思维的竞拍者会意识到这一点，并且想道："如果我赢了，那就意味着其他99个竞拍者的估价比我低。那么，我应该从中学到什么？我该如何来调整出价？"答案是，降低你的出价。计算降价幅度的数学原理很复杂，实际上许多竞拍者没有做出正确的推断，于是经常出现意外的结果：成功赢得矿物和原油开采权的人发现他们付出的代价太高；或者，成功签下超级明星的运动队发现他的实际表现不如预期。这样的现象被称为"**胜利者的诅咒**"。

此外，还有"失败者的诅咒"，这种假想的情形没有得到太多关注。假设有100个竞拍者在拍卖中竞争99件物品，而你是最终的那个失败者。这意味着你的估价非常低。你应该问自己："如果我输了，那就意味着其他99个竞拍者的估价比我更高。我应该从中学到什么？我该如何来调整出价？"这时你应该提高出价来避免失败者的诅咒。

现在考虑中间范围，假设标的物数量与竞拍者数量的比例处于中间位置：既不是接近0（1个标的物和100个竞拍者），也不是接近1（99个标的物和100个竞拍者）。这样一来，胜利者的诅咒和失败者的诅咒没有多大区别，每个竞拍者都可以忽略其他人，不用去考虑他们基于各自的估价是否会有不同的信息和出价。这是一种非常微妙但很有帮助的做法，我们因此可以理解有着大量买家和卖家的竞争性市场如何有效运作，即便相关信息在所有参与者中广泛散布。我们从市场出发，随后讨论了其他的平台和制度，最后又圆满回到起点。

第七章

什么才是有效的？

　　如果你希望读到的大结局，宣告市场的胜利，或者资本主义的终结，那么你注定会失望。我在第四章中已经说明，竞争性市场在运行良好的情况下如何实现帕累托效率。你不妨回想一下相关定义：帕累托效率意味着，其他任何结果都无法做到在不损害他人的情况下，为一些人带来更大的经济利益。然而，帕累托效率可能会造成非常不公平的福利分配。我在第五章中分析了垄断、外部性和信息不对称等因素如何妨碍市场产生有效结果，哪怕只是有限的帕累托效率。还有另一个坏消息，那就是政府通常不会带来任何更好的结果。由于政治事务的特性，无论是民主政府还是独裁政府，都必然遭遇它们自身的失灵。它们有自己的喜好和服务对象（比如，现有的生产者、其他的利益相关组织、竞选资助者），这些人都想着牺牲公众利益，为自己谋取好处。

　　鉴于市场和政府存在诸多缺陷，当今世界的发展并不算太糟糕。混合经济包括两个部分：一部分是市场和类似的制度，它们依靠激励和自利来运行；另一部分是公共制度和政府，用于组织集体行动，提供监督，限制市场权力的滥用，借助税收或其他政策来纠正市场失灵。在许多国家，混合经济已经取得合理的经济成果和增长。我认为这样的混合模式是我们最希望实现的目标。

在我看来，要想取得合理的良好成果，最大的风险是，在局面失控并造成严重损害之前，没能注意到相关错误并予以纠正。当某个人或某个组织控制所有决策时，风险达到最大值。只要竞争对手能发现决策者的失误，并且出于自身利益或其他动机来纠正错误，那就能取得良好成果。因此，究竟该选择市场还是政府，我并没有现成的答案，但我反对任何一种形式的垄断。

垄断影响决策的一个极端例子是第二次世界大战后的城市规划和公共住房。受法国建筑师勒·柯布西耶和其他人的影响，政府设计并建造了像巴西利亚这样被荒漠包围的都市，还有像圣路易斯市普鲁伊特—艾戈项目那样糟糕的住宅区。如果城市住房的供给方是彼此竞争的私人建筑商，其中一些人很快就会注意到这些项目的缺陷，并提出替代方案。然而，政府坚持它们的计划。更糟糕的是，麦卡锡主义在美国制造恐怖氛围，污蔑许多人有叛国嫌疑，并禁止他们谋求政府职位，许多人（虽然并非全部）甚至无法在私营企业工作。作为20世纪最顶尖的五位经济学家之一，保罗·萨缪尔森在一篇文章中（该文于1983年发表于《美国经济学家》杂志）描述了自己的人生哲学：

> 我从麦卡锡事件中得到的教训是，只有一位雇主的社会非常危险。当你被政府辞退时，市场上还有数以万计的

匿名雇主等着你，这会带给你巨大的安全感。这就是我近来提出的观点，我倡导的并非自由放任式的资本主义，而是混合经济。

在混合经济中，竞争性市场或类似制度会生成有关稀缺性的信息，并创造激励措施，以合理有效的方式来缓解稀缺性。反垄断政策始终保持市场的竞争性，同时政府和其他社会组织有助于克服外部性的效率低下。政治竞争作为一种纠正机制，用于制约权力滥用，纠正严重的判断错误。因此，我认为混合经济是组织微观经济活动的最佳方式。

索 引

（条目后的数字为原文页码，
见本书边码）

A

adverse selection 逆向选择 83, 96
Affordable Care Act (Obamacare)《平价医疗法》(奥巴马医改) 83
Airbnb 爱彼迎公司 106
Akerlof, George 乔治·阿克洛夫 77, 79
Aliber, Robert Z. 罗伯特·Z. 阿利伯 122
Amazon 亚马逊公司 106
Angelides, Phil 菲尔·安吉利迪斯 93
antitrust policy 反垄断政策 41—42
Arnott, Richard 理查德·阿诺特 71
auction 拍卖 111—115
all-pay 全支付 112—113
asymmetric information in 信息不对称 113
    first-price 首价竞拍 113—114
    revenue-equivalence in 收益等价 114
    second-price 次价竞拍 113—114

B

babysitter effect 保姆效应 16—17
bankruptcy 破产 93, 100
Baron, David 戴维·巴伦 121
Barzel, Yoram 约拉姆·巴泽尔 124
Bear Sterns 贝尔斯登公司 97
beekeeping 养蜂业 74
behavioural economics 行为经济学 23
Bernheim, Douglas 道格拉斯·伯恩海姆 119, 121
Bernstein, Lisa 丽莎·伯恩斯坦 103
Bernstein, William J. 威廉·J. 伯恩斯坦 119
Bird, John 约翰·伯德 123
Birnbaum, Jeffrey H. 杰弗里·H. 伯恩鲍姆 123
Blundell, Richard 理查德·布伦戴尔 12—13, 120
boom-bust cycles 繁荣与萧条周期 62—63
Botsman, Rachel 蕾切尔·博茨曼 125
Brill, Steven 史蒂文·布里尔 123
Buchanan, James M. 詹姆斯·M. 布坎南 123

C

carbon emission trading 碳排放交易 76
Carlyle, Thomas 托马斯·卡莱尔 50
cartel 卡特尔 41
    diamond 钻石 45
    lysine 赖氨酸 43—44
    petroleum 石油 44
Catch-22《第二十二条军规》87
Cheung, Steven N. S. 张五常 122
China 中国 92
Christie, Agatha 阿加莎·克里斯蒂 93
Coase, Ronald 罗纳德·科斯 46, 73,

121—122
collective action 集体行动 73, 96
　bottom-up 自下而上 73—74
　in political participation 在政治参与中 89
　top-down 自上而下 73
collective goods 集体产品 86—88
　exclusion 排除 88
　government provision 政府提供 87—88
　private provision 私人提供 88
Common Agricultural Policy 共同农业政策 64—65
Congo, The 刚果 92
complement 互补 7, 14
congestion tolls 交通拥堵费 75
consumer surplus 消费者剩余 52—53
cost 成本
　first-copy 初版成本 29, 85
　opportunity 机会成本 18, 29
　marginal 边际成本 30, 44
　sunk 沉没成本 29, 44
　transaction 交易成本 47—48
cost-of-living index 生活成本指数 14—16
Craiglist 克雷格信息分类列表 106

D

dairy price supports 乳制品价格支持 65
demand 需求
　curve 曲线 8, 50—51, 53
　elastic 有弹性的 10

inelastic 缺乏弹性的 10
shift of 变化 9—10, 56—58
law of 定理 5, 14, 25
market 市场 6
dead-weight loss 无谓损失 67
Deaton, Angus 安格斯·迪顿 120
deferred acceptance algorithm 延迟接受算法 109
Diamond Merchants' Club 钻石商人俱乐部 103
Dixit, Avinash 阿维纳什·迪克西特 123, 125
disequilibrium 不均衡 63

E

eBay 美国 eBay 公司 106
efficiency 效率 53
　loss of 效率损失 60, 参见 inefficiency
eminent domain 国家征用权 100
empathy 共情 25
endowment effect 禀赋效应 24—25
Epstein, Edward J. 爱德华·J. 爱泼斯坦 121
equilibrium 均衡 50—51, 55
　efficiency of 均衡效率 53
　shift of 均衡变化 56—61
equity 平等 25
European Union 欧盟 64, 76
externalities 外部性 70
　in financial crisis 在金融危机中 95, 97
　in firms' profits 在企业利润中 84—85
　Coasian solutions 科斯式的方法 73—74, 76, 97

索引

121

costs of 成本 71
informational 信息 80—81, 83, 95
Pigouvian policies 庇古式的方法 74—76

F

fairness 公正 25
favour exchanges 互惠 101
Federal Reserve Board (US) 联邦储备委员会（美国）98
financial crisis 金融危机 92
　　and economic crisis 与经济危机 97
fisheries 渔业 73—74
Fortune, John 约翰·福琼 123
framing 框架 24, 26
Friedman, Milton 米尔顿·弗里德曼 119, 121—122
Friedman, Rose 罗斯·弗里德曼 121

G

Gale, David 戴维·盖尔 108
Gambetta, Diego 迭戈·甘贝塔 101, 104, 122, 125
Glass-Steagall Act《格拉斯—斯蒂格尔法》98
Godfather, The《教父》102
gold rush 淘金热 105
governance institutions 治理制度
　　arbitration 仲裁 103, 106
　　communities 共同体 102—104
　　family and friends 亲朋好友 101—102
　　state 国家 101

trade fairs 大型集市 104
government 政府
　　authoritarian 专制 92
　　collective action 集体行动 87—88
　　democratic 民主 89—90
　　externality policies 外部性政策 71, 74—76
　　failures 失灵 88—92
　　financial regulation 金融管制 97—98
　　institution of 政府的建立 87
　　price controls 价格管控 63—65
　　taxes and subsidies 税收和补贴 59—60
Greenspan, Alan 艾伦·格林斯潘 98
Greif, Avner 阿夫纳·格雷夫 103, 125

H

Harford, Tim 蒂姆·哈福德 120
Harper, David 戴维·哈珀 122
high-fructose corn syrup(HFCS) 高果糖谷物糖浆 90, 92
honour code 荣誉守则 102

I

impatience 缺乏耐心 25
incentive 激励 2, 72
　　and financial crisis 与金融危机 96
income effect 收入效应 11
Independent Commission on Banking (UK) 银行业独立委员会（英国）98
India 印度 92
inefficiency 效率低下 55

caused by a tax 税收导致 60
of monopoly 垄断 67—69
information 信息 2, 72
    asymmetric 不对称 79—83, 113
    and financial crisis 与金融危机 95
intermediary 中介机构 93
internet 互联网 2, 39, 105—106

K

Kahneman, Daniel 丹尼尔·卡内曼 23, 120
Kindleberger, Charles 查尔斯·金德尔伯格 122
Klemperer, Paul 保罗·克伦佩雷尔 xiii, 121, 125
Krugman, Paul 保罗·克鲁格曼 124

L

law merchant 商人习惯法 104
Lee Kuan Yew 李光耀 92
Lehman Brothers 雷曼兄弟公司 97
Libecap, Gary D. 加里·D. 利贝卡普 124
liquidity 流动性 94—95
lobbying 游说 90, 92
loser's curse 失败者的诅咒 114—115
loss-aversion 损失规避 18, 24, 26
luxury 奢侈品 12

M

McCarthyism 麦卡锡主义 117
McMillan, John 约翰·麦克米兰 119, 121

macroprudential regulation 宏观审慎监管 98
Maghribi merchants 马格里布商人 103
make-or-buy decision 自制或购买决策 47
market 市场
    collapse of 崩溃 3, 77—78
    design 设计 105—107
    efficiency of 效率 53
    equilibrium 均衡 50—51, 55
    failure 失灵 3—4, 67—85
    -maker 做市商 51—52
Marks, Stephen A. 斯蒂芬·A. 马克斯 123
Marshall, Alfred 阿尔弗雷德·马歇尔 50
Mary Poppins 《欢乐满人间》94—95
Maskus, Keith E. 基思·E. 马斯库斯 123
matching markets 匹配市场 107—111
    hospitals and doctors 医院和医生 110—111
    kidney donation 肾脏捐赠 111
maturity transformation 期限转换 94
Maynard-Smith, John 约翰·梅纳德—史密斯 122
Merrill Lynch 美林证券 97
Milgrom, Paul 保罗·米尔格罗姆 125
Mirrlees, James 詹姆斯·莫里斯 121
Mobutu Sese Seko 蒙博托·塞塞·塞科 92
monopoly 垄断 41, 67
    and innovation 与创新 69

索引

costs of 代价 68—69
moral hazard 道德风险 82—83, 96
mortgage interest deduction 住房按
　　揭贷款利息抵扣 60—61
Muellbauer, John 约翰・米尔鲍尔
　　120
Murder on the Orient Express 《东方快
　　车谋杀案》93
Murray, Alan S. 艾伦・S. 默里 123
Musgrave, Richard A. 理查德・A. 马
　　斯格雷夫 123
Myerson, Roger 罗杰・迈尔森 121

N

Nalebuff, Barry 巴里・奈尔伯夫 121
necessity 必要性 14
Newman, Barry 巴里・纽曼 123
North, Douglass 道格拉斯・诺斯 124

O

oligopoly 寡头垄断 41—42, 67
Olson, Mancur 曼瑟・奥尔森 122
Ostrom, Elinor 埃莉诺・奥斯特罗姆
　　73, 122

P

Pareto, Vilfredo 维尔弗雷多・帕累托
　　54
Pareto efficiency 帕累托效率 54, 72, 89,
　　108, 116
peer-to-peer (sharing) economy 点

对点(分享)经济 106
Pesendorfer, Wolfgang 沃尔夫冈・佩
　　森多费尔 125
Pigou, Arthur 阿瑟・庇古 74
Pindyck, Robert 罗伯特・平狄克 119,
　　121
policy 政策
　　failure 失灵 88—92
　　nudging 推动 26
pro-business 亲企业 90
pro-market 亲市场 90
Porter, Michael 迈克尔・波特 120
price discrimination 价格歧视 37—40
price floors and ceilings 价格上限和
　　下限 64
pricing strategies 定价策略 36—39
　　airlines 航空公司 37
　　computer software 电脑软件 38
　　with first-copy costs 考虑初版成本
　　　　85—86
　　hospitals 医院 68
　　insurance 保险 38
prisoners' dilemma 囚徒困境 42—43,
　　74, 87, 101
producer surplus 生产者剩余 52—53
pure public goods 纯公共产品 88

Q

quantity controls 数量管控 75

R

R&D competition 研发竞争 43

Rajan, Raghuram 拉格拉姆·拉詹 124
reference point 参照点 23
Reinhart, Carmen M. 卡门·M. 莱因哈特 124
rent, economic 经济租 90—91
rent-seeking 寻租 91—92
Ramzy, Austin 奥斯丁·拉姆齐 121
Reiley, David 戴维·赖利 120
Reisch, Lucia A. 露西娅·A. 赖施 120
rent controls 租金管控 64—65
risk 风险
　-aversion 规避 18
　counterparty 交易对手 95, 98
　diversification 分散 21
　independent 独立 19—20
　hedging 对冲 21
　pooling 汇集 19
Rogers, Roo 鲁·罗杰斯 125
Rogoff, Kenneth S. 肯尼斯·S. 罗格夫 124
Roth, Alvin 埃尔文·罗斯 108, 125
Rubinfeld, Daniel 丹尼尔·鲁宾菲尔德 119, 121

S

St Augustine 圣奥古斯丁 25
Samuelson, Paul 保罗·萨缪尔森 117
screening 筛选 38—40, 81—82
security 保障
　of contract 合同 100
　of property 财产 100
Shapley, Lloyd 劳埃德·沙普利 108, 125
Shiller, Robert 罗伯特·席勒 124
signalling 释放信号 4, 79—82
　cost-difference property 成本差异特性 80
Singapore 新加坡 92
Skeath, Susan 苏珊·斯基丝 121
Small, Kenneth 肯尼斯·斯莫尔 71
Smith, Adam 亚当·斯密 55
social surplus 社会剩余 52
solvency 偿付能力 94
span of control 管控范围 47
Spence, Michael 迈克尔·斯彭斯 79, 122
Spulber, Daniel 丹尼尔·施普尔伯 122
Stigler, George 乔治·斯蒂格勒 122
Stiglitz, Joseph 约瑟夫·斯蒂格利茨 79, 121
subsidy 补贴 60
　incidence of 归宿 60—61
solar or wind power 太阳能或风能 74
substitute 替代 5—6, 14
Sunstein, Cass 卡斯·桑斯坦 120
sugar, US policies in 美国的糖制品政策 90—92
supply 供给
　chain 供应链 45—46
　curve 曲线 31—32, 50—51, 53
　elastic 有弹性的 33—34
　inelastic 缺乏弹性的 33—34
shift of 变化 33, 56—57
Swinkels, Jeroen 杰伦·斯温克尔斯 125

System I 系统 I 23—24
System II 系统 II 23—24

tax 税收 59
 incidence of 归宿 59—60
 Social Security 社会保障 60
Tett, Gillian 吉利安・泰特 124
Thaler, Richard 理查德・塞勒 120
time-budget 时间预算 17
Tirole, Jean 让・梯若尔 123
top-trading cycle 首位交易循环 108
trading platform 交易平台 106

ultimatum game 最后通牒博弈 24

urban planning 城市规划 117

V

Vickers, John 约翰・维克斯 124

W

Wells, Robin 罗宾・威尔斯 124
Whinston, Michael 迈克尔・惠斯顿 119, 121
Williamson, Oliver 奥利弗・威廉姆森 46, 121, 124
winner's curse 胜利者的诅咒 114—115

Y

YouTube 美国优兔视频网站 124

Avinash Dixit

MICROECONOMICS

A Very Short Introduction

Contents

Preface i

List of illustrations v

List of tables vii

1 What and why of microeconomics 1

2 Consumers 5

3 Producers 28

4 Markets 50

5 Market and policy failures 67

6 Institutions and organizations 99

7 What works? 116

Further reading 119

Preface

Non-economists think economics is about unemployment, inflation, growth, competitiveness of nations, and other matters pertaining to the economy as a whole, or in economists' jargon, about *macroeconomics*. They rarely mention, and perhaps are not even aware of, the whole nexus of choices and transactions behind the larger picture: people's choices of where to live and work, how much to save, what to buy, and so on; firms' decisions about location, investment, hiring, firing, advertising, and many other dimensions of business; and government policies with regard to infrastructure, regulation of industries, structure and rates of taxes on goods and services, and so on. Citizens' relative ignorance and neglect of these fine-level, or *microeconomic*, issues is partly explained by the fact that things often work pretty well at that level, and when they don't work so well, each failure seems small in the larger scheme of things. But many such small failures can add up to a large economic cost. They can have large ramifications at the macroeconomic level too. Therefore it is important to understand why things work pretty well in the microeconomy much of the time, when and why they fail in little and big ways, and what to do to guard against and cope with such failures. In this book, I attempt to present this way of thinking about economics, and some of the conclusions it yields. I hope to convince non-specialist readers that microeconomics is important, and connects as closely with their daily life as unemployment and inflation. I hope to give them some aha moments, where they say, 'I have often seen this; now I understand why!' For more lasting value, I hope to equip them with some basic concepts and tools of microeconomic analysis for use in their own thinking and actions, and leave them eager to do the further reading that I recommend.

Three caveats before you begin. First, in this *Very Short Introduction* you should not look for anything like a comprehensive treatment of the subject. I had to leave out many topics, ideas, and methods, not because they are unimportant, but because in my opinion others have a stronger claim in a brief introduction. If you are a microeconomist and your favourite topic is missing, blame my tastes.

Second, economics has an unavoidable quantitative aspect that requires a little numeracy, for example reading tables and graphs. I have kept these topics as simple as I could, but readers who have occasional trouble with the graphs or numbers can usually just skip those parts and read the rest.

Third, while I hope the subject is fascinating and my treatment readable, such a book cannot be a page-turner. If you are new to the subject, do not try to read too much at one go. Stealing from P. G. Wodehouse's preface to his collected Jeeves short stories, I advise: Do not attempt to finish this volume at one sitting. It can be done—I did it myself when correcting the proofs—but it leaves one weak and is really not worth doing just for the sake of saying you have done it. Take it easy. Spread it out. Assimilate it little by little. Take one small section with each meal. Should insomnia strike, add another section or two at night.

Drafts of a book intended for intelligent non-economist readers should be tried out on intelligent non-economists. I am fortunate to have just the right friends: my breakfast group at Small World

Coffee. I am very grateful to Frank Calaprice (physicist), Julie Jetton (lawyer), Bill Shaffer (financial adviser), Connie Shaffer (high-school French teacher), and Cathy Smith (hypnotherapist) for their patience and generosity in reading early drafts and telling me what needed clarification, rewriting, or even deletion. Andrea Keegan at Oxford University Press and her colleagues also provided valuable feedback on matters of style as well as substance.

Fellow economists were also generous with their time and advice, correcting my errors and suggesting better examples and explanations. Karla Hoff has my eternal gratitude for combining this role with that of an eagle-eyed copy-editor. I am also very grateful to Dilip Abreu, Paul Klemperer and John Vickers for their perceptive comments and useful suggestions.

My biggest *Thank You* goes to all the teachers, colleagues, and students from whom I have absorbed and improved understanding of microeconomics over my whole career. Much of what is good in the book is your doing; the defects are mine.

List of illustrations

1 Representation of a point **8**

2 A market demand curve **9**

3 Shift of the demand curve **10**

4 More and less price-responsive market demand curves **10**

5 A market supply curve **32**

6 Shift of the supply curve **33**

7 More and less price-responsive market supply curves **34**

8 An illustrative short-run supply curve for crude oil **35**

9 Equilibrium of supply and demand **51**

10 Efficiency of supply–demand equilibrium **53**

11 Examples of shift of equilibrium **56**

12 Effect of fashion shift in the short- and long-runs **58**

13 Effect of a tax **59**

14 Incidence of mortgage interest deductibility **61**

15 Price fluctuations **62**

16 Price floors and ceilings **64**

17 Inefficiency of monopoly **68**

18 Economic rent **91**

List of tables

1 Substitution, complementarity, and income responsiveness **13**
Adapted from 'Consumer Behaviour: Theory and Empirical Evidence—A Survey', Richard Blundell, *The Economic Journal*, 98(389), March 1988, 16-65. With permission from Wiley

2 Reducing risk of loss by diversification **21**

3 Crude oil lifting costs and capacities, 2009 **35**
Cost data from <http://www.eia.gov/tools/faqs/faq.cfm?id=367&t=6>, capacity data from <http://www.eia.gov/forecasts/steo/data.cfm?type=tables>, Tables 3b and 3c

4 Example of matching with two-sided preferences **109**

Chapter 1
What and why of microeconomics

A wake-up call

Every morning I choose among several alternatives for my jolt of caffeine. I can brew coffee at home, go to a national chain coffee shop like Starbucks, or to go to Princeton's local Small World Coffee. If I choose to go out, I can walk, bike, or drive. With my coffee I can have healthy bran and berries, indulge in a muffin full of carbs and fat, or binge on fats and salt with eggs and bacon.

What I choose depends on many considerations: whether it is raining or snowing, whether I overindulged at dinner the night before and need exercise, whether my friends have congregated and I feel like socializing that morning, sheer whim or desire for variety, and the quality and prices of the coffee and eats at the different places (including the value of my time if I make coffee at home). As these conditions change from day to day or month to month, my choices also change. But never have I arrived at a coffee shop only to be told, 'Sorry; we don't have any coffee today'. Nor has the supermarket ever run out of coffee when I went to buy some to brew at home. How did they know I would come, and why were they ready and willing to serve me? Examining my choices one step back, when I went to buy a car that (among other trips) I would drive to the coffee shop or the supermarket, how did someone anticipate my demand and have the car available?

Microeconomics studies how millions of consumers choose what goods and services to buy, how producers make decisions to meet these demands, and how the two sides interact. Much of the time the transactions work fairly smoothly. That is why microeconomics is often a story of the dog that did not bark in the night, which in turn explains why non-economists are often unaware of any microeconomic problems. But from time to time things do go wrong. At a trivial level, the coffee shop does run out of muffins on a few days when I am late (although I can then get a scone or some other carb fix instead). But some failures are more drastic, like the gasoline shortages in the 1970s and the housing bubble and its collapse in the 2000s. Therefore it behooves all intelligent people to get some basic understanding of microeconomics: when and how transactions go well, when and why they fail, and what can be done when they do fail or threaten to fail.

Information and incentives

In most societies, consumers and producers interact in markets—not necessarily traditional bazaars and marketplaces, but shops, restaurants, other venues like bargaining tables and auctions, and increasingly the internet. In a market, buyers pay a price to sellers for the good or service. This price serves a twofold purpose. First, if something is scarce, its price rises; thus a high price conveys *information* about scarcity. Second, when a price is high, a supplier of that good or service can profit by producing more of it, and buyers will buy less or switch to something else; thus a high price also provides a natural *incentive* for actions that alleviate the scarcity. Information and incentive mechanisms to coordinate transactions between producers and consumers, and specifically whether and how prices work in this dual capacity, are the main subject matter of microeconomics.

The focus on information and incentives also tells us when and why the price mechanism can fail: it may convey inadequate or wrong information or incentives, or responses to these signals may not occur. The most frequent failure of this kind arises when one person's actions have spillover effects on others. Every car driver contributes to air pollution, which increases the scarcity of clean air. But there is no market or price for clean air, so no one gets a signal of that scarcity and no one has a profit incentive to alleviate it.

The price mechanism can also fail if responses to its signals are suppressed. Price controls suppress them. So do barriers to entry of new producers: whether natural barriers, strategic ones erected by entrenched producers, or those created by government policies. Further, existing producers can conspire to preserve some scarcity so as to drive up the price for their own greater profit. In socialist countries where production and supply are in the hands of the state, its functionaries have little to gain personally by satisfying consumers and suffer few penalties by neglecting them. Without markets the functionaries even lack good information about scarcity. That is why those systems have chronic shortages and poor quality.

More subtly, the price mechanism may fail by conveying information about matters besides scarcity. Suppose you know that used 2010 Toyota Camrys are listed for around $15,000, but don't know the quality of the particular car you are contemplating buying. You infer that the car cannot be worth much more than $15,000—otherwise the previous owner, who has had plenty of opportunity to observe its quality, wouldn't be selling it. But it could be worth less—much less. That depresses your willingness to pay. When all buyers think this and hold back, the lower demand leads to a lower price, driving even more owner-sellers out of the market. In the worst-case scenario, the whole market can collapse. Of course sellers of good cars and buyers who want good cars can both benefit by enabling credible communication of information about quality. The signals they use for this purpose are also subjects for microeconomic analysis.

A different kind of market failure arises from a moral or ethical perspective. The signals and incentives of the price mechanism are ineffective if would-be buyers don't have the purchasing power to back up their desire. The Pieman said to Simple Simon: 'Show me first your penny,' and Simon had to reply: 'Indeed I have not any'. This is a trivial example, but we may legitimately regard some wants such as health and education as meritorious or basic human rights, regardless of a person's private ability to pay for them. Deciding and implementing policies to fulfill such wants become an issue in political economy.

Prices and payments don't have to be in conventional money. One thing may be exchanged for another; payment may be deferred either as a loan or as a general favour owed. Depending on the context, one form of 'currency' may be more appropriate and effective than another. Money is crass and inappropriate in many social situations; informal arrangements of reciprocity and favour exchanges prevail among families and friends. Elaborate algorithms and organizations have evolved for matching hospitals and freshly graduated doctors, and for multilateral exchanges of organs, for example kidneys, when most people would regard their sale for money as abhorrent. Interpreted broadly and adapted to fit the context, economic analysis can be applied with considerable success to all these many and varied interactions and transactions.

So much to tell, so little space! Therefore, enough introductory chat and motivation—let us begin with the end-users of economic activity, namely consumers.

Chapter 2
Consumers

Substitution

Consumers make their decisions using some combination of calculation and instinct, and taking into account many aspects, of which the price of what they are considering buying is only one. Microeconomics pays attention to other aspects too, but focuses on prices to study the interaction of each consumer with the rest of the economy. A very broadly valid property of consumer choice, almost general enough to merit the name *law of demand* that is sometimes attached to it, is that when the price of something rises, other things being equal, less of it will be purchased.

The main explanation for this empirical regularity is *substitution*. Consumers respond to a price increase by buying less of that commodity, instead they satisfy their desires, perhaps imperfectly so, by substituting it with something else relatively cheaper. As an example, suppose the price of lager rises while that of ale stays unchanged. Consider a consumer who chose lager at the original prices. At the new prices the preference for lager is to some extent outweighed by its increased cost, so the consumer may settle for drinking less lager and more ale, that is, he or she may substitute ale for lager. If the preference for lager is not very strong, or if the price rise is very large, the consumer may switch completely to ale.

Elementary textbooks illustrate substitution using a few commodity groups (aggregates) such as food and clothing. Readers may rightly wonder how one can substitute clothing for food. If the price of food rises, can wearing more clothes on a cold day to reduce the loss of body heat adequately make up for eating less? In reality the choice is not between broad commodity groups. Instead it is between subcategories such as chicken and fish, or cotton and wool—and the narrower the categories, the greater the possibility of substitution. Actually, a little substitution occurs even at the level of broad categories, as we will soon see in an example of statistical estimation of demand.

Ability to substitute depends on time scale. A consumer with fixed habits will need time to change the mindset or cultivate taste for the substitute commodity. A coffee addict will not switch to tea unless the price of coffee rises by a lot and for a long time. The owner of a house heated by an oil-burning furnace, seeing the price of natural gas fall, may not switch to a gas furnace until the old furnace breaks down. If a price increase is expected to be temporary, the consumer may choose to ride out the increase; many consumers literally do so in their fuel-guzzler cars when the price of the fuel rises.

The relationship between the price of something and its quantity demanded is useful for economic analysis only if it is reasonably stable and can be estimated or forecast. Any one person's demand is influenced by many idiosyncratic chance factors. Luckily for the study of markets, we need only know the total or aggregate response of consumers. This makes the market demand more stable and predictable.

Aggregating demand over consumers has two effects. First, the random part of individual consumers' decisions, whether due to whim or to some idiosyncratic change in circumstances, gets averaged out to zero by the law of large numbers. Second, one consumer's substitution may be sudden, shifting from buying one type of car to another, or from car-driving to bike-riding; this gets smoothed out because different consumers shift at different prices and each of them is only a tiny part of the market. Therefore overall market demand becomes a smoother and more stable relationship than that for an individual.

The quantity of any one commodity that is demanded in the market depends not only on its own price but also on other factors. This is not a problem as long as these can be estimated and predicted. Some factors affect the market as a whole, such as advertising and seasons of the year. Most important for market analysis are prices of other related commodities. For example, if the price of lager increases, consumers will substitute it with ale; therefore at any given price of ale, more of it will be demanded than before.

Complements

However, suppose most consumers eat fish and chips together. If the price of fish increases (while that of chips stays unchanged), this increases the price of the fish-and-chips combo, so less of it is bought. Therefore for any given price of chips, their quantity demanded decreases when the price of fish rises. Consumers do not substitute away from fish toward chips: the two commodities are not substitutes for each other, but *complements*. This distinction proves important for organization of markets for such pairs, as we will see in Chapter 5 when we examine profit externalities among firms.

Demand curves

The relationship between the price of a good and its quantity demanded is best illustrated graphically. For readers unfamiliar with this representation of a relationship between two entities, here is a brief explanation (see Figure 1). The vertical and horizontal lines are called 'axes'. In our context the vertical line is

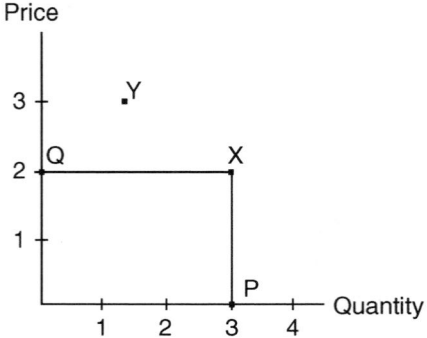

1. Representation of a point

the price axis, and the horizontal line the quantity axis. Any point in the area enclosed by the two axes represents a price–quantity combination. In Figure 1, from any point such as the one labelled X, look at the lines parallel to the two axes: XP parallel to the price axis and XQ parallel to the quantity axis. Then X represents a combination of price equal to the length XP and quantity equal to the length XQ. Thus in the figure, X represents price = 2 (dollars per bottle of lager, say) and quantity = 3 (million bottles of lager).

To reinforce your understanding, draw similar parallel lines from the point labelled Y and check that it represents the combination price = 3, quantity = 1.5. For more details, see <http://www.mathopenref.com/tocs/coordpointstoc.html>.

Figure 2 uses this method to show how the price of a good influences the total demand for it. This is called a (market) *demand curve*; it is best thought of as a sum of many different individuals' choices at each price. Suppose the good in question is the one in our opening example—namely, lager. The upper left hand portion of the curve, where the price is high and quantity small, comes from those few people with the strongest preference for lager who are willing to pay the highest prices. At lower prices

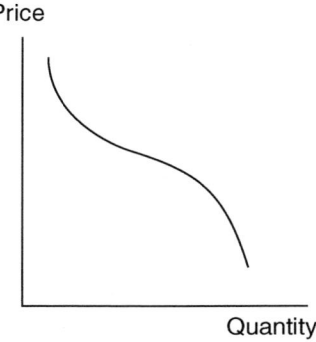

2. A market demand curve

of lager, the quantity demanded increases as the lager-lovers drink even more, and more importantly, as ale-drinkers and some wine-drinkers substitute away from those into the now-cheaper lager. Finally, at very low prices, perhaps even some tea-drinkers may try lager.

As new consumers enter the picture at successively lower prices, the added quantities are actually horizontal lines in the graph and the demand curve consists of steps. But there are thousands or millions of consumers, so each step is tiny in relation to the whole market, and the demand curve looks smooth to a sufficient degree of accuracy.

The market demand curve shows the relationship between the quantity demanded of something and its own price. This relationship changes when some third thing in the background— the price of a substitute or complement, or consumers' incomes— changes. Figure 3 shows such a shift. Suppose the demand curve is for coffee. When the price of tea (a substitute) rises, the quantity of coffee demanded increases for any given price of coffee; the demand curve for coffee shifts to the right. A similar shift to the right occurs if consumers' incomes increase. Or suppose the figure shows the demand curve for fish; it shifts to the right when the price of chips (a complement) falls.

3. Shift of the demand curve

To understand the effects of changes such as taxes or technical progress, as we will do later, we will need to know the price-responsiveness of market demand. Figure 4 shows two possibilities: high responsiveness (the technical term in the jargon of economics is *elastic* demand) on the left, and low responsiveness (*inelastic* demand) on the right. Demand is likely to be more responsive if (i) good substitutes for the commodity in question are available, (ii) the time span is sufficiently long that consumers can adjust their habits or acquire

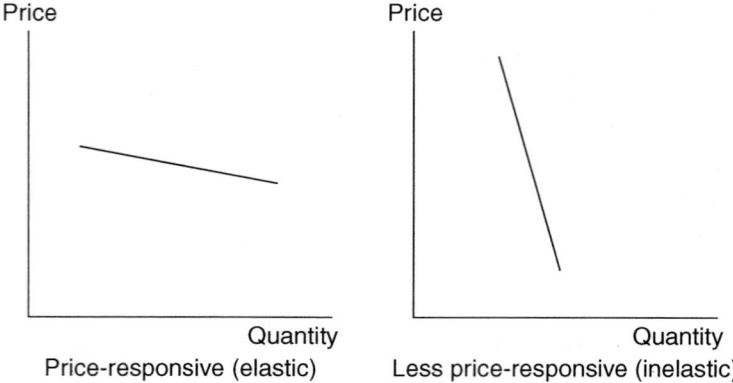

4. More and less price-responsive market demand curves

new tastes, or (iii) the price decrease is expected to be temporary so consumers seize the opportunity to buy. I drew these demand curves as straight lines only to bring out the concept of responsiveness in the simplest way—in reality, responsiveness can vary along the length of the demand curve, as in Figures 2 and 3.

Consumers as workers and savers

Excepting the few who live off inherited wealth, most of us earn the income that we spend as consumers. We also spread out consumption over our lifetimes, perhaps borrowing for education or home purchase in our youth, saving during our peak earning years, and winding down our savings after retirement. These decisions are amenable to analysis similar to that of demand for lager or coffee. An increase in the wage rate creates an increase in the incentive to work, substituting away from leisure; and an increase in the rate of return to savings increases the incentive to save, substituting away from immediate consumption in favour of future consumption.

However, another effect of price changes becomes important in these contexts. If your wage rate increases from $20 an hour to $25 an hour, you will probably increase your hours of work somewhat, say from 40 hours a week to 45 (to the extent that you have such flexibility). However, if your wage rate increases to $1 million per hour (you can always dream), you may choose to work for just a few hours each year: at that huge wage rate, your potential income is so large that you may choose to enjoy more leisure. This is called the *income effect* of the change in the price of your labour services. Similarly, if the rate of return to savings becomes very high, you are much wealthier, and may choose to use more of this wealth for immediate consumption, thus saving less.

Any price change has an income effect, but for commodities you buy, it normally only reinforces the substitution effect. For example, an increase in the price of meat, holding your income constant, makes you worse off; you respond by consuming less meat (and also less of other things). Only for so-called inferior goods, of which you buy more when you are worse off, can the income effect offset the substitution effect, and those are mostly curiosa for economics exams.

Statistical estimation

Many statisticians and economists have researched the relation in actual data between consumer demands and prices, incomes, and other relevant magnitudes. The broad concepts of substitution, complementarity, and income effects stand up quite well, although more refined hypotheses, especially those based on the assumption that consumers are perfectly rational calculators of their self-interest, have less success. I illustrate the general ideas using an influential survey of research on consumer behaviour by Richard Blundell of University College, London.

This work estimated the income and price responsiveness of demand for some broad commodity groups, based on the annual United Kingdom Family Expenditure Survey of households with children for the years 1970–84. Table 1 shows the effects of a 1 per cent increase in income, or in the price of a group listed in the left hand column, on the demand for the group listed at the top of each of columns 2–7. For example, when income rises by 1 per cent the consumption of alcohol rises by 2.014 per cent, and when the price of fuel rises by 1 per cent quantity of transport demanded goes down (negative number) by 0.480 per cent.

If a 1 per cent rise in income increases the consumption of something by more than 1 per cent, then richer households will spend a greater proportion of their income on this good than poorer households; in other words, it is regarded as being a luxury. Thus, alcohol is a luxury. (Many undergraduates would

Table 1. Substitution, complementarity, and income responsiveness

Effect of 1% increase in	On demand for					
	Food	Alcohol	Fuel	Clothing	Transport	Services
Income	0.668	2.014	0.329	1.269	1.212	1.654
Price of						
Food	−0.246	0.032	0.110	0.066	0.021	−0.004
Alcohol	0.210	−1.869	1.043	0.080	0.999	0.218
Fuel	0.464	0.671	−0.718	0.027	−0.480	0.223
Clothing	0.231	0.042	0.023	−0.716	0.163	0.045
Transport	0.048	0.345	−0.257	0.106	−0.475	0.197
Services	−0.012	0.114	−0.181	0.034	0.298	−0.587

Source: Table 2 in Blundell, *Economic Journal*, March 1988

do well to remember this!) Conversely, food and fuel, for which the income-responsiveness numbers are 0.668 and 0.329, constitute a larger proportion of the expenditure of households with lower incomes; these goods are necessities.

All numbers for the effects of an increase in the price of a commodity on its own quantity are negative; this confirms the law of demand, which says that demand curves slope down. If an increase in the price of item A increases the quantity demanded of item B, the two are substitutes (a positive number in the cell); this is the case for many category pairs in this study. Observe that food and clothing are substitutes, although the effect is small. Transport and fuel are complements; when the price of one goes up, the quantity demanded of the other goes down, as shown by the negative number in those cells.

Such tables underlie demand curves like the one shown in Figure 2 and its shift shown in Figure 3. For example, the demand curve for food will show its quantity and price, with the quantity decreasing by 0.246 per cent for each 1 per cent increase in the price. An increase in income, an increase in the price of alcohol (a substitute), or a decrease in the price of services (a complement) will shift the demand curve for food to the right.

Cost-of-living indexes

Probably the most important application of the principle of substitution is to cost-of-living indexes. To illustrate this in a simple way, limit the scope to the choice of two beverages: tea and coffee. Suppose the price of each is $10 per kilogram (kg), and you use 1kg of each per month. Your total monthly cost of beverages is $20. Now suppose the price of coffee doubles. At the new prices, buying 1kg of each would cost a total of $30. But you can do better by substituting tea for coffee. At the old prices you chose 1kg of each. You could have bought 900 grams of coffee and 1,100 grams of tea, but you chose not to. At the new prices, if you give up 100 grams (g) of coffee you can buy 200 g more of tea, thus getting 900g of coffee and 1,200g of tea. Suppose you like this better than your choice of 1kg of each at the old prices. Thus the combination of 900g coffee and 1,200g tea is better for you than that of 1kg of each, which in turn is better than 900g coffee and 1,100g tea. In between the two extremes, then, there must be a mix that is just as good in your preference scale as 1kg of each. Suppose this is 900g coffee and 1,150g tea. That costs 0.9 * $20 + 1.150 * $10 = $29.50. So you need only $29.50, not $30, to leave you just as satisfied with your beverage consumption at the new prices as you were at the old ones.

Cost-of-living indexes calculate the cost of buying a given bundle of consumer goods, usually the one actually chosen at an original set of prices. In this example, your beverage cost index would go up from 20 to 30, an increase of 50 per cent. But your actual cost of obtaining the same level of satisfaction increases by only $9.50, or 47.5 per cent. The conventionally calculated index overstates the effect of the price change.

The overstatement arises because the *relative* price of tea and coffee changes. If both prices had doubled to $20 per kilo, you could substitute between them one-for-one just as you did at the old prices, and you would have no reason to do so if you had none before (although you may choose to switch from beverages to other things whose prices have not risen so much).

Huge changes in relative prices occur over time. In the last several decades, prices of goods like medical care have risen far more than those of food, and prices of many electronic goods have fallen dramatically. Many wage contracts and public retirement schemes are tied to cost-of-living indexes that neglect substitution. This overcompensates workers and retirees when relative prices change and is costly to firms and governments. The solution is frequent adjustment of the quantities in the cost calculation as substitution changes choices. For example, the increase in the cost-of-living index from 2000 to 2001 is calculated using the 2000 quantities, that from 2001 to 2002 using the 2001 quantities, and so on. The increase from 2000 to 2012 is obtained by chaining together the 12 successive annual increases. But the solution is politically difficult to implement. Senior citizens resist attempts to link pension payments to a chained index. They like the overcompensation they now receive based on the fixed-weight index, and their votes matter to politicians.

Many travel and business sites offer comparisons of the cost of living in different cities, using the quantities appropriate to one base city (usually New York). This ignores substitution responding to relative price differences. For example, it ignores substitution away from expensive beef toward excellent and cheaper fish in Japan. Therefore all the other cities look more expensive relative to be base city than they should. I am sure you have noticed this when you travel.

The economy-wide consumer price index may not be appropriate for specific groups. For example, senior citizens spend more on age- and health-related items than does the population in general. Therefore their cost-of-living adjustments should be made on an index based on these quantities, not on general population aggregates. Of course there are practical limits to how fine distinctions of this kind can be made.

The babysitter effect

The principle that relative prices govern substitution also gives rise to the *babysitter effect*. Consider a childless couple deciding between a $20 pizza dinner and a $200 dinner at a top-end restaurant—a 10:1 price multiple. Later, when they have a child, they will have to hire a babysitter. Suppose this costs $40. Then the total cost of going to the pizzeria becomes $60 and to the restaurant $240—only a 4:1 price multiple. The couple will probably dine out less because of the added childcare expenses.

But whatever dining out they can manage is likely to shift toward higher-end restaurants.

The babysitter effect operates at larger scales, too. Consider a country exporting cars. Shipping costs are almost the same regardless of the quality of the car. So they raise the price of low-end cars relative to that of high-end cars in the destination country. Buyers respond to this; therefore high-end cars constitute a larger proportion of exports than those of the home market.

Time—and other budgets

Price is an important consideration in most people's budgeting decisions. Price may be irrelevant for a lucky few, but everyone faces some kind of other constraints on choice, notably time. The rich may be able to hire others to do chores, but they can't hire anyone else to enjoy a music concert or sport event for them, or to spend quality time with their family. Everyone must choose between competing demands on limited time, just as most people must choose between competing demands on limited income. Indeed, one can think of allocating time using the same ideas of substitution and complementarity as outlined above for allocating money. For example, when washing machines speeded up and simplified home laundry, people cleaned their clothes more often than they had done in the bad old days, but they still spent less total time on laundry work than they used to.

Opportunity cost

The thought process involved in budgeting decisions can be summarized in one general principle. When deciding whether to spend money (or time) on one good or activity, you compare it to other things you could be doing with that money (or time). With a limited income, when you buy a latte at your local coffee shop, you cannot spend that $4 on alternatives like beer or a magazine. This forgone opportunity to do alternative things is the true cost of the latte; that is why in the jargon of economics it is called *opportunity cost*. When making any decision, not just for consumers but also for firms, and often not just in an economic context but also in social, political, and other contexts, the question should be: 'Is this action worth its opportunity cost?'

This relentless insistence on comparing alternatives has made economists the butt of several jokes. Perhaps the oldest of these goes: two economists meet after a long time and are catching up on each other's news. One asks: 'How is your wife?' The other answers: 'Compared to whom?'

This discussion contains another general lesson: almost all of our choices must be made within certain limitations, whether they pertain to money, time, or our networking and information processing ability. Attempting to do one's best within such constraints is the essence of the economics of decision-making.

Risk

Risks pervade our decisions. Allocation of savings among different assets such as equities, bonds, and foreign securities, buying a home, and choices of education, career and spouse, are the biggest risky decisions most of us face. The quality of many goods cannot be perfectly known in advance, so many purchases are also risky. And there are risks of accidents, illness, theft, and so on.

In most contexts, people dislike risk. Not many people would accept a simple bet of winning or losing $100 on the toss of a fair coin. To induce them to accept the bet, either the sum they stand to win must be sufficiently larger than the one they stand to lose, or the odds of winning have to be sufficiently better than 50:50. In other words, their behaviour shows risk-aversion. Risk-aversion is greatly strengthened by *loss-aversion*: most people strongly dislike suffering losses relative to the status quo or some other reference point.

I will mention some other features of decisions under risk later, but I begin with an important consequence of risk-aversion. When faced with a risky prospect, people are willing to pay a premium to insure against it. For example, given a 5 per cent probability of incurring $10,000 in medical bills during the coming year, most people would be willing to pay something more than $500 (statistically, the average loss they would suffer) for insurance that would cover this bill in full.

Suppose Mr A is willing to pay $550. Suppose Ms B takes on Mr A's risk in exchange for a premium of $525. This means Mr A pays Ms B $525 up front. At the end of the year if Mr A has incurred the $10,000 bill, Ms B pays it; otherwise she pays nothing. There is a 95 per cent chance that Ms B simply gets to keep the $525 premium, but a 5 per cent chance that she has to pay the $10,000 thus losing $9,475. As a statistical average, Ms B makes a profit of 0.95 * 525 − 0.05 * 9475 = 498.75 − 473.75 = $25, although of course this is a risky prospect. If Ms B is sufficiently less risk-averse than Mr A, she may like this trade-off between the profit possibility and the risk. Then Mr A and Ms B have the basis for a mutually beneficial trade.

Indeed, this idea of transferring risks to those who are most willing to bear them is probably the most useful role that financial markets play in the economy (although I must admit that in recent years they have played other, less socially useful, roles). We will have occasion to see this in other contexts later.

Ms B might simply dislike risk less than Mr A does, but in practice there are other reasons why Ms B may accept the risk at a lower price than Mr A is willing to pay to avoid it. The most common reason: Ms B actually represents an insurance company *pooling* similar but independent risks for a large number of clients like Mr A. 'Independent' means that there is no common influence on the risks facing different individuals; therefore it is very unlikely that the bills for all or even too many of them will come due at the same time. Very roughly speaking, the 'law of large numbers' says that adding together many independent random outcomes averages out their uncertainty. Using our example, when the company (Ms B's) has many insured clients (like Mr A) with independent risks, close to 5 per cent of the insured clients will incur the large medical bills. Then the company will, with near-certainty, make a profit close to $25 per customer.

The requirement of independence is crucial; common influences that affect all insured risks jointly can defeat pooling with disastrous effects. The great housing bust of 2007–8 in the United States and many other countries exemplifies this. Homeowners may default on their mortgages because of illness or job loss or a family emergency. If default risks are independent across homeowners, they can be insured using pooling. Banks and other mortgage lenders insured their risks using instruments like default swaps. But when the Great Recession struck and house prices fell everywhere, too many homeowners defaulted simultaneously, and mortgage lenders and their insurers faced bankruptcy. Severe recession was the common factor ruining independence, and it had not been adequately recognized or provided for.

The independent risky prospects that can be combined to reduce overall risk don't have to be identical, as with the risks of many similar homeowners above. For example, suppose you have $2 million in savings (very prudent or very lucky you!). You could invest the money in blue-chip stocks, which are due to go up by 60 per cent if the economy as a whole does well, but down by 50 per cent if recession hits. Suppose the two scenarios are equally likely, then you face a 50 per cent risk of losing $1 million. Or you could invest your money in a biotech venture fund, which could double or halve your money with equal chance, so again you have a 50 per cent chance of losing $1 million. Suppose the two risks (a general recession and the success of a specific biotech project) are independent, then you can reduce your overall risk by *diversification* of your portfolio: holding a mix of the two. Suppose you invest $1 million in each. Now you will lose 50 per cent only if both outcomes are bad, which happens with only a 25 per cent chance, like two fair coins independently tossed both coming tails up. Table 2 shows the results of the three investment strategies in each of the four possible scenarios. Observe how the downside—your wealth falling to $1 million—has been reduced from two scenarios to one, reducing its probability from 50 per cent to 25 per cent. Of course the upside is now smaller: you will never reach $4 million. But if you are risk-averse (and perhaps also loss-averse), as you should be with all your retirement savings at stake, you will probably accept the trade-off. Note that blue-chip stocks have a role in your portfolio because they provide diversification, even though on their own they look worse than does the biotech fund: the two have the same downside risk (50 per cent loss), while blue chips have a smaller upside gain than biotech (60 per cent against 100 per cent).

Finally, one risk can be reduced by taking another risk that is negatively correlated with the first, in other words, one that has a bad outcome when the first has a good outcome and vice versa. The good and bad of the two partly offset each other, leaving you with less risk overall. This is called *hedging*. As a trivial example, at the next Super Bowl or World Cup Final, you can bet against the team you favour, so if it loses you at least have the consolation

Table 2. Reducing risk of loss by diversification

Portfolio	Both up	Blue chip up, biotech down	Biotech up, blue chip down	Both down
Blue chip	3.2	3.2	1.0	1.0
Biotech	4.0	1.0	4.0	1.0
Mix	3.6	2.1	2.5	1.0

of money won from your bet. More seriously, if your job and income depend on the success of one sector of the economy, your portfolio should have assets that do well when this sector does poorly. Investing your pension fund in the stock of the company where you work exposes you to great risk—loss of both income and wealth—if the company does badly. For diversification you should do the opposite: sell short some of its stock, in other words, commit to selling the stock at an agreed future date at an agreed price, so you will profit if the stock falls below this agreed price. Similar effects can be achieved using options, which give you the right but not the obligation to sell. Of course, owning your company's shares may have offsetting good effect on incentives, which can be important for top management, but less so for ordinary workers or even middle managers in the firm, each of whom can do little to affect the share price. I discuss this further in Chapter 3 in the section 'Firms as organizations'.

Are consumers rational?

Conventional economic theory assumed that consumers (and indeed all participants in the economy, including managers of firms, etc.) make their decisions rationally. This means that they know their own preferences, and given the choice among any alternatives, they calculate which one they like best and choose it. Psychologists and other social scientists always found this difficult to believe. For a long time the standard economic counterargument was that the rational choice approach works: it gives good explanations of market behaviour of aggregates of consumers over reasonable time-spans, and can be thought of *as if* the consumers were acting rationally. But evidence of departure from conventional rationality (actual or as if) has mounted from widely different sources including laboratory experiments, field observations, and imaging of brain activity in the decision-making process, and this is found to affect outcomes of transactions and markets in many contexts. Therefore mainstream economics has accepted and internalized many of the criticisms. The new view, often called 'behavioural economics', has supplemented conventional theories and in some cases modified and replaced them.

Definitive consensus has yet to emerge, but the most broadly accepted framework is one developed and advocated by psychologist Daniel Kahneman, who shared the 2002 economics Nobel prize for his work. He recognizes two systems the brain uses for making decisions. He calls these System I and System II to avoid prejudicial connotations. System I is fast, instinctive, and uses heuristics (trial-and-error-based automatic decision rules) instead of explicit calculation for each situation. System II is slower and makes explicit calculations, closer to the picture in conventional economics. System I has obvious merits. It saves calculation cost and time in routine decisions–and also in emergencies such as fleeing from predators. Therefore it may have emerged in the process of human evolution by natural selection. It may also play a role in impulsive decisions. The systems do not exist in separate watertight compartments: the heuristics of System I are modified over time as a result of experience and calculation, and use of System II in repeated situations generates new heuristics that are then incorporated into System I.

Even when someone wants to think about a decision in the consciously calculating framework of System II, the required information and the complexity of the calculation may prevent him or her from doing a perfect job of it. This may be especially important in decisions of the poor, who have too many things to think about: juggling multiple jobs, how the cost of every single item can fit into their limited budgets, and so on.

Perhaps the most important finding of Kahneman and others is that consumers care not only about what they finally ended up with, but also how it compares to some *reference point*, which depending on the context can be their status quo level of income or consumption, the level they regard as normal in their community, or some other standard of comparison. People regard falling below the reference point by say $100 as far more serious than an equal gain above it; this is the phenomenon of *loss-aversion*. This may occur because the loss hits System I emotions harder, but it could also figure in System II calculations because the status quo or comparisons with peers do genuinely affect preferences.

The status quo also plays a role in the *endowment effect*, where people place an extra value on something they own by the mere fact of ownership. Laboratory experiments have shown that people's willingness to pay for a small object like a coffee mug (where the status quo is no ownership) is significantly less than their willingness to accept money to give it up after owning it for as little as 20 minutes. This is probably a System I feature; habitual traders who have less attachment to objects they trade are found to be less prone to the endowment effect.

Reference points can be created and manipulated by *framing* choices in different ways. The most dramatic example is where people regard two disasters, one in which 400 lives are lost and the other in which 600 lives are at risk but 200 are saved, as different. This is probably another System I feature; slower logical thought would make them recognize that the difference is not substantive.

Many people turn down economic gain because of perceived unfairness or because the situation provokes emotions like anger. This could be cold calculation in System II, but functional magnetic resonance imaging (fMRI) studies of people making such decisions show activity in parts of the brain normally associated with System I and deep emotions. The prime example is the 'ultimatum game'. Of two players A and B, one, say A, is chosen at random to propose division of a sum like $10 between the two. If B accepts A's proposal, it is implemented; if B rejects it, neither gets anything. Cold economic logic suggests that B's choice is between something and nothing, and so B should therefore accept whatever A offers, even if it is just one penny. In fact many Bs reject anything short of about $3. And anticipating this, or driven by their own sense of fairness, most As offer more, quite often an equal split. If the role of proposer is not randomly assigned, but based on scores in a prior puzzle-solving contest, many B's are willing to accept smaller shares—presumably because they think A's success in the contest has earned him or her the right to a higher share!

In decisions involving time, people often exhibit inconsistency. They show high impatience in decisions over the immediate future, while claiming to be more patient in matters farther off. They will consume right now, planning to save or diet next year. Of course, when next year comes, immediate impatience kicks in again. In this they are just following the example of St Augustine, who asked of god: 'Give me chastity and continence, but not yet'.

Finally, people are not purely selfish; their behaviour shows empathy and concern for fairness and equity. They make choices that benefit others—certainly for family and close friends, but also for strangers—at some cost to themselves. This behaviour may have been hardwired in an evolutionary process for group survival, or deliberately instilled by socialization and education, or some combination of the two. People's preferences are heavily influenced by the society and culture in which they live and were brought up, by what their immediate friends think, and so on.

Given the space constraint, I must limit myself to listing these few departures from the economist's picture of perfect individual rationality, and turn to discuss some consequences. The new findings do not generally contradict very broad features of aggregate behaviour in markets for most everyday commodities. Instinctive behaviour usually does not contradict the 'law of demand' that when a price of something rises, less of it is demanded, but the magnitude and time-lag of the response can be affected. And loss-aversion and other features of decisions under risk can affect the properties of financial markets in significant ways.

When analysing transactions involving two or more individuals, behavioural aspects become more important. Participants in such transactions must think how their partners or opponents would actually behave, and not assume conventionally rational responses, if they are to do well in the game of strategy that is played out in such contexts. Some problems of market design, for example auctions, also involve game-theoretic considerations, and good understanding of participants' behaviour becomes essential for good design.

Policy-makers can use research on framing, immediate impatience, and limited will-power to 'nudge' the population into actions that would be in their own System II interest, such as healthy lifestyles and prudent saving. For example, many people find it mentally costly to evaluate multiple plans for saving, or are affected by immediate impatience, and end up choosing none. Making some basic plan the status quo or default option (instead of no plan) can overcome the calculation cost problem, and getting people to commit now to a saving plan that starts at a later date can counter their immediate impatience. Experiments have shown that such policies are more effective than educating people about the importance of saving or subsidizing saving. Framing and nudging can also be effective in getting people to make 'green' choices that are better for the environment. If green choices are the default option, some consumers will stay with it. Loss-aversion, where a loss in relation to the reference point looms bigger than an equal gain, also comes into play. Green choices are often somewhat more costly than non-green ones. If the default option is non-green, then making a green choice would mean accepting a loss; consumers are likely to avoid this. If the default option is green, switching to a non-green choice would bring an equal gain, but consumers are less likely to go for it.

Thus behavioural economics helps policy-makers design default options cleverly to alter consumer behaviour. This is paternalism, but of a mild or soft kind: it can help consumers overcome their short-term or System I temptations, and thereby achieve outcomes that may be in their own best calculated long-run or System II interests. However, we must recognize the potential for abuse—the state may use the same methods to encroach dangerously on individual freedom. Here as in all public policy matters, citizens must exercise eternal vigilance on policy-makers.

Chapter 3
Producers

Costs

At its most general, production is an activity that transforms inputs—raw materials and other produced goods, as well as services of labour, land, and capital—into outputs. Anyone organizing this activity must pay attention to the costs of these inputs—the prices of inputs that are used up, as well as wages, rents, and costs of capital (interest and depreciation). A producer seeking profits wants to keep costs low; non-profit and public-sector producers also want to be cost-effective and have limited budgets. Decisions of whether to produce, how much to produce, and the appropriate mix of inputs to be used, all depend on costs.

Most production decisions have multiple stages. At the earliest stage, costs must be incurred to set up the organization, usually a firm, which will carry out the production activity. In most advanced countries this cost is trivial, but as a World Bank report (<http://www.doingbusiness.org/rankings>) shows, in many less-developed countries it can be very substantial, in both money and time. Next comes the cost of acquiring land, office space, machinery, etc. The amount varies greatly depending on the nature of the activity. A petrochemical plant needs huge capital investment; a small garment-making shop can rent a room and a few sewing machines. Next, in some businesses, large expenditures are needed before anything can be produced at all. For example, software for operating systems, browsers, application programs, and games must be developed and tested before a single copy can be sold; hence the name first-copy costs. Finally, actual production involves costs of labour, materials, and so on, followed by those of marketing; these are a large part of the costs of garments, but a small part for computer software.

Decisions at each stage—whether to enter this business, the scale at which to enter, and so on—must look ahead to the prospects of recovering the costs, or making a profit. At each stage, some of the costs must be committed or *sunk*, in the sense that they cannot be recouped if something goes wrong and the subsequent stages have to be aborted. Therefore the decisions at the remaining stages should consider only whether the costs not yet sunk can be recovered.

For example, a retail garment store must rent its premises, keep some stock on hand, and hire some staff. If it fails to make any sales, it cannot recoup these costs (unless it has some return privileges for the stock). Therefore at this point all these costs are sunk, and the extra cost of the actual act of selling a dress, say, is almost zero. Should the owner therefore be willing to sell the dress to you if you offer $1 for it? No; other customers willing to pay more might show up tomorrow. Every action must be compared with all possible alternatives, and taken only if it is better than all the rest. Therefore the true cost of selling the dress today is an opportunity cost: the cost of giving up the opportunity to sell it tomorrow or later. That is uncertain; therefore if you try to bargain with the owner for a better price, the owner's decision involves some intricate estimation and calculation of these opportunities and risks. That is one reason why stores have non-negotiable fixed prices and rarely give lower-level employees any power to bargain with customers. The garment store may discount its merchandise drastically at the end of the season, as do sellers of perishable fruit or vegetables in farmers' markets at the end of the day, because the opportunity cost of forgoing future sales is very low at that point.

This brief general discussion suffices to show that cost calculations are not simply matters of arithmetic to be totted up in a ledger or a spreadsheet; they involve much judgement about uncertain prospects.

How costs enter into firms' decisions depends on the nature of the market. Let us consider various possibilities.

Small firms: supply curves

Producers in some markets are so small that individually they cannot influence the price, which is determined by larger forces of supply and demand in the whole market. Farmers in most agricultural markets, and most mining and petroleum producing firms, are in this situation. Each such firm has only one basic decision to make: how much to produce at the going price.

For profit-seeking firms, one general principle governs this decision: expand the operation so long as the addition to revenue from the added quantity exceeds the extra cost of supplying it (the technical term in the jargon of economics is *marginal cost*). But correct interpretation of marginal cost depends on the context, in other words, on the precise 'margin' at which the decision is being made. At a final stage when all costs have been sunk, the marginal cost may be zero or very small; as a train or airplane is ready to depart with some empty seats, the marginal cost of another passenger is virtually zero. But at an earlier stage, when the decision is whether to schedule that train or the flight, the marginal cost includes all the crew and fuel costs and any opportunity cost of using the equipment for this purpose rather than on some other route. Finally, at the earliest stage when considering whether to set up or expand the rail company or the airline, the marginal cost includes the opportunity cost of using capital for this purpose rather than another, say a pharmaceutical firm.

In many cases, the marginal cost rises with the quantity. For example, a mining operation starts with the most easily accessible or richest deposits, and only then moves on to the ones that are more difficult and therefore more costly to extract; a farmer cultivates the best land first, and expands output by gradually turning to less productive land. This process naturally brings expansion to an end at any given price. Eventually the marginal cost catches up with the price, making further expansion unprofitable. That determines the firm's choice of quantity (its supply) at that price. We can then show the relationship between price and the total quantity supplied in the market, in other words a (market) supply curve, just as we graphed a market demand curve coming from buyers' decisions.

In other cases marginal cost decreases (or at least does not increase) as quantity increases, so further expansion becomes even more profitable at a given price. For example, once the first-copy costs of software development are sunk, the marginal cost of printing and mailing a CD are minimal, and the marginal cost of a web-based download is almost zero; the cost of building a petrochemical plant increases less than proportionately with its capacity, so the marginal cost of successively larger capacity decreases. In such cases one or a few firms grow to the point where they constitute a large fraction of the market, and each has some influence over the price. Then the strategic analysis of the next section becomes relevant. For now, let us stay with the case where each firm's quantity at a given price is such a small part of the market that it has no power to influence the price.

The construction of the market supply curve is simply a mirror image of that of the market demand curve we saw in the previous

5. A market supply curve

chapter. Figure 5 gives an example. The curve slopes upward, because at higher prices more firms find it profitable to enter this market, to expand their plants, run more shifts, or engage in more selling efforts, depending on the time span involved and on the specifics of production and selling in their industry. At a very low price, just a few firms with superior proprietary technology, land, or other resources may be able to supply, so the lower left portion of the curve has low price-responsiveness. At somewhat higher prices, many firms with standard general technologies enter the picture, so the price responsiveness is higher and the curve is flatter. Finally, at the right hand end, the industry hits capacity limitations and price-responsiveness decreases again.

Just as a market demand curve shifts because of changes in some background variables such as consumer incomes or prices of substitutes or complements, a supply curve can shift because of changes in costs of inputs or technical progress. Figure 6 gives an example of the latter. The shift is bigger on the right hand side of the curve than on the left: the idea is that the left end of the curve corresponds to firms that are already at the technological frontier and do not benefit much from further advances, while other firms benefit by catching up as well as from new advances, so their costs decrease more.

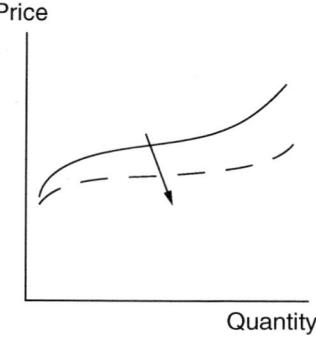

Quantity

6. Shift of the supply curve

We can also develop some general ideas about when supply curves will be flatter, in other words more price-responsive (elastic) as in the left panel of Figure 7, or steeper, in other words less price responsive (inelastic) as in the right hand panel. Some examples of high price-responsiveness are: (i) If the time span is long, more firms can enter or exit, and existing firms can make more adjustments in their production plans. (ii) In industries with standard technologies to which all firms have easy access, a small price increase around their common level of unit cost will generate a large quantity response. (iii) If a price increase in extractive industries is believed to be temporary, firms expect to profit by producing more right now and will respond rapidly to the increase. Low price responsiveness arises in the opposite circumstances, and in some other situations. For example, if the whole industry hits a capacity constraint (limit to available land or a transport bottleneck) then the price incentive cannot bring forth greater supply.

These examples are not meant to be definitive or exhaustive; they are merely intended to spur your thinking about situations you may have experienced or observed. In Chapter 4, I will put together the ideas about demand and supply curves to help you understand the operation of markets.

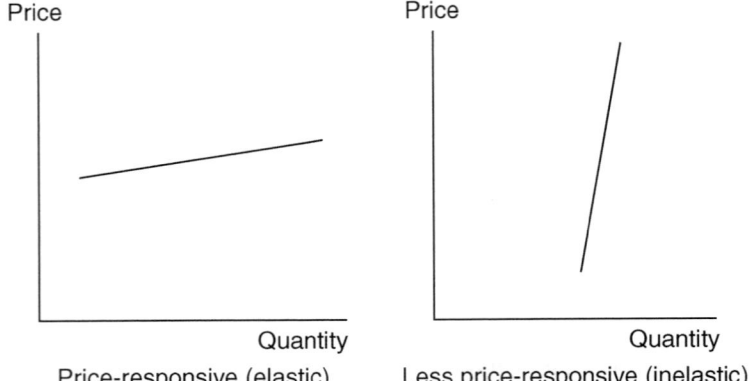

7. **More and less price-responsive market supply curves**

In Chapter 2, the concepts were illustrated using a statistical estimation of aggregate consumer demand. A similar economy-wide supply curve would be less meaningful in microeconomics. Industry-specific, statistically estimated cost curves do exist, but even they fail to bring out the role of individual firms. Therefore I will illustrate cost and supply curves using an example based on reality but without supporting statistical evidence.

Consider the short-term supply curve for crude oil. At this stage, new exploration and development of reserves is not a consideration, and those costs are sunk. The marginal costs of production are those of maintenance and operation of the existing wells and related equipment and facilities to bring the oil to the surface (these are called *lifting costs* in the jargon of the industry), and supply is limited by the capacity of the existing wells. Cost and capacity data are available for some countries; these are shown in Table 3.

Figure 8 shows the same information graphically in a supply curve, where each country or region is willing to produce a quantity up to its capacity when the price exceeds its marginal cost.

Table 3. Crude oil lifting costs and capacities, 2009

Country or Region	Lifting costs per barrel	Capacity (million barrels/day)	Total capacity upto this cost
Central and South America	6.21	10.28	10.28
Middle East	9.89	24.27	34.55
Africa	10.31	9.36	43.91
United States	12.18	8.62	52.53
Canada	12.69	3.40	55.93

Source: Cost data from <http://www.eia.gov/tools/faqs/faq.cfm?id=367&t=6>, capacity data from <http://www.eia.gov/forecasts/steo/data.cfm?type=tables>, Tables 3b and 3c

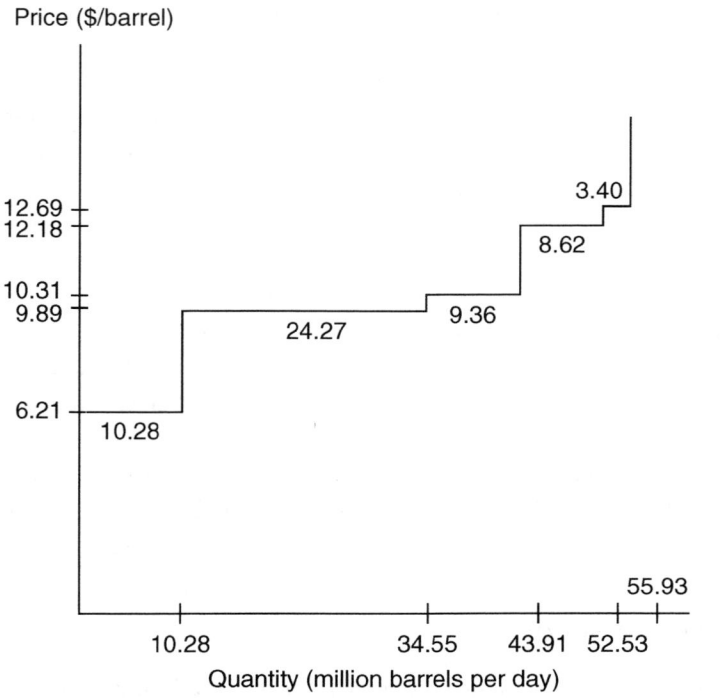

8. An illustrative short-run supply curve for crude oil

Although this example makes the idea of a supply curve stand out vividly, it is merely illustrative. First, data are not available for all countries; for example Russia and China are omitted for want of cost data. Second, countries or regions are not the right unit of analysis. Ideally we should have data on lifting costs and capacities for all the thousands of individual wells. These differ greatly within a country; they would generate a smooth supply curve instead of the large steps shown. Finally and most importantly, lifting costs are not correct short-run marginal costs. Firms that operate the wells have the choice of leaving oil in the ground, thus producing at less than full capacity, if they believe that prices will rise in the future. In other words, opportunity costs are the correct measure. But these are based on expectations and calculations done within firms, and are not available in reported data. Therefore this example can be used to improve understanding of the ideas, but should not be taken literally.

The decision of how much to produce or supply is subtle and complex in many ways. Except for custom production to order, the decision must be made without knowing the exact demand. If you produce too much, you run the risk of failing to sell all; if too little, you run the risk of disappointing and alienating some customers. Firms would not be willing to produce more unless they could expect to recoup the costs. In affluent market economies consumers are willing to pay a higher price to get assured availability, and competitive firms profit from catering to them. That helps explain why my local coffee shop almost never runs out of goodies. In socialist economies, producers suffer no penalty for disappointing customers; on the contrary they enjoy some power by being able to allocate scarce goods to favoured customers. That helps explain why those economies always suffer shortages.

Pricing strategies

When a firm can influence the price in its market, it must devise pricing strategies for its interaction with customers as well as with competing firms. I will focus on private-sector firms whose main objective is profit; related but different analyses apply to non-profit or public enterprises.

The customers of any firm differ in the satisfaction they get from its products relative to other things on which they could spend their money, and therefore differ in their willingness to pay for its products. A profit-seeking firm would benefit by serving any customer who pays more than the marginal cost of the service. But it does not want to give the same deal to other customers who are willing to pay more. Firms' attempts to extract from each customer the full amount that he or she is willing to pay explain many pricing strategies we observe.

Airlines provide the best-known example. Business travellers are willing to pay higher prices than are tourists or people visiting family. Airlines would like to attract the latter types with low fares without offering the same deals to business types, but cannot do so directly. Blatant discrimination probably would be illegal and is certainly impractical. Any obvious indicators—having your company's travel office make the reservation, wearing a suit, and so on—can easily be circumvented. So airlines exploit other differences between the types: business travellers want flexibility, while tourists and family travellers are willing to make advance purchases and commit themselves to a schedule; business travellers (actually, their companies) are more willing to pay for the comfort of business- or first-class on long hauls; and so on. Therefore airlines offer different types of tickets: cheap, advance purchase, non-refundable economy (cattle-class) tickets, and high-priced, business- or first-class, unrestricted tickets. When the prices are calculated and set in just the right way, each type of traveller selects the type of ticket and service the airline intends for him or her.

This strategy of separating or 'screening' different buyers with different willingness to pay by offering different versions of the product at different prices and letting them select one is called *screening by self-selection*. Once you understand this method of price-discrimination you will see it everywhere. The following are just a few examples.

Computer software often comes in a professional or business version and a lite or student version. The latter is lower priced but has fewer features. Companies usually buy the first kind: they believe their employees need all the features, or that they should have them just in case they need them later. Price is less of a concern for them. Casual users paying out of their own pockets are more likely to be satisfied with only the basic features. Vendors can profit by separating the two types and charging each a price closer to the buyers' willingness to pay. How is the lite version made? Usually by taking the full version and disabling the advanced features! So the price difference has nothing to do with any additional cost of programming the advanced features; its sole purpose is to achieve more profitable screening.

Coffee shops serve two types of customers, regulars and transients. Regulars are more likely to respond to price differences among different coffee shops in town, because over the year their savings will amount to quite a lot. Transients are likely to go to the first one they find on the street and not spend time searching for a lower price. To separate the two, the shop sets a high price and gives 'buy 10, get one free' loyalty cards. More generally, quantity discounts can serve a similar purpose.

Insurance companies would like to charge higher premiums per dollar of coverage to the applicants whose risks are higher. Some risks can be assessed and premiums charged accordingly: smokers, homeowners in flood-prone areas, and so on, pay more for insurance. Other risks require screening by self-selection. People often have a better idea of their own risk than does the insurance company, and those with higher risk are less willing to bear the risk themselves. Therefore versions of insurance policies can help separate them. Policies with high deductible or co-insurance but low premiums are more appealing to the low-risk types who don't expect to have to use the service often. The high-risk types are keener to avoid having to pay more or they are more often out of pocket, so they prefer policies with fuller coverage even though the premiums are higher. With suitably designed premiums and co-pays in separate packages, insurance companies can separate the two types and enjoy higher profits.

Issuers of credit cards have three types of potential customers. From their perspective, those likely to default are the worst, but those who pay off the whole account every month are almost equally bad. Those who run revolving balances and pay a lot of interest are the best. The issuers developed a clever strategy to attract selectively these profitable types: an offer to transfer balances from another card at an attractively low interest rate for the first few months. Obviously this appeals to those who have run up balances and are paying higher interest charges elsewhere.

Such strategies have limitations. They do not extract from each and every buyer his or her full willingness to pay, usually for the simple reason that sellers do not have this information. The strategies must be coarser, like the airline's two-fare strategy above. Within each type there is heterogeneity of willingness to pay. For example business fliers' (or their firms') willingness to pay for flexibility and comfort will vary between top- and middle-level managers, and from one company to another. The two-fare strategy does not exploit such fine detail, but it works well enough for airlines to increase their profits (or reduce their losses). Vendors on the internet now have so much information about individual buyers from their previous purchases and other databases that they can attempt perfect price discrimination: when you log into their site, they instantly estimate your willingness to pay and display an individually tailored price to extract it all. Car insurance companies can use data from 'telematic' devices (see <http://en.wikipedia.org/wiki/Telematics>) in the car to monitor the driver's actions in great detail, and find premiums precisely tailored to his or her skill and care.

There are further limitations. First, discrimination is not possible if buyers can easily resell the good or service—so anyone can pretend to be a low-paying customer and then resell to others undercutting the price the firm wants to charge them. Next, discrimination based on some observable differences among consumers, such as age or gender, may be illegal or socially unacceptable. Third, screening by self-selection cannot go so far that buyers with higher willingness to pay settle for the cheaper version. For example the difference between business and economy fares cannot exceed the extra value business fliers place on the extra comfort; therefore the firm may be unable to extract their full willingness to pay. But some profitable discrimination is feasible, and is frequently used.

Some pricing strategies exploit insights from behavioural economics. Recall Kahneman's finding that people often make decisions using the instinctive System I. In purchase decisions they focus on the most visible major item of information about a product without taking the time and effort to investigate other seemingly minor matters. Therefore sellers highlight a bargain price, hiding other charges that customers discover only when it is too late. Airlines publicize low fares, concealing baggage fees, payments for inflight food and drink, and so on. One airline even planned to charge passengers for using lavatories on its aircraft, but retreated when that attracted too much bad publicity. Many hotels advertise attractively low room rates. Only when guests are settled in do they discover how much more they must pay for internet access, use of the fitness room, and so on.

Firms' responses to inflation exploit the behavioural trait that prices are more visible than some other attributes of products.

A price rise, even if justified by cost increases, might deter some consumers. Instead, where possible firms keep the price and outer appearance of the package unchanged, but quietly and gradually reduce the contents: fewer or smaller cookies, for example. When this has gone too far to pass unnoticed, they raise the price in a jump, using as their justification an increase in contents (actually only back to the original level!).

Rivalry among large firms

Unless a firm is so small in its market that its sole decision is how much to produce at the going price, it must be aware of its rival firms and strategize against, or sometimes jointly with, them. The first step in such strategic thinking is the recognition that rival firms are strategizing similarly and simultaneously.

First, let us look at a little of the terminology you will meet, not only in economics books but also in business newspapers and magazines. A market with only one firm is called a *monopoly*, from the Greek *monos* (single, alone); *poleein* (to sell). (Its mirror-image, a single firm on the buying side of a market, is a monopsony.) Governments grant monopoly rights for limited periods to inventors through patents, and to authors and creators of software through copyrights, but also to favoured firms or in exchange for political contributions or bribes. A market with a small number of firms (usually fewer than ten) is called an *oligopoly* (Greek *oligos* (little, few)). If oligopolists collude to keep prices high and new competitors out of their market they are said to form a *cartel*. Such practices, at least if carried out explicitly, are illegal in most countries, and antitrust policies try to keep markets competitive. It is not easy to define what constitutes 'a market' because most things have some substitutes and ultimately everything competes for the consumer's budget, but approximate and porous boundaries can be drawn for purposes of economic analysis and antitrust policy.

Strategic interaction in oligopoly can be understood using game theory. The game of competition among such firms is usually a *prisoners' dilemma*. In the story that gives the game its name, the police have arrested two people whom they could convict of a minor crime, but suspect them to be guilty of a much more serious crime. They interrogate the two separately, and invite each to confess also implicating the other. Each will get leniency if he or she confesses while the other holds out, but an especially harsh sentence if matters are the other way round. Therefore each finds it in his or her own interest to confess, regardless of what he or she thinks the other will do. But when both confess they are both convicted of the bigger crime, which is worse for both than the sentence for the minor crime that they would get if neither confessed.

In an oligopoly, each firm is tempted to compete to win customers at the expense of other firms by offering a lower price, a better product, more after-sales service, advertising, and so on. If the other firms do not use such competitive strategies, the one that does gets a big advantage; if others do, the one that does not is left behind. But when all compete, their actions defeat each other. They become prisoners of a dilemma: all end up with lower prices or higher costs, and lower profits. Of course the consumers benefit from price competition, and as we shall see in Chapter 4, competition promotes overall social efficiency. But the firms do lose. To resolve their dilemma, they must devise ways to promise credibly to one another not to compete so hard. Conversely, if antitrust policy has the overall social interest as its objective, it should anticipate and prevent attempts by firms to collude.

Firms compete with others that are already *in* the relevant market; they compete as hard or harder *for* the market. When a dominant position in a lucrative market is at stake, for example when airwave spectrum for mobile phones in a big city is being sold, competing firms bid aggressively for that right, dissipating the profits they stand to make. Some such dilemmas may also hurt overall social benefit. If one firm beats another by one day in a race to invent and patent a mass-market drug to treat a condition like high cholesterol or erectile dysfunction, the benefit to society is small—because the treatment is simply available for one extra day—but the benefit to the patent-winning firm is huge: 20 years of monopoly profit. Therefore such R&D competition is often carried to excess. Competition for lucrative illegal markets, such as territories for drug-dealing or gambling, can be literally cut-throat.

Can firms avoid these prisoners' dilemmas? A primary requirement is an ongoing and stable interaction. Suppose the firms in an industry have reached an agreement to keep prices high. Such agreements are mostly unenforceable at law; in fact explicit collusion is illegal under most countries' antitrust laws. Therefore any implicit agreement has to be self-sustaining. Each firm is tempted to undercut the agreed price and increase its own profit at the expense of other firms. But it risks tit-for-tat retaliatory price cuts by the others, leading to a collapse of the arrangement and then lower profits for all including itself. It must weigh the immediate profit gain against the risk of future loss. If it expects a stable and ongoing interaction, the long run will be more important in its calculation, and it is likely to desist from breaking the agreement. But if the industry is declining or likely to be rendered obsolete by technical change, or if the agreement is likely to be upset by newcomers who are not part of it, then the firm may go for the short-run advantage by cutting its price. Of course when all firms do this, the dilemma strikes.

Firms do try explicit collusion in violation of antitrust laws; probably the best-known recent example, vividly described in *The Informant* by Kurt Eichenwald, was the market for lysine, a chemical widely used in animal-feed. Executives of the leading firms, Archer Daniels Midland of the US and Ajinomoto of Japan, met to negotiate, keep prices high, and divide up the market. Of course the customers suffered. The conspirators' private slogan was: 'The competitors are our friends, and the customers are our enemies'.

Firms also think up some ingenious devices for implicit collusion. For example, in a round of US mobile telephone spectrum auctions in multiple area codes, bidders communicated their special interest in particular areas by adding the last three digits of that area code to bids; for example $10,000,415 says to other bidders that I am willing to fight hard for area code 415 (San Francisco), so you had better stay out. Other firms might have special stakes in other areas. The messages enable them to divide up the whole market and avoid competition in each area.

Entrenched monopolists or oligopolists wish to deter new entrants, who would dilute their market power. They can threaten to start a price war that would make entry unprofitable. But mere words may be seen as empty threats; they have to be made credible. One device is to set a price lower than the existing market power would justify, the aim being to convince a prospective entrant that the incumbent firms' costs are very low, so the entrant would find the competition too fierce. The incumbent firms can also maintain a large capacity, so they can easily expand output and start a price war should a new entrant appear. This strategy manipulates costs: by making the commitment to high capacity, in other words sinking the capacity cost, the firm lowers the marginal cost of future expansion.

The record of success in creating and sustaining cartels over a long haul has not been very good. The crude petroleum cartel OPEC achieved notoriety in the 1970s. But cheating by some of its smaller members, increased production from nonmembers, and buyers' actions to decrease their oil-dependence reduced OPEC's market power within a decade. Attempts of other commodity and mining industries to mimic OPEC were nonstarters or very short-lived. China recently tried to exert monopoly over rare-earth elements, which are vital for cutting-edge technologies including computers, smartphones, and weaponry. But supplies from other countries are quickly emerging, technological improvements are reducing the amounts of the elements needed in these devices, and recycling is reducing the need for new supplies, thereby eroding China's market power. The diamond cartel organized by the firm of De Beers is probably the only one to have survived and flourished for almost a century. That required eternal vigilance to absorb some new producers and deter others, create and sustain a market by imaginative advertising, and to avoid competition from sales of pre-owned diamonds by inducing a mindset in diamond owners never to resell, or making it possible to sell only at a great loss.

Supply chains

Buyers are not always final consumers. Production of most goods involves several stages and assembly of different components. The output of one stage is sold to another firm that will process it and combine it with other inputs; firms buy components made by other firms. As containerization and air-freight lowered transport costs and international trade regimes became more liberal, supply chains went global in the 1990s and early 2000s, although recent years have seen some retreat from extreme outsourcing. Transactions where both buyers and sellers are firms constitute at least as important a part of the overall market economy as do sales to final consumers. Management of supply chains is almost as important a part of firms' activities as organization of their own production.

If the items one firm sells to another are standardized commodities, for example fuel or RAM memory chips, then the transactions fall within the scope of standard supply and demand analysis. The demand curve in this case comes from firms, not consumers, but the principle of substitution applies and the law of demand holds. But more often the items are not standardized; the buying firm has specific requirements, for example a machine to serve a particular purpose or custom software, and the items must be designed to meet them. The transaction requires a contract between the two firms, and its terms are subject to bilateral negotiation. The price can be affected by their relative bargaining powers, which in turn depend on their alternative opportunities: the buying firm may have other potential sources and the selling firm other potential contracts it could enter into. Once the contract is made, the two firms are to some extent stuck with each other. No contract can anticipate and cover all possible contingencies. Therefore each firm has some wiggle room, which it can opportunistically exploit to its own advantage and at the expense of the partner. All this makes the operation and the analysis of inter-firm transactions much more complex than simple supply and demand. In this brief introduction I cannot develop details, but one important implication follows.

Firms as organizations

Firms buy some inputs to their production from other firms and make some inputs in-house. The choice is theirs, and thinking about it raises some intriguing and basic questions.

As I mentioned in Chapter 1 and will discuss in more detail in Chapter 4, the market provides good information and incentives through the price system. Then why not leave everything to the market? Why not produce each tiny link of the supply chain in a separate firm, which sells its output in a market to another firm that makes the next link? Or why not do exactly the opposite: make everything in-house? Carrying this thought to its logical limit, why not have just one firm, Gross Domestic Products Inc., for the nation's economy?

Ronald Coase suggested the answer, and Oliver Williamson enriched and developed it; both won Nobel prizes for their contributions. The key idea is that using markets entails significant costs. Most goods transacted between firms have to be

tailored to the specific needs of the buyer. Therefore the buyer must locate a suitable supplier, and negotiate a contract.
The contract cannot specify every contingency in detail. Then each party can engage in opportunistic behaviour, for example cutting costs and shading quality a little, or demanding alteration of the terms of the contract in its favour when the other party can no longer find a new partner. Therefore contractual performance must be monitored, disputes negotiated or ultimately settled in court, and so on. All these things are costly. In some countries the court may be slow, inefficient, biased, or corrupt; then contracts must be self-enforcing based on long-term reputations and relationships, which require costly build-up and maintenance. All such costs, called *transaction costs*, can be just as important as ordinary costs of production.

In-house production also involves transaction costs, but of a different kind. The information and incentives that would be contained in the market price have to be replicated internally. The firm as a whole profits by responding to a higher price: expanding production and doing so in a cost-efficient way.
To transfer this incentive to individual managers, their compensation has to include some profit-sharing. That is a cost to the firm's ultimate owners, the shareholders. Workers' performance may have to be monitored. Such internal transaction costs of corporate governance rise rapidly with the size and depth of the managerial hierarchy. Incentivizing the managers, monitoring the workers, monitoring the monitors, preventing collusion among the lower tiers of workers and managers to defeat upper tiers' strategies to make them work harder and smarter—all these get harder and costlier, limiting the firm's span of control. Running the whole economy as one firm becomes virtually impossible and hugely counterproductive; failure of central planning in communist countries gives conclusive proof of this.

A firm's make-or-buy decision has to consider transaction costs of the two modes in addition to the ordinary costs of internal production and the price of buying from another firm, and choose the mode that has lower overall cost. The result will vary depending on the context. Therefore we see some highly integrated firms that make almost everything in-house, some who merely design their products and do some final assembly, outsourcing almost all manufacturing, and many somewhere between these extremes. Many petroleum companies exemplify integration. An oil field and a refinery connected by a pipeline are stuck with each other; it would be very costly for one to switch to a relationship with another firm. Therefore risks of opportunistic behaviour are large; they are most easily mitigated by bringing both operations within one company. Some makers of desktop computers and many garment and shoe companies exemplify the opposite extreme: 'hollow' companies that do almost no manufacturing. Their components are standardized, the quality of their suppliers can be monitored relatively easily, and they can relatively easily switch to other suppliers even in other countries if necessary. Therefore transaction costs are low, and they can outsource manufacturing to the lowest-wage sources.

Firms don't always get the make-or-buy decision right; many have sent manufacturing offshore to low-wage countries only to find that the advantage of low labour costs was wiped out by quality problems, costs and delays in transporting the product to markets back home, greater risks of supply disruption, risks in contract enforcement, and loss of synergies of proximity between R&D, design, production, and business processing. Labour cost advantage of countries like China is also eroding as their wages rise faster than those in the US.

The transaction cost perspective also helps explain the large conglomerates we find in many less-developed countries. These are often family-owned, and span things with little in common: textiles, chemicals, cars, beverages, hotels, information technology services, and more. A rationale can be found in the defective legal system of these countries. Formal contract enforcement is unreliable; business dealings are governed by reputation and relationships. If your company has accumulated profits but the best new investments are in some other line of business, you cannot lend out the capital to an unconnected firm and hope for honest return on your investment. Instead you bring that activity under the umbrella of your own family firm, where relational aspects are strongest. The conglomerate need not create any synergies or conventional efficiencies in production. Instead it reduces governance costs.

Chapter 4
Markets

Supply and demand

Thomas Carlyle supposedly said: 'Teach a parrot the terms supply and demand and you've got an economist.' As with many such glib sayings, this gets at only the starting point of an intricate and even beautiful mechanism, but it is a good place to start. Although economics has become much more mathematical, the simple diagrammatic apparatus of supply and demand curves, which goes back a century and owes much to the writings of the British economist Alfred Marshall, remains the basic tool in most economists' thinking.

In Chapters 2 and 3, we met demand and supply curves. Now put together the demand and supply curves for some commodity, say coffee, into one diagram, as shown in Figure 9. The two curves meet at the point labelled E, which corresponds to price P and quantity Q. If price P prevails in the market, the quantity demanded by consumers equals the quantity supplied by the producers, namely Q. Supply equals demand; the market clears; we have equilibrium.

What process or mechanism might bring about this price? The simple answer goes as follows. If the price is higher than P, then at that price the quantity that producers are willing to supply will

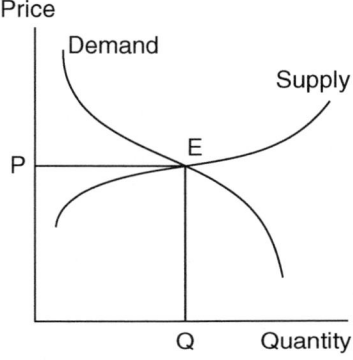

9. Equilibrium of supply and demand

exceed Q along the rising supply curve, and the quantity that consumers demand will be less than Q along the downward-sloping demand curve. Therefore at this high price there will be an excess of supply over demand. Then producers will accept a lower price, and consumers will respond to the lower price. The opposite chain of events will unfold if the price is less than P. Thus from either direction the price will move toward P.

The trouble with this answer is that in the logic of supply and demand curves each consumer and producer responds to 'the prevailing price,' which is outside the control of any one of them. Who, then, adjusts the price toward equilibrium?

Some financial and commodity markets do have explicit market-makers who set the price. Market-makers maintain an inventory of certain assets or commodities, from which they sell to buyers and to which they add what they acquire from sellers. If they see their inventory shrinking, they raise the price; if it is growing they lower the price. Thus the price adjusts to equate the flow into and out of inventory, thereby equating supply and demand. The incentive for market-makers comes from a spread between their buying and selling prices, but in a 'thick' market, in other words one where the volume and number of transactions is large, the spread is small and the outcome is close to the story of the intersection of supply and demand curves.

Most markets lack market-makers; then the processes of matching buyers and sellers and setting prices are more complex and differ from one situation to another. Whether the outcome can be described and studied *as if* it occurs at the supply–demand intersection is unclear, and can only be decided from experience. In Chapter 6 we will meet some examples of other mechanisms, but for now I focus on supply-and-demand as this is the simplest to explain, as well as the source of most common beliefs about markets, some valid and others not.

Efficiency

Figure 10 shows a supply–demand graph; each curve is drawn as a straight line purely for visual simplicity. Imagine the resulting equilibrium at price P and quantity Q as arising from successive decisions to increase quantity starting at zero. The buyer of the very first unit is willing to pay the price indicated by the height A, but only has to pay P. Therefore this buyer derives an extra benefit (the technical term in the jargon of economics is *consumer surplus*) equal to the height AP. The first unit is produced at marginal cost B, but the producer gets price P for it, thus deriving an extra benefit (*producer surplus*) equal to the height BP. Adding the two, the first unit of quantity yields an extra benefit to the economy as a whole (*social surplus*) equal to the height AB.

Proceeding to successively higher quantities, the willingness to pay falls and the marginal cost rises. For the unit of quantity at X, the buyer is willing to pay C and gets consumer surplus CY; the producer incurs marginal cost D and gets producer surplus YD. Therefore this unit of quantity contributes social surplus CY + YD = CD. Finally, at the quantity Q, the buyer pays what he or she is willing to pay, and the producer recoups his or her marginal cost; each gets zero surplus.

For any quantity beyond Q, the buyer's willingness to pay (measured along the falling demand curve) would be less than the producer's marginal cost (measured along the rising supply curve). Such a unit would contribute negative social surplus; it would be inefficient to produce it.

In other words, the supply–demand mechanism produces just the quantity that contributes positive social surplus, and no more. The outcome maximizes the total social surplus; it is economically efficient.

This property of efficiency of markets can be validated in far more general contexts, and constitutes a basic 'theorem' of economics. Of course conclusions of any theorem are valid only so far as its underlying assumptions are valid, and I will have more to say on this. Begin with clarification of the concept of efficiency.

Most importantly, the concept says nothing about how the maximized social surplus is divided among people in the economy. In Figure 10, the total consumer surplus is the area

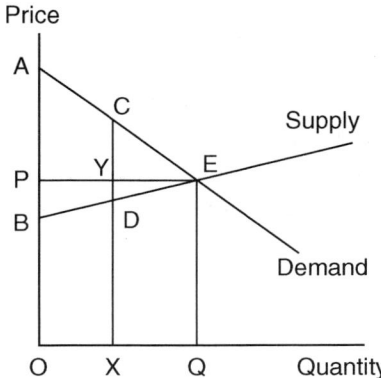

10. Efficiency of supply–demand equilibrium

swept by the heights like AP and CY, namely the area of the triangle APE; the total producer surplus is the area of the triangle BPE. Their relative magnitudes depend on the accidental shapes of demand and supply curves, and say nothing about the merit or justice of the split. Producer surplus contributes to the firms' profit, and goes to their owners as dividends or capital gains. The ethical merit of this is unclear. You may think that owners of firms are always the undeserving rich, but they may include shareholders like your grandparents or parents who get only a modest retirement income from their pension funds.

Economic efficiency of an outcome means merely that any change that benefits one person hurts someone else. It says nothing about distributive justice or ethical merit. The concept is named *Pareto efficiency* for its inventor Vilfredo Pareto, a nineteenth–twentieth-century engineer, sociologist, and economist. To give an extreme example, an outcome is deemed Pareto efficient if any change that benefits a homeless person on the streets of New York hurts Warren Buffett.

Economists' sometimes heartless emphasis on Pareto efficiency has produced some sharp jokes at their expense. My favourite: a businessman, a priest, and an economist are a golf threesome held up by a very slow group ahead of them. After cursing the slowpokes for a long time, they discover that those players are all blind. The businessman is mortified and promises to contribute $10,000 to the Foundation for the Blind. The priest vows to pray to restore their sight. The economist says: 'Wouldn't it promote Pareto efficiency—be better for us, and no worse for them—if they played at night?'

In my opinion efficiency should not be the sole criterion, or in some instances even the primary criterion, to judge economic outcomes; some efficiency should be sacrificed if that yields sufficient improvement in terms of some other social or ethical criterion. I believe Warren Buffett would agree, even though some libertarian or extreme right-wing politicians would not. I said 'should be sacrificed'; whether that happens depends on political institutions and processes.

But wait; the news gets worse. Market outcomes can fail to be efficient even in the limited Pareto sense. When one buyer's or one seller's actions affect others through channels outside the market, adversely as with pollution and congestion and beneficially as with vaccination, market outcomes are not Pareto efficient. And actions to remedy these inefficiencies may be easy for economists to specify on paper but difficult to implement in the real political world. I discuss these issues in the next chapter. Right now let me just warn you against a common pitfall. The word 'equilibrium' misleads people into thinking that everything is for the best in the best of all possible worlds. That is not always or necessarily so: the word merely signifies that the price clears the market; it equates supply and demand. Any other properties, even limited ones like Pareto efficiency, may be valid but must be established separately.

Now for some good news. Many well-meaning policy activists condemn markets using slogans like 'Food for people, not for profit.' Our study of the market mechanism shows that people and profit need not be in conflict. When markets work well (which may need vigilant oversight and regulation), producers' private pursuit of profit efficiently serves the purpose of supplying consumers with their wants for food and other things. High prices signal the wants, and profit provides the incentive to fulfill the wants. In fact this was one of the earliest insights of economics, and was brilliantly expressed by Adam Smith in *The Wealth of Nations*, which is arguably the founding text of economics: 'It is not from the benevolence of the butcher, the brewer, or the baker that we expect our dinner, but from their regard to their own self-interest.'

Shift of equilibrium

If underlying conditions of demand and supply change, market equilibrium will shift from the old intersection to the new one. Whether the price and the quantity increase or decrease depends on the type of shift of demand and supply that has occurred. There are four basic types of such shifts, illustrated in Figure 11. When you have seen and understood these, you will be equipped

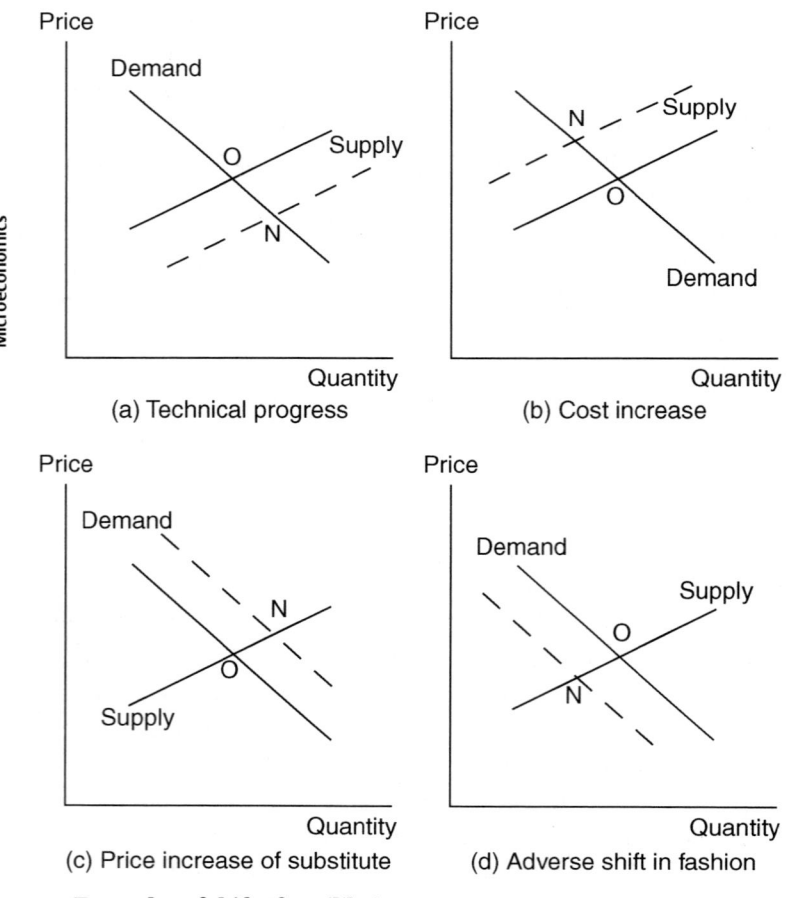

11. **Examples of shift of equilibrium**

to interpret changes in prices and quantities that you observe in many everyday markets.

The figure has four panels, labelled (a)–(d). In each, the original supply and demand curves are shown as solid lines, and one of the curves shifts to a new position shown as a dashed line. (Once again, the curves are shown as straight lines purely for visual simplicity.) The old equilibrium is labelled O and the new one N.

In panel (a), technical progress reduces the cost of production, shifting the supply curve downward. The new equilibrium has lower price and higher quantity than the old one. Flat panel TV sets are the most prominent recent example.

Panel (b) shows the effect of a cost increase, for example the jump in crude oil prices that occurred in 1973 and again in 1979. That increases the marginal cost of producing gasoline, and therefore shifts up its supply curve. The result is an increase in price and a decrease in quantity, as people drive less or switch to more fuel-efficient cars. Of course such responses take time; therefore we should expect the initial impact to be mainly on the price. Gradually as the quantity responds the price will climb back down to some extent. That is exactly what happened in the two episodes of crude oil price shocks.

In panel (c) the source of the shift is an increase in the price of a substitute. Suppose the demand and supply curves shown are those for lager, and the price of ale goes up. Then at any price of lager more of it is bought than before, so the demand curve for lager shifts to the right. The result is more lager sold, and at a higher price as the marginal cost of producing the extra lager goes up.

Panel (d) shows an adverse shift of demand, for example a shift of fashion away from a type of dress. This reduces the quantity and also the price, as the marginal cost goes down along the supply curve.

Consider the fashion shift case a little further. In the short-run, production runs are already committed and stocks are in the stores. Therefore supply is less price-responsive (inelastic or steep), and the brunt of the shift is on price as stores hold clearance sales. Gradually producers shift their lines to producing other now-fashionable garments, the supply curve becomes more price-responsive (elastic or flat), and the main effect is a decrease in quantity of the now unfashionable item. Figure 12 shows these cases separately; the new equilibrium is labelled S in the short-run panel on the left and L in the long-run panel on the right.

Thus price and quantity may each rise or fall by a little or a lot depending on the circumstances. You have probably seen all combinations at different times in different markets, and wondered why price and quantity move together at some times and not others, and why sometimes price changes a lot and sometimes it is the quantity that changes. Now you can understand each episode by thinking about an underlying cause that shifts the supply curve upwards or downwards, or the demand curve to the right or to the left, and the length of time over which the equilibrium adjusts.

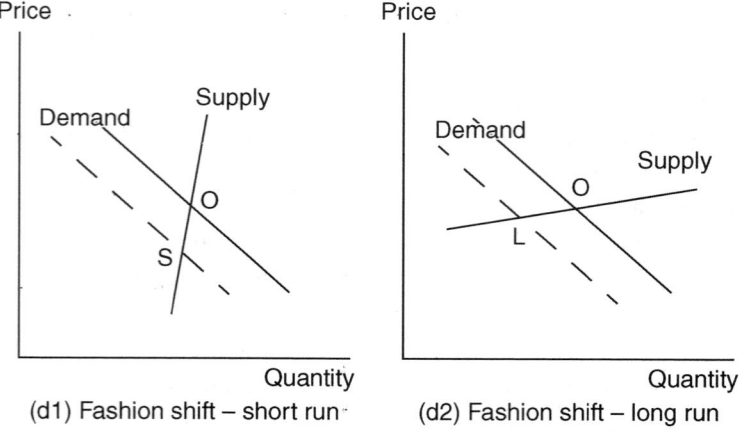

(d1) Fashion shift – short run   (d2) Fashion shift – long run

12. Effect of fashion shift in the short- and long-runs

Taxes

One cause of equilibrium shift merits special attention: imposition of a tax. As the simplest example, consider a tax of a specified amount per unit of quantity. Suppose the seller is required to keep records and pay the tax to the government. Then the seller's tax-inclusive marginal cost rises by the amount of the tax, and the supply curve rises vertically. Figure 13 shows the result. The new equilibrium is at N, and the price buyers pay is given by the height of B. Of this, the government gets the tax, which equals the height of the shift of the supply curve and therefore equals BS. Sellers get only the price given by the height of S. Before the tax was imposed, buyers paid and sellers received the same price, namely the height of P. The tax has raised the price buyers pay from P to B, and lowered the price sellers receive from P to S. We can say that of the total tax BS, buyers pay BP and sellers pay PS. These effects are called the *incidence* of the tax.

Even though the sellers hand over the tax to the government, buyers end up paying part of it through the higher price. In fact,

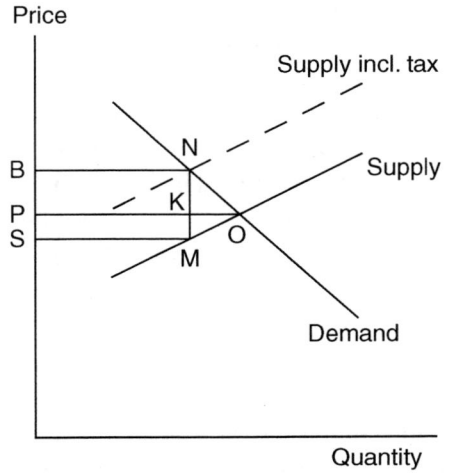

13. Effect of a tax

who initially pays the tax is irrelevant; as the effects of the tax work their way through the market equilibrium, the eventual incidence is the same. There may be only transitory differences as the market moves to its new equilibrium.

This point is often not understood. Consider the US social security tax. Formally, employers pay a part of it, and workers pay the rest. But this eventually works its way through the labour market with the same consequence for wages as when one side initially pays all the tax. The policy debates we see frequently about whether it is unfair to ask workers to pay part of the tax, or whether taxing employers will be bad for employment, are mostly immaterial.

The tax reduces the quantity traded in the market; the new equilibrium N has a smaller quantity than the old equilibrium O. Quantities between N and O could have been traded to the mutual benefit of the buyers and sellers: absent the tax, buyers are willing to pay more than the sellers' marginal cost. The tax creates inefficiency: total surplus equal to the area of the triangle NMO is lost, of which NKO is consumer surplus and KMO producer surplus. But these efficiency losses should not automatically condemn the tax: if the revenue it raises serves some socially useful purpose, that benefit can outweigh the loss.

Subsidies have similar incidence effects. Deductibility of mortgage interest in the US and many other countries is such a subsidy, usually justified as a policy to spread benefits of homeownership to the masses. Figure 14 shows its effects under different conditions of supply in the housing market. In both panels the subsidy raises the demand curve for housing: anyone who was willing to pay x for a house before is now willing to pay x plus the subsidy because the government is picking up the subsidy part leaving the individual to pay the same x as before. The equilibrium shifts from the old O to the new M. The nature of the shift depends very much on the conditions of supply. In the left-hand panel the supply is unresponsive to price (inelastic); that is so in

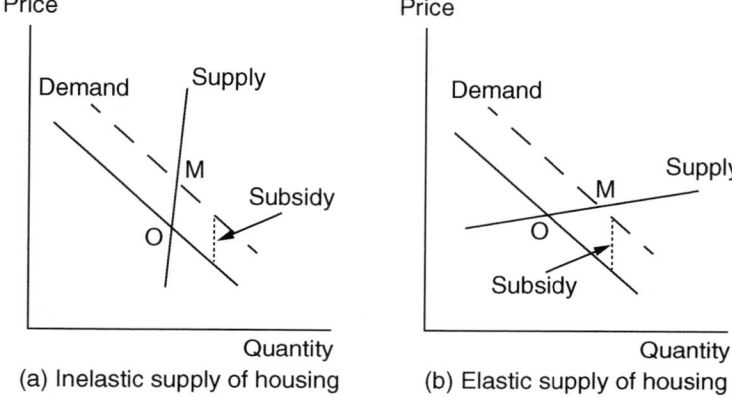

14. Incidence of mortgage interest deductibility

the short-run, and can be so even in the long-run if local government regulations restrict new construction. The price rise from O to M is almost equal to the subsidy and the quantity increase is small: the subsidy gets almost entirely swallowed up in price increases of existing housing with little expansion of home-ownership. Existing homeowners are the main beneficiaries; no wonder the deduction is politically so popular. New buyers willing to pay the higher price are mostly rich; spreading homeownership to them is not the stated intention of the policy. In the right-hand panel supply is price-responsive (elastic); here the quantity increases and the price rises only a little, which is more in keeping with the intent. But for this to happen, the government should not restrict construction of new housing by zoning or other regulations.

The budget deficits and debt accumulation of governments in the United States and elsewhere has led them to think of eliminating or restricting the mortgage interest deduction from their income tax laws. You can run the above analysis backwards and see that such a reform will mainly hurt existing homeowners, at least in the short-run. That explains the strong political opposition to these proposals.

Cycles of booms and busts

As I mentioned earlier and re-emphasize now, most markets do not have market-makers to equate demand and supply and keep the market continuously in equilibrium. There may still be tendencies toward equilibrium. For example, if a price is too high, there is excess supply and some producers are unable to sell. They will eventually resort to clearance sales to attract buyers, so prices will fall. However, this may be a slow process. In other situations, adjustments may be too rapid, leading to cycles of prices shooting above and below the equilibrium level. Here are a couple of examples.

In some markets, such as housing and commodity mining, supply is fixed in the short-run but responds to prices with a time delay. Before that happens, price is determined so as to equate demand and the available fixed supply. The left-hand panel of Figure 15 shows what can then happen. Suppose initially the price is too low, and the supply responds to put the market at the point labelled 1. Pressure of demand raises the price, moving the market to the point 2. After some delay supply responds to this higher price, taking us to the point 3. To absorb this excess supply, the

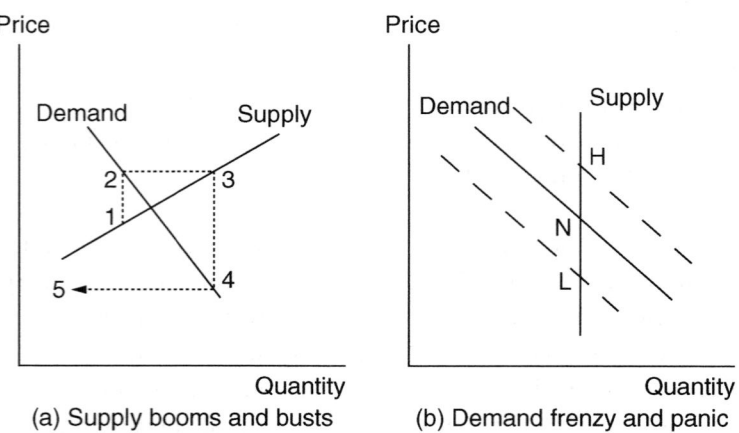

15. **Price fluctuations**

price must drop, resulting in the point 4. And so on. The demand and supply curves shown are such that this process is actually unstable; with other shapes the cycles could gradually dampen down but disequilibrium may persist for a long time.

One would think that over time producers would understand the nature of the price fluctuations—look further into the future and not respond to the last price observed. But that does not seem to happen; we do observe such fluctuations and even instabilities in housing and mining.

The right-hand panel of Figure 15 shows price fluctuations that occur in many financial markets when demand chases the trend. Without such behaviour by investors, equilibrium would be at N (for normal). But suppose the price rises a little above N for some accidental reason. Investors interpret this as a trend; they expect the price will rise even higher and they will profit if they buy now. Demand shifts up and price rises to a point like the one labelled H. This may create even more pressure of demand—you could call this greed or frenzy. Eventually new buyers are scarce; the price rises slowly or even falls a little. This sets up the opposite reaction—which you could call fear or panic. That shifts demand downwards and price collapses to a point like L. Once again, if investors understood the whole process they might not be moved to such extreme reactions, but individuals and even markets collectively have short memories, and every few years we see alternating booms and busts.

Price floors and ceilings

Sometimes governments keep markets away from equilibrium by imposing upper or lower limits on prices. The motive may be to benefit some politically favoured special interests at the expense of others, or it may be to address some need or want that is deemed socially more important or urgent enough. (Or it may be the first motive masquerading as the second!) In both cases, the policies have side-effects that are often harmful, sometimes even to the intended beneficiaries.

The European Union's (EU) Common Agricultural Policy aims 'to ensure a fair standard of living for farmers and to provide a stable and safe food supply at affordable prices for consumers'. For almost five decades the EU pursued these lofty goals by stipulating minimum prices for various farm products. The left-hand panel of Figure 16 shows the result. At the price P, producers wish to supply the quantity corresponding to the point labelled B while consumers demand only the quantity A. Suppliers could have been restricted, but the EU usually allowed and purchased the excess supply AB. The media gave these surpluses colourful names like the 'butter mountain' and the 'wine lake'. Some of the surpluses were sold at very low prices to countries outside the EU; the loss incurred by paying farmers high prices and reselling at low prices was borne by EU taxpayers. Countries with large farming populations were net beneficiaries; the more industrialized member countries were net losers. This created much political conflict in the EU. Recently the policy has been reformed to give farmers direct income support not linked to their production. That has

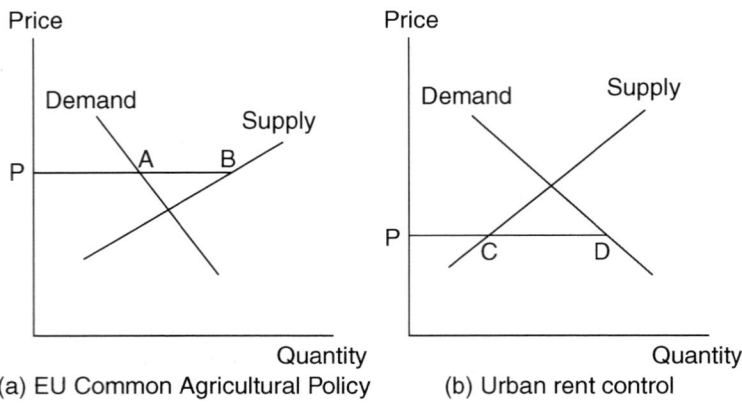

16. **Price floors and ceilings**

eliminated the surpluses, but conflicts arising from different allocation of benefits and costs across countries remain.

From the 1930s to the 1980s the US had a similar policy of dairy price supports. The result: an abandoned mine full of cheese growing mouldy, accumulated at a cost of $4 billion per year, and maintained at a cost of $1 million per day.

As cities grow, the pressure of demand shows up in rising rents. Incumbent tenants dislike having to pay more. Some city governments respond by imposing rent controls. New York after World War II was a prime example but there are others; you may have lived in one and experienced the consequences. The right-hand panel of Figure 16 shows the direct effect. With price not allowed to rise above the point P, demand is at D and supply at C, creating excess demand equal to DC. That sets in motion a whole chain of events, most of them inefficient or even pernicious. Landlords or their agents engage in favouritism or discrimination when renting, or extract payments like 'key money' from prospective renters. People sublet rooms, often illegally, causing overcrowding. Landlords provide poor services and skip maintenance, so the controlled rent eventually gets renters a low quality of housing. Builders find new construction unprofitable at the controlled rents; this aggravates the scarcity over time. The city government responds by relieving new construction from rent control, but that precludes efficient allocation of space. For example an old couple who raised their family in a large rent-controlled apartment would now like to move into a smaller new one but cannot do so because the rent there is much higher; in the meantime a young family that needs a large apartment cannot find one. In extreme cases these side-effects may wipe out the benefits of even the intended beneficiaries of the policy, namely the original occupiers. But the policy persists, because politicians fear the immediate impact of any repeal: rents of the controlled apartments will rise, creating adverse media coverage and a political backlash.

Here we have examples of policies that may have started out with good intentions—to ensure decent incomes for farmers and affordable housing for city-dwellers—but ended up creating very costly side-effects and in the long-run sometimes hurting even the intended beneficiaries. In the next chapter we will see more examples of market failures and policy failures alike, leading me to conclude that perfection is unattainable and that we must accept the least imperfect among feasible solutions to economic problems, mixing market-based and governmental solutions as appropriate for each problem.

Chapter 5
Market and policy failures

Monopoly and oligopoly

The efficient outcome at the intersection of the demand and supply curves requires price to be outside the control of any one producer. If a firm is large enough to influence the market price, it can profit by curtailing supply to drive up the price along the demand curve. Several firms may be able to collude and achieve the same result. Exactly how much the supply is curtailed will depend on the context, and the details of that analysis are not important in this brief introduction. But the consequences are.

Figure 17 reproduces Figure 10 with some modification. Suppose monopoly or oligopoly reduces quantity to a point such as X, less than Q. Then the social surplus contributed by quantities between X and Q, namely the excess of the willingness to pay over the marginal cost of these quantities, amounting to the area CDE, is lost. This measures the inefficiency of the monopoly or oligopoly (the technical term is *dead-weight loss*).

If all the buyers of the quantity X pay the same price, namely C along the demand curve, then an amount equal to the area of the rectangle MCYP, which would have been part of the consumer surplus under perfect competition, now becomes a part of the firms' profits. Any successful price discrimination

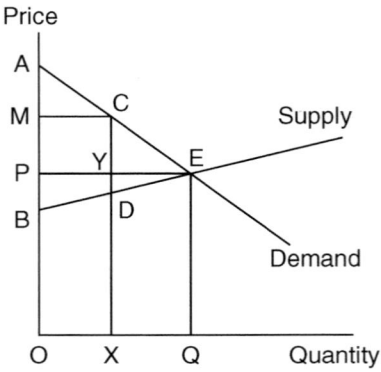

17. Inefficiency of monopoly

can extract even more surplus from the consumers. This raises the possibility that firms may expend resources to facilitate acquisition of monopoly power—deter entry of competitors, pay political contributions or even bribes to obtain and sustain their monopoly power, sometimes in the guise of 'national champions'. These resource expenditures also do not contribute to overall social welfare, and must count as inefficiencies.

How big are the effects of monopoly power? Hospital treatment in the US provides an extreme example. Patients have few or no competing alternatives in their area, they lack information about prices and cost-effective treatments, and they have neither time nor ability to make rational choices in urgent or emergency situations. And rationally calculating patients with good insurance coverage are undeterred by high prices. Therefore providers can charge prices ten or more times costs. For example, the maker of a spinal stimulation device that cost about $4,500 to produce sold it to a hospital for about $19,000, which then charged the patient $49,237 for it! (That did not include the doctors' and hospital's charges for installing it; the total bill for a day's outpatient procedure was $86,951.) As a general principle, the less price-responsive the demand, the greater the potential to raise price above cost.

What about economy-wide efficiency losses due to monopoly and oligopoly? Estimates for the US vary from 0.1 per cent to 7 per cent of gross domestic product (GDP); in countries where antitrust laws and their enforcement are less stringent, the fraction may be higher. Even 1 per cent of GDP is sizeable: in the US this is about $150 billion per year, or $500 per US citizen. Seen from another angle, a 2 per cent drop in GDP is similar to the average for recessions in the years 1947–2006; the Great Recession of 2007–9 had a GDP drop of about 5 per cent. But the loss due to monopoly occurs every year, not just one–two years out of every four–five as with recessions. Thus inefficiency of monopoly is a problem of magnitude comparable to that of recessions in macroeconomics. Effective antitrust policy is correspondingly important, but the political process may be captured by existing and would-be monopolists, as pointed out above.

Might some monopoly power be necessary for innovation and growth? Both theory and evidence are unclear on this point. The prospect of temporary monopoly profits resulting from a new idea or product, whether protected by a patent or simply because other firms need time to imitate and produce rival products, might spur research and development. Profits from previous monopoly power might also generate internal financing for these activities. But a secure monopoly may blunt the incentive to innovate; firms may hesitate to develop new products that cannibalize the market for their own existing products. In my opinion the most important thing is to preserve freedom of entry into markets. Then entrepreneurs with new ideas and products can put them to the test of consumer acceptance, and incumbent firms will also continue to innovate for fear of losing out to some newcomer.

Externalities, negative, and positive

Many actions of consumers or firms have side-effects, beneficial or harmful to others. When you drive your car you pollute the air, which harms other people's health, and you add to congestion on the roads, which increases others' driving time. When you get vaccinated, you reduce not only your own risk of catching the disease, but also that of passing it on to others. If you keep your front yard beautiful, you increase the pleasure of your neighbours and passers-by. Toxic discharges and greenhouse gas emissions of mining companies and power plants can harm people's health and perhaps endanger the future of human life on earth.

In many such situations, people and firms lack the incentives to take into account the by-product effects when making their choices. Alas, most of us are not sufficiently other-regarding to include the harm or benefit to others automatically in our calculations. When we ignore the harm our action imposes on others, we carry the action beyond the level that would be best for aggregate social efficiency; when we ignore the benefits to others, we do too little. That is why we see too much congestion on our roads, and sometimes dangerously low vaccination coverage of the population. Economists call such effects *externalities*, positive when they are beneficial to others and negative when they are harmful.

It is important to emphasize that not every good or bad by-product of an action is an externality. When you buy something, you use up the labour, materials, and other resources that went into making it, leaving less for others. But the price you pay for your purchase in a well-functioning competitive market equals the marginal cost of production. Therefore you face the correct scarcity price of your action, and have the correct incentive to economize on the use of society's scarce resources. Only when you do not face the correct scarcity price, as in cases like clean air and roads, will your actions create externalities. What is an externality therefore depends on whether a market puts the correct price on that action. Unfortunately many such markets are missing or malfunctioning, and externalities are ubiquitous.

What is the total social cost of externalities? They arise in too many and too varied contexts to allow calculation of a reliable overall number, but an important instance will serve to illustrate the magnitude of the problem. In their 1994 *American Scientist* article, Richard Arnott and Kenneth Small calculated that, in the US, traffic congestion caused delays of 6 billion vehicle hours. Assuming the average number of people was 1.5 per vehicle, and valuing the average person's time at $12 an hour (the average wage that year), the cost of traffic congestion was $108 billion. It has surely risen since. Other instances can be even more costly. If the effects of global climate change prove as bad as some fear, the externality costs of carbon emissions could be huge.

How can these inefficiencies be remedied? Two approaches exist: one market-based the other government-based. Each has its merits and drawbacks—which works better depends on the context. Neither is ever perfect, but separately and together they offer significant improvement over doing nothing.

We have seen how prices create incentives to produce goods and services that someone is willing to pay for, and to economize on consumption of high-priced goods and services. The market-based approach applies these insights to things like clean air or toxic waste, for which no market or price would otherwise exist.

For a market to operate, what is being transacted must be clearly defined, and someone must have an 'alienable' right to it: a right that can be sold to someone else. Suppose society awards all citizens a right to clean air. Then a firm that pollutes the air as a by-product of its activities must buy the right from them. It is willing to pay a price up to the extra profit that activity will generate. For a price, the citizens may be willing to sell the right, if in their judgement the money they get is worth more than the damage from pollution they will suffer. If the price the firm is willing to pay exceeds the total that the citizens demand, the two sides have the basis for a trade. By making both sides better off (each by its own judgement) the trade promotes Pareto efficiency.

Alternatively, firms can be given rights to pollute, and allowed to make enforceable contracts with citizens promising not to pollute in exchange for a price. That also increases efficiency (to reinforce your understanding, I recommend that you do the reasoning for this case). Distribution of the efficiency gains differs in the two cases: each side is better off when it has the right than when the other has it.

If such markets can be established and function well, prices will exist and will convey information and incentives efficiently in the usual way. For example, if clean air is very scarce, citizens will demand a high price to allow pollution; if firms have to pay this price in order to pollute, they have strong incentives to use or develop less-polluting technologies. This is the motivation behind markets for carbon emission trading that exist, for example, in Europe and California.

Unfortunately, well-functioning markets of this kind are difficult to create and operate. Perhaps the greatest difficulty in the emissions market is that clean air is a collective good, in contrast to a private good like bread of which each buyer consumes what he or she buys. The same air affects everyone in a locality, and carbon emissions may affect everyone on earth. The market has to find out what price every affected person is willing to accept for allowing more emissions, and add this up over them all. People can game this system. Each thinks that if he or she overstates the price it will make very little difference to the outcome; when they all do so, the total price gets so high that firms are not willing to pay it and the market collapses. Worse, in the case of long-lived pollution and emissions that can cause permanent damage like global warming, the future generations who will be adversely affected are unable to participate in today's market. Other difficulties arise in other contexts. More generally, Ronald Coase's insight that markets have transaction costs is valid here just as it was in the discussion of firms' decisions to make or buy, which I discussed in Chapter 3.

Indeed, Coase himself developed this idea in his pioneering analysis of the market approach for coping with externalities. He argued that *if* there were no transaction costs, markets would yield efficient solutions without any need for government intervention (except in its usual roles of defining and enforcing property rights and enforcing voluntary private contracts). This has subsequently often been misunderstood: the big *if* at the opening of Coase's argument is often forgotten, and the implication—efficient markets—is wrongly thought to be a universal rule.

Among small stable groups where actions are easy to monitor and enforce using long-term relationships and reputations, Coasian efficient outcomes can be sustained without top–down governance. Indeed, the local information available to insiders makes bottom–up group action superior. Consider the benefit homeowners provide to their neighbours by keeping their houses and gardens beautiful. Condominium associations can handle this perfectly well by devising norms and sanctions; even informal social pressure to conform to a neighbourhood's norm can have the right effect. A government bureaucrat would find it very difficult to elicit a group's tastes in these matters and devise and enforce appropriate laws.

Elinor Ostrom demonstrated the potential and limits of bottom–up collective action in her Nobel-prize-winning research of original case studies and meta-analysis of other studies. Fisheries are a good example. Each person's fishing reduces what is available to others. This negative externality can lead to overfishing or even extinction of the stock, to the detriment of all.

The fishermen are all aware of the problem, but each of them has only a negligible effect on the risk of extinction and they personally benefit by fishing more. Thus they are trapped in a prisoner's dilemma. Small stable groups, for example a lake-fishing community, can draw up rules for the size and allocation of the catch, and enforce these by using threats of punishment including social ostracism. But it is harder for ocean fisheries to do this, as fish migrate far and the fishermen come from many localities and countries. Overfishing has indeed endangered or made extinct populations of Atlantic cod, Chilean sea bass, Bluefin tuna, and other ocean fish species.

Sometimes the Coasian solution can work beyond small, tight social groups. A beekeeper benefits orchard-owners by providing pollination services. This was one of the earliest examples of a positive externality mentioned in economics. In reality private arrangements resolve it very well: beekeepers hire their services to orchard owners. This goes beyond local deals; beekeepers maintain mobile hives on trucks, and travel from south to north following the flowering seasons in different regions.

Next consider government-based approaches. These can include incentives with effects similar to those of prices, namely taxes or subsidies. Such policies are called Pigouvian after Arthur Pigou, a twentieth-century British economist who pioneered their analysis. A tax on carbon emissions increases firms' incentives to use clean technologies; a subsidy for solar or wind power generation increases the incentive for power companies to use more of those methods.

The tax or subsidy for an action should equal the by-product damage or benefit the action confers on others. For a quick illustration to understand this, observe that car drivers' violations of traffic laws are monitored more carefully and punished more severely than pedestrians' violations of jaywalking laws. This makes good sense: a car driver's mistake creates a much bigger negative externality than that of a pedestrian.

Costs of externalities can be difficult to assess. Objective measurements are often not feasible. Asking the parties may not yield honest answers. If the government compensates people and firms for harm they suffer from pollution created by others, they may overstate their harm; if it taxes or fines them for toxic discharges, they may attempt to evade the tax by diverting the discharges into other even more harmful outlets. Prospects are better if the needed information is purely statistical, pertaining to the aggregate of the population and not to individuals or particular firms, because then it can be obtained by anonymous sample surveys (provided people believe that their anonymity will be respected!).

Modern technology has made it easier to gather the needed information in some cases. For example, many cities now impose tolls on cars to access their congested centres, using cameras placed all around the periphery of the central areas to photograph licence plates of entering cars and send bills to the owners, or by using more advanced transponder devices placed in the cars. These charges can be varied according to the time of day, or even the actual level of congestion continuously monitored by cameras placed at many locations in the city centres.

Governments can also attempt quantity controls—restrictions or bans on emissions, requirements of minimum fuel efficiency for cars, and so on. But such policies require information that is not usually directly available to the government agencies that promulgate and enforce the controls, and firms lack the incentives to supply honest information. For example, suppose a limit on the country's total emissions has been decided, and it remains to allocate this quota among firms. A firm that does not have a permit has to find other ways to reduce or eliminate its emissions, and this is costly. Therefore it is efficient to give emission quotas to the firms whose cost of abating emissions is highest. Then each firm wants to overstate its costs in order to win more permits. It would be better to use a market-like solution that makes firms put their money where their mouths are: auction the quotas, so firms that find it hardest to do without will bid most for the quotas.

Determination of the aggregate quotas is also difficult and often becomes politicized. Indeed, the European Union's carbon emission trading market is beset by such problems. Too many permits were awarded, the price collapsed, and the scheme has lost much of its purpose.

To sum up, each of the approaches—Coasian market-based and Pigouvian government-based—has its problems. Luckily the two have different problems. The Coasian approach works better in small and stable groups; the Pigouvian one works better in large populations when anonymous statistical information can be used. Even then government policies are likely to work better if they have market-like features, for example auctioning emission quotas instead of awarding them by a bureaucratic process. In some instances a mixture of the two approaches may work best; for example, quotas that are auctioned but can be traded in secondary markets. Shifting equilibrium in these markets preserves efficiency as conditions change over time. Even jointly the two methods will not resolve all externalities perfectly, but nothing is perfect and we must accept the least imperfect solution that is available.

An example will help you remember the relative merits of the two methods. I apologize for its impropriety, but that is what makes it memorable. If you are more skilled at sex, your partner gets more pleasure from the act. How should this externality be handled? In monogamous societies, couples can achieve the Coasian optimum by private agreement. But in promiscuous societies, the government can do better by giving Pigouvian subsidies to education in 'marital arts'!

Information asymmetries

An important, but often unstated, requirement for a market to function well is that the parties to the transaction should have a clear idea of what they are buying or selling. But in many instances one party is much better informed than the other: sellers know product quality better than do buyers, and buyers of insurance policies know their own risks better than do the companies that issue the policies. Strategies to interpret, elicit, conceal, or reveal information play key roles in such interactions, and affect market outcomes.

George Akerlof's Nobel-prize-winning analysis of the market for lemons (cars with serious defects) dramatically alerted economists to such effects, including the possibility of a complete collapse of the market. I mentioned this briefly in Chapter 1; here is a fuller outline.

Consider the following scenario. Each car can be either peach-perfect, worth $15,000 if its quality could be credibly guaranteed, or a worthless lemon. In the total population of cars, 2/3 are peaches and 1/3 are lemons. Each seller knows the type of his or her own car, but prospective buyers cannot know the quality of any individual car. Buyers are willing to pay what they believe to be the average value of cars on the market.

Could the market price be 2/3 * $15,000 + 1/3 * $0 = $10,000? Yes, if cars on the market were a representative sample of the population. But they are not. A seller who knows his or her car to be a peach is reluctant to sell it for $10,000. Some may sell because they are moving, are in financial trouble, or for some such reason. Just to be definite, suppose half of peach owners are willing to sell for $10,000. All lemon owners are of course glad to get this price. Therefore the mix of cars on the market consists of the 1/3 of the population that are lemons, and half of the 2/3rd that are peaches. The market is an equal mix of peaches and lemons, so the value of the average car is only 1/2 * $15,000 + 1/2 * $0 = $7,500.

But that is not the end of the story. At this lower price, even more peach owners drop out of the market: the movers may decide to take their car, or those in financial trouble persuade their relatives to help. Suppose only 1/4 of peaches remain. Now the market consists of the 1/3 of the population of cars that are lemons, and 1/4 of 2/3rds, that is 1/6, that are peaches. This is a 2:1 mix of lemons and peaches: of the used cars on the market, 1/3 are peaches and 2/3 are lemons. So the average value drops to 1/3 * $15,000 + 2/3 * $0 = $5,000.

The process could go on until all peach-owners drop out and only lemons remain on the used car market. But even short of such complete market collapse, the used car market becomes an unrepresentative sample of the population of cars; lemons are overrepresented and peaches are rare.

Although dramatic, is a market collapse realistic? Anyone who has bought a used car knows that the process is fraught with uncertainty and worry about quality. But a market exists, and high-quality used cars are traded. Owners of good used cars have ways of giving credible assurances to buyers.

Reputation is an important device of this kind. In the private market, if the seller is a friend, or a friend of a friend, or even a friend three or four steps removed in a chain, the seller wants to remain in the good books of the whole friendship network, and is more likely to be forthcoming about any known defects in the car. A warranty would be a good device, but the buyer can't be sure that the seller will be available and will fulfill the warranty if and when this is needed, so it ultimately relies on the reputation of the seller.

What about professional dealers? Used car dealers may make a quick buck by cheating a few customers, but their bad reputation will spread and they won't last long in the business. But how do you know whether the dealer you are negotiating with is in the business for the long haul or a fly-by-nighter? You look for evidence of stability. Does the dealer simultaneously sell new cars of an established brand? Has the dealership been at the location for a while? Do the premises convey an aura of permanence or do they look as if everything could be dismantled and the storefront converted into a restaurant in a couple of days? Such indicators of stability are costly; an unpaved parking lot and a hut for an office would be a lot cheaper than a fancy storefront and well-maintained car lot. It is precisely this cost that makes the indicators credible. A dealer who means to be in the business for a long time can amortize the cost over many years and so can afford it; a fly-by-nighter cannot. The same principle also helps explain why banks have large and impressive premises; they are proclaiming, 'We are here to stay, so your money is safe with us.'

Michael Spence developed this idea of costly signals in work that won him a Nobel prize jointly with Akerlof and Joseph Stiglitz; these three launched the whole field of the economics of asymmetric information. Spence's theory is best explained in the labour market. Imagine yourself interviewing for a job. The conversation goes as follows:

EMPLOYER: This job requires high quantitative skills and strong work ethic.
YOU: Sure, I have plenty of both of these.
EMPLOYER: Why should I believe you? Anyone can say that.
YOU: Look at my college transcript. I took tough maths, statistics, and economics courses, and got As. That requires not only first-rate quantitative skills, but also the willpower to work every night completing all problem set assignments.
EMPLOYER: Wouldn't everyone do the same to qualify for this high-paying job?

YOU: No. A non-quantitative student couldn't handle the work; one lacking true dedication would succumb to the temptations of campus social life.

Words are cheap; the employer wants you to 'put your money where your mouth is', so to speak. You offer your educational achievement as a *signal* that you have the qualities the employer wants. The signal is costly: you have to spend time and effort and resist temptations in order to acquire the signal. But more than that: the cost of the signal—in terms of time, effort, and giving up campus parties—would be prohibitively high to someone who lacked the qualities you are signalling. It is this *cost difference*— you, with the right qualities, can afford the cost of the signal but someone without them cannot—that distinguishes you from a would-be mimic or pretender and makes credible your assertion of quality.

Signals can thus solve the asymmetric information problem, but at a cost. Who pays this cost depends on the context. In the education example, those who lack the quantitative skills and the work ethic would like to get the high-paying jobs (at least for a year or so until they are found out and thrown out), and will mimic the actions of the truly skilled, unless the bar is set high enough. The hurdle must usually exceed the level of education that genuinely improves your productivity on the job. The innately skilled and dedicated must therefore spend some time and effort in getting education that is productively wasteful, solely for its signalling purpose. The mere existence of dummies and slackers creates a cost for the better students to prove credibly that they are not dummies or slackers!

We can relate this to the discussion of externalities in the previous section. The dummies and slackers, by their mere existence, are imposing a negative externality on the skilled and dedicated, who must invest excessively in education in order to prove that they are not one of the undesirable types.

Indeed, many effects of information asymmetries can be seen through the lens of externalities, and the market failures resulting from these externalities can be remedied, albeit only imperfectly, by Coasian or Pigouvian methods as appropriate. I will discuss and illustrate this approach in the concluding section of this chapter.

The screening devices for price discrimination we met in Chapter 3 are a mirror-image of signalling. Firms comprise the less informed side of the interaction, and choose pricing strategies to separate and attract those buyer types that yield them the most profit while discouraging the rest. Signalling is initiated by the informed side, but in many cases could instead be implemented as screening by the uninformed side. In the education example, employers can (and often do) stipulate qualifications tough enough that only the truly skilled and dedicated workers will achieve them; then they are screening applicants instead of the applicants signalling to them.

Once you understand the concept, you start to see signalling and screening everywhere, not only or primarily in markets, but in all kinds of social interactions. Here is a tiny sample.

Mafias have initiation rites that require new recruits to perform specified criminal deeds, often murders. These serve as measures of the requisite toughness and ruthlessness, but they are also effective devices to screen out police infiltrators or investigative reporters: someone like that might comply if the test was merely one of toughness, but not if it requires criminal acts.

The theory of sexual selection in evolutionary biology says that females choose mates with special attention to genetic superiority, because given their limited number of breeding opportunities, they must seek to maximize the fitness of each offspring. The large antlers of stags, or the heavy and elaborate plumage of peacocks and birds of paradise, are a handicap to carry and defend.

Therefore they serve as credible signals of genetic quality: only an exceptionally fit male can afford the resources needed to develop and maintain these features.

Finally an example from ordinary life. You are on a first date with someone you find attractive. You know you won't get a second chance to make a good first impression. But you also know that your date will watch out for fake first impressions. In other words, you are signalling and your date is screening. If the date finds you attractive, there may be traffic in the other direction too. What are good signals in this context, and what are good screening devices? Both are likely to be situation-specific, so I leave you to think what can work in your context. I only emphasize the importance of careful thinking. It is too easy to lose a lifetime's happiness by being unaware of the information game that is going on: failing to give a credible signal or failing to screen effectively.

Moral hazard and adverse selection

Two important types of information asymmetries can be illustrated using insurance markets. People can mitigate many health risks by diet and exercise. An insurance contract may specify that the insured is required to do this, but the company can only very imperfectly monitor adherence by the insured. People may then be tempted to shirk exercising or order the calorie-laden dessert; to some extent the temptation may be greater in the knowledge that they have insurance to cover their medical expenses. Insurance companies of course regard such behaviour as immoral. That industry coined the term *moral hazard* for such situations; it has now become standard economic usage for situations of transactions where one party's actions are not observable to the other party, or not demonstrable to a third party that may be called upon to enforce the contract.

The insured may also have better knowledge of their own innate risks than does the insurance company. Then any given insurance contract is most attractive to the worst risks, and the company selectively attracts them to its offering. This is called *adverse selection*. Again the term is used more generally for situations where one party to a transaction knows some relevant attribute better than does the other. Akerlof's market for lemons is a great example. Current owners of used cars know their quality better than do prospective buyers; therefore at any price the market attracts sellers of relatively low quality cars.

We saw how the used car market can potentially fail. A similar problem can arise with health care. The Affordable Care Act in the United States (the so-called 'Obamacare') makes coverage available at a stated price to all applicants. Older and relatively unhealthy people are more likely to want the coverage; the young and healthy may choose to stay uninsured, even if they have to pay the small fine that the law imposes for this. The insurance pool thus adversely selects the worst health risks; premiums must be high enough to cover their costs if the policies are to be financially self-sufficient.

Informationally disadvantaged parties in transactions have various ways of coping with their disadvantage. The screening devices we saw in the previous section are ways of coping with adverse selection. Moral hazard in insurance can be mitigated by providing incomplete insurance using deductibles and co-pays; this leaves the insured facing some risk, and giving them some incentive to expend care to reduce the risk. Moral hazard in the workplace can be reduced by making the employee's compensation depend on observable consequences of his or her actions. For example, if output or profit is observable to the employer and is affected at least in part by the quality or quantity of the employee's effort, then output-based payments or profit-sharing will mitigate moral hazard. But none of these devices can achieve an outcome as efficient as the hypothetical possibility with full and symmetric information. The inefficiency that remains is akin to an externality; I will illustrate this later in this chapter using examples from the recent financial crisis.

Profit externalities between firms

One firm's actions affect demand for substitutes and complements to its products, and therefore profits of firms selling those products. Such interactions have implications for market structures and therefore economic consequences to the consumers of these products.

Suppose coffee and tea (a pair of substitutes) are made and sold by different firms, each with some market power. Let us call the firms Java and Assam, respectively. If Java raises the price of coffee, demand shifts toward tea (for a reminder, see Figure 3 in Chapter 2 and the associated text). With a stronger demand for tea, Assam can raise its price and make more profit. This is as if Java is bestowing a positive externality on Assam. But Java is not concerned with Assam's profit; it ignores the externality. Therefore it does not raise its price as high as the combined interest of the two firms would warrant. Assam's pricing decision has the same issue. Both firms would do better to merge into one—let us call it Caffeine—which would then raise prices of both products and make more profit than the sum of profits of the separate firms. Of course the higher prices hurt consumers. Thus makers of substitutes have incentives to merge, and antitrust policy should be on guard for any resulting price increases that harm consumers.

Next consider a pair of complements, computer hardware and software, made and sold by firms called Chips and Codes, respectively. If Chips raises the price of its hardware, demand for software declines, hurting Codes' profits. This is a negative externality. In any activity like pollution that has a negative externality, private choices lead to excess. Here Chips pushes its price rise farther than the joint interests of the two firms warrant.

So does Codes. If these two firms merged into one, it would increase total profit by reducing both prices: the lower price of each product sufficiently stimulates demand for the other. The lower prices also benefits consumers. This is a rare win-win-win situation; merger benefits the two firms *and* consumers. Antitrust policy should not prohibit mergers of complements; on the contrary it should encourage them!

A difficult trade-off

Many products have high first-copy costs, and after these have been incurred, the marginal cost of supplying each unit is small. The best examples come from the tech sector. Creation and debugging of software for operating systems, browsers, and major application programs takes many programmers' time over many months and millions of dollars; once the programs are ready, they can be disseminated almost costlessly over the web. The pharmaceutical industry is similar. The cost of research, development, and testing of each new miracle drug is huge, especially since many failed trials lie behind each success. Once the drug is available and approved, the cost of production and delivery is tiny.

How should such products be priced? Consider the situation once they are available and are being marketed. Efficiency at this point requires expanding supply until the willingness to pay for the next unit equals its marginal cost. That would imply a very low price—almost zero for software. Indeed, many idealists advocate exactly this. They say that information can be disseminated to everyone for free (or almost free), so there should be no charge for it. They argue that charging more for a life-saving drug than the tiny cost of making it is morally reprehensible.

But at such low prices the makers of these products will not recoup the high first-copy costs. And if precedents are established for selling existing products at low prices leaving the makers to bear the first-copy costs, that will deter future drug researchers and software developers, which will hurt future consumers too. There is truth to this argument, although sometimes firms disingenuously advance it to justify monopoly prices out of all reasonable proportion to the first-copy costs and the need for incentives.

Social policy therefore faces an unavoidable dilemma or trade-off between promoting new research and development on the one hand, and disseminating the results at low marginal cost on the other. The resolution is a compromise: firms or individuals who develop or create such products are given a monopoly over their sales for a limited period: patents for drugs and other innovations, copyrights for software and books.

Why not pay first-copy costs from general tax revenues and let producers charge only the low (perhaps near-zero) marginal? Such a system would create bad incentives. No one knows in advance whether a new drug will be effective, or a new book worth reading, or a piece of software worth using. Charlatans and politically well-connected people would make a nice living by persuading the authorities to pay them as they wasted time and finally confessed to failure. The tiny number of potential consumers of a rare drug or a highly specialized computer program would agitate to get taxpayer support for their special needs. The patent and copyright system reduces such risks by making developers and consumers put their money where their mouths are. It is not perfect but, once again, nothing is perfect.

Collective goods

When they function well, markets supply individuals' wants in economically efficient ways. Other institutions that we will examine in the next chapter do likewise in some other circumstances where markets are less effective. But many goods and services are collective in nature. Leaving payment for them to individual decision generally fails. Each person will usually aim to minimize his or her contribution towards the cost of a good or service, hoping to get a free ride on the contributions of others. When too many people try this, the total contributions fail to cover the cost and the good or service cannot be provided. This is a bad equilibrium of a prisoners' dilemma game: not contributing is privately the best strategy for each person regardless of what others are doing, but when they all do this, the result is bad for them all.

It doesn't suffice to educate people about the dilemma and ask them to be less selfish. True, if people were sufficiently other-regarding, they would not try free riding. But despite the finding of behavioural economics that people are not totally selfish, the degree of altruism observed is generally too low to achieve adequate provision of most collective goods and services on a purely voluntary basis in economies involving millions of people. Remember Yossarian in *Catch 22*, who did not want to be among the last to die in a war that was almost won. When his superior officer argued 'But suppose everyone felt that way', he replied 'Then I'd certainly be a damned fool to feel any other way, wouldn't I?'

Collective action to resolve such dilemmas is one reason why, as the preamble to the 1776 American declaration of independence says, 'governments are instituted among men, deriving their just powers from the consent of the governed'. The government can levy taxes or other charges to finance the provision of collective goods and services.

I say 'can' deliberately, because provision by the government using taxes may not be the only or even the best method of supplying many collective goods. We must distinguish two aspects of such a good. One is its collective nature: it can be consumed or used simultaneously by several people, unlike say a slice of bread: when one person eats that, no one else can then consume it. The other is the impossibility of excluding non-payers from consuming or benefiting from the good or service. National defence may be the ultimate example: when a country is attacked, the military defends all citizens; those who have failed to pay their taxes cannot be selectively offered to the enemy to be captured or killed! Collectively consumed and non-excludable goods and services are called *pure public goods*.

In reality, collective consumption and exclusion are both matters of degree. A road can accommodate many drivers, but gets congested and therefore available at a lower quality if too many drivers arrive simultaneously. Exclusion may be possible to a sufficient degree to allow a private entity to finance provision of many collective goods. Even lighthouses, seemingly available for free to all ships passing by, could be and were financed from fees charged to ships using nearby harbours. Toll roads have existed for centuries. Gated communities hire private guards to protect residents. Services with widespread public benefit like education, health care, and rubbish collection can be privately produced even if they are paid out of taxes, and often that works better than public production. With all these qualifications, the government does have a role in provision of goods and services that come close to the conceptual category of pure public goods.

Political economy of policy

We have seen several reasons why markets fail to deliver the magic their most fervent believers expect. The main categories of market failures are monopoly power, externalities, collective goods, and costs of asymmetric information. In each case, a government can design and implement policies to improve market outcomes or sometimes even replace markets altogether. In fact an opposing group of fervent believers expects miracles from governments. In my judgement matters are more subtle and complex. Governments have their own failures, distinct from failures of markets. Judicious selection would let each institution operate in domains where it delivers better outcomes, but there is no reliable mechanism for such selection either. In practice societies must muddle through, accepting some inefficiencies but hoping to detect and correct them before they become too severe.

Why do many people believe in the magic of markets? Usually because they mistakenly believe that the outcome will always be (Pareto) efficient, without any of the qualifications and limitations that I have stressed. Why do extremists on the other side believe in the magic of governments? Usually because they picture themselves as benevolent planners who can order everything in the economy for the best according to their own criteria of efficiency, equity, fairness, sustainability.... This picture is far from the reality of the process of making and implementing economic policy. The actual process falls short of the ideal in many respects. Here I outline just a few prominent issues.

Even in the best of circumstances, namely a democracy where everyone's vote counts equally, political science tells us that policy outcomes will represent the preferences of the median voter—one who ranks exactly at the fiftieth percentile in the political spectrum in the relevant dimension, for example left to right, or rich to poor. This may or may not reflect the sum of everyone's well-being, let alone concerns like fairness or sustainability.

In fact the process differs from an idealized representative democracy. Access to legislators and officials, voice in the media and public forums, lobbying and political contributions, and in some situations outright bribery, all vital parts of the process of making and implementing policy, are unequally available. The rich have an obvious advantage; so do the organized. For a group with common interests, organizing for political participation is a collective action problem. Contributing money, time, and effort are all matters in which each individual may hope to free ride on others in the group. Different groups succeed in solving this collective action problem to different degrees. As a broad generalization, groups that are relatively small in size, and involve large stakes per member, are better organized than large groups with diffuse interests. US sugar import and price support policies give a dramatic example. These policies keep sugar prices high in the US, benefiting domestic sugar farmers and producers of sugar-substitutes like high-fructose corn syrup (HFCS). It has been estimated that in the mid-1980s the consumers' loss was about $3.9 billion and the producers' gain $2.8 billion, so the net loss to the US economy was $1.1 billion. But with a population of about 250 million at that time, the loss to each consumer was only about $15, not worth agitating or organizing over. The gain to sugar-beet farmers averaged $50,000 each, and the gain to sugarcane farmers averaged $500,000 each! Therefore they organized and lobbied in favour of the restrictive policies.

Individuals, firms, or groups with privileged access to the political arena lobby for policies that favour them at the expense of the citizenry as a whole. Firms and industries benefit by restricting competition, so they can keep prices high and enjoy the profits of monopoly or oligopoly. They want regulation and licensing that deter new domestic firms, and tariffs, quotas, or other barriers to imports. In the latter they are supported by organized labour. Such policies are often said to be pro-business, but that usually means that they favour existing businesses. They discriminate against new entrants who would bring in new ideas, products, and methods, creating competition to incumbents. What benefits the country as a whole is not *pro-business* policy, but *pro-market* policy. That means fostering competition, which brings cost-saving and product-improving innovation, and leads to efficient outcomes.

Any scarcity creates a gain, called *economic rent*, to the scarce item. Figure 18 shows a market where at the price corresponding to the point N the supply would be at the point D corresponding to quantity X. If policy restricts the quantity supplied to X,

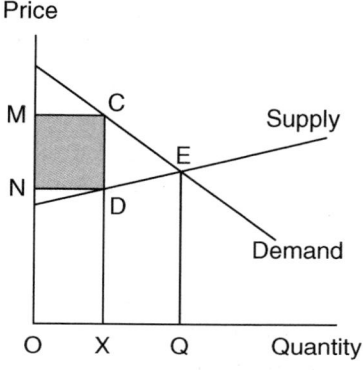

18. Economic rent

demand and supply are equated at C with price M higher than N. Therefore the height MN is the extra gain to each unit of quantity from O to X, and MN times OX, or the area of the shaded rectangle MNDC in the figure, is the total gain or economic rent from the scarcity. Producers of this commodity stand to benefit by creating such scarcity and reaping the rent. If they cannot coordinate to organize the industry as a monopoly or oligopoly, they can lobby the government to institute a scarcity-creating policy under some pretext. Such rent-seeking political activities are common, indeed ubiquitous, and despite the supposedly beneficial motives of the policy sought, are usually detrimental to the interests of the economy as a whole just as private monopolies would be. Barriers against imports are of this kind. So are some certification requirements that restrict entries into professions, limits on the numbers of taxicabs that can operate in a city or the number of restaurants that can serve alcoholic beverages with meals. Existing professionals, cab owners, and restaurateurs benefit at the expense of potential newcomers and the general public.

Effects of bad policies are compounded by the fact that they create special interests that then fight for their continuation. For example the US sugar import restrictions were what made it profitable to produce sugar-substitutes like HFCS. Corn farmers and HFCS firms then became a powerful lobby for preservation of the import restrictions, hurting US consumers economically, and perhaps even in matters of health if claims about the especially unhealthy nature of HFCS are true. The bureaucracies and agencies that implement policies are also a powerful interest resisting policy reforms.

Lobbying and rent-seeking activities are most visible in democracies. That may lead some readers to think that authoritarian or dictatorial regimes would be better for economic efficiencies. Such thinking would also fit with a tendency to think that authoritarian regimes are better for economic development because they are more decisive. For example, many commentators have observed how India's democratic processes slow down the rate of infrastructure construction, and how China proceeds faster by stifling opposition to land acquisition, etc. But authoritarian regimes have their own internal politics and inefficient policies that favour some special groups, often the rulers and their kin, or their ethnic or regional people. Here is the stark and blunt question. Suppose you are convinced of the merits of decisiveness and would like to get an authoritarian ruler for your country. Can you ensure that he or she will turn out to be a Lee Kuan Yew, who brought prosperity to Singapore, and not a Mobutu Sese Seko, who impoverished the Congo?

The financial crisis

The financial crisis started in 2007–8 with a drop in house prices in the US and in many other countries, leading to defaults on home mortgages, and threatened or actual bankruptcies of the financial firms that held these mortgages or mortgage-backed securities. The crisis led to what has come to be called the Great Recession; its effects arguably still persist, despite some recovery in some countries in 2013 at the time of this writing.

This might not appear to be a topic for microeconomics. Its main manifestations, namely high unemployment and a large drop in the gross domestic product (GDP) in many countries, are indeed macroeconomic. But these phenomena were driven by microeconomics—multiple market failures and policy failures of the kind discussed in this chapter. Phil Angelides, chair of the US Financial Crisis Inquiry Commission that met in 2010, hit the nail on the head when he compared the crisis to Agatha Christie's novel *Murder on the Orient Express*, where 'everybody did it'—bankers were greedy, homeowners were gullible, policy-makers pandered to special interests, and so on. I can only touch on a few aspects in this brief account, and have chosen those that provide good examples of market failures and policy failures.

Most financial firms are *intermediaries*: they channel funds between parties that have a surplus of saving or profit (call them 'depositors'), and parties that have a deficit because of needs of spending or investment (call them 'borrowers'). When borrowers promise a higher return on the money they receive than depositors require for the money they supply, the intermediary can carry out a transaction that benefits everyone. It makes a profit for itself while giving each of the two parties the return they offer or require. Of course these activities entail many forms of risks.

First and foremost, the borrower may not deliver the promised return, and in the event of bankruptcy may return nothing, not even the principal. Random shocks such as price fluctuations, natural disasters, and political shifts may destroy the firm's value. But the borrower's incompetence, negligence, or outright fraud may also play a part. The intermediary should develop the skill to judge the borrower's quality, and should exercise due diligence over the borrower's actions. Indeed this is one of the justifications for the existence of the intermediary. The intermediary may also reduce the depositors' risk by lending to several different borrowers with uncorrelated risks. None of these can eliminate the risk entirely.

Second, many financial intermediaries perform *maturity transformation*. This enables depositors to reclaim their money at short or zero notice, which individual borrowers are often unable or unwilling to deliver. Each intermediary deals with many depositors, and only a small fraction of them are likely to want their money back at the same time unless something panics the depositors en masse. Therefore the intermediary is able to hold a relatively small fraction of the deposits as liquid assets or capital reserves, lending the rest at higher returns for longer terms. However, there remains some *liquidity risk* that the intermediary cannot meet the immediate redemption demands of depositors even though it may eventually be able to deliver a high enough return—in other words, it remains *solvent*.

An added complication comes from the fact that depositors' perceptions of liquidity or solvency depend on their beliefs, which may be driven by factors other than the objective circumstances of borrowers or the intermediary. The best example comes from fiction. In *Mary Poppins*, Jane and Michael's father works in a bank. The children are visiting him there, and Michael is carrying two pence to buy food for the birds in Trafalgar Square which they are to visit later that day. Their father's boss wants Michael to deposit the money in the bank, where it will grow. He snatches the two pence from Michael's hand, and Michael shouts 'Give me back my money!' A lady at one of the counters hears him and thinks the bank is running out of money. She asks to withdraw all of her own account at once. Others hear her and do likewise, and there is a run on the bank.

The story shows how liquidity risk can create two equilibria in banking. In one, people believe the bank to be safe. Therefore they are willing to leave their money there, the calls for immediate redemption are low, and the bank is indeed safe. In the other, people doubt the safety of the bank and each tries to get his or her money out at once before it is too late, so the bank fails. The outcome can tip from the former to the latter in response to accidental and mistaken fears, as in the episode from *Mary Poppins*, or to real fears, as when house prices fall and a bank is known to have a large portfolio of mortgages—but real fears get magnified by the process of spreading panic.

Bad loans may create solvency risks for banks, not just liquidity risks. Any carelessness, negligence, or fraud by the borrower raises the risk to the bank and in turn to its depositors. Any carelessness or negligence by the bank in its lending adds to this risk. If all parties had full information about borrowers' or banks' quality and actions, they could enter into a contract with appropriate conditional clauses. For example, depositors could stipulate that the bank should exercise optimal vigilance in its choice of borrowers. But that is clearly unrealistic; information is very asymmetric. Then a bank's carelessness in choosing or monitoring borrowers creates costly risks to depositors, and borrowers' incompetence or negligence creates costly risks to the bank and in turn to its depositors. These are spillovers or externalities caused by information asymmetries. They can be mitigated by vigilance following the dictum 'know your counterparty'. But there are limits to that. Moreover, risks of default can spread in a chain; if A fails to pay what he owes to B, then B may be unable to pay what he owes to C, and so on. Therefore the dictum must be expanded: 'know your counterparty's counterparty; know your counterparty's counterparty's counterparty; and so on'. This is of course impractical. Therefore one bank's actions may create costly risks to other banks and their depositors: information asymmetries can spread and create widespread spillovers. The financial crisis provides many examples.

Home mortgage lending to people with inadequate incomes was perhaps the starting point and driving force of the crisis. Lending decisions were made by bank officers and mortgage brokers who did not expect any penalties if their loans went sour: that would not happen for years, or ever, if commonly held expectations were valid that house prices would never fall. The increase in prices would cover the high future mortgage interest. So the lenders did not care about adverse selection, namely the low quality (low incomes and other indebtedness) of the borrowers. Many homeowners were happy to take these loans in the belief that house prices would rise for ever; many used their homes as cash cows to buy luxury cars, plasma TVs, and other consumer goods that were of low value to banks if repossessed. Governments wanted to extend home-ownership to lower income citizens; therefore regulators overlooked and even encouraged these risky 'subprime' loans. The mortgages were packaged into securities that were rated highly by credit-rating agencies, whose incentives should have been suspect because they were paid by the very firms whose products they were evaluating.

Incentives of intermediaries to exert due diligence in selecting high-quality securities and monitoring them were also lacking. No single depositor had the ability to hold the intermediary to account for lack of diligence. Depositors would have to act collectively, which is difficult. In the case of bank deposits with explicit or implicit government insurance, depositors have no reason to worry about the banks' care in investing their money. In fact they do better when the bank takes big risks: if the risks pay off, they get high returns; if the risks go sour, deposit insurance kicks in and taxpayers bear the loss (as long as the government's full faith and credit is not in doubt). Bank executives likewise prefer risk: they do well if their loans go well and get government bailouts if they go badly. Thus the whole chain of asset holding and transformation was replete with moral hazard and adverse selection poorly controlled by incentives, and made worse by government policies.

The risk inherent in financial intermediation was amplified when retail or commercial banks also engaged heavily in investment banking, and all types of intermediaries traded on their own account, often using debt to leverage their investments. If you use $1 of your own equity and $9 of borrowed money to make a $10 investment, then a mere 10 per cent drop in the value of that investment makes you insolvent. Some banks and other intermediaries such as hedge funds had debt/equity ratios as high as 50.

These risks spread along the whole chain of counterparties. And one failure shakes the public's belief in the soundness of other institutions. Thus externalities arise not only through the direct channel of insolvency, but also through a general loss of faith in, or reputation of, all related financial institutions. For example, when Bear Sterns, an investment bank, was bailed out in March 2008, market speculation against Lehman Brothers increased; when the latter failed in September 2008, the soundness of Merrill Lynch came into question.

The financial crisis quickly spread into an economic crisis. Banks facing risks to their liquidity or solvency cut back on their lending. Firms unable to borrow or even get lines of credit were unable to expand or even sustain employment. The loss of income led to lower demand in the economy, and in turn to lower production and employment. Monetary easing and fiscal stimulus had to be used on an unprecedented scale to prop up demand and prevent the whole economic machinery grinding to a halt for lack of the lubrication that finance provides. Thus microeconomics of the financial sector—bad incentives and externalities—was the root cause of the macroeconomic effects—loss of output and high unemployment.

Financial institutions claim that regulation is unnecessary and even harmful. This could be just a blind and misplaced faith in the magic of the market. On a more generous interpretation, the assertion is they can govern themselves, handling the externalities by Coasian methods. These claims were strongly supported by

Alan Greenspan when he was Chairman of the US Federal Reserve Board, and accepted by successive presidents. Few outsiders hold this belief after the financial crisis. The need for some form of regulation is widely accepted, although the design of the best form of regulation is a matter for debate, and different countries have taken different approaches. Most involve some constraint on debt and risk-taking by retail banks. At one time the Glass-Steagall Act in the US imposed total separation of retail and investment banking. Few support a return to that now, but some separation—installing 'firewalls' or 'ring-fencing' riskier investment banking activities—is often recommended, for example by the UK Independent Commission on Banking. Other proposals include 'macroprudential regulation', which consists mainly of Pigovian measures to control externalities inflicted by the excessive risk-taking of one intermediary on others. Such measures include requiring certain minimum ratios of equity capital or liquid reserves by banks, or other forms of taxing debt and leverage. Regulators can also establish procedures for orderly resolution of insolvencies that are bound to occur from time to time because of risks inherent in investments; this can minimize the risk of failure spreading along a chain of counterparties. Almost no one advocates much greater government role, which would probably result in lending governed by political priorities rather than economic merit, and stifle good innovation along with bad.

Most insiders in financial institutions oppose reforms that increase government regulation, perhaps in the belief that they are better off with the status quo: they get to keep risky profits secure in the knowledge that governments will come to their rescue when the risks go bad, so taxpayers bear the losses. I think they are mistaken to resist all regulation. Making themselves subject to effective regulation is a commitment and a signal that they are of good quality and will behave prudently. This will increase the public's confidence, reduce the risk of panics and liquidity crises, and therefore serve the long-term interests of all banks better.

Chapter 6
Institutions and organizations

Humankind has moved farther away from self-sufficiency for thousands of years. Specialization according to comparative advantage, whether based on resource endowments or skill differences, organization of production in large volumes and long runs, and accumulation of capital equipment have all yielded huge increases in productivity. And decreases in transport costs have made it possible to trade the resulting goods and services for the benefit of consumers across the globe.

Each of these developments entails increasing numbers and complexity of transactions among the specialized individuals and firms. These transactions in turn require an infrastructure of institutions and organizations. Markets are the most common and best known of such institutions—that is why they have been the focus of microeconomics and of this book. But other arrangements for transacting do exist, and can be better than markets for some purposes. We saw in Chapter 3 how firms can use internal organization to save on transaction costs of using markets. Families, social groups and networks, industry associations, and governments work better in other contexts. Study of these institutions enriches microeconomics, and builds bridges between it and other social sciences that study these institutions from their own perspectives.

Property rights and contract enforcement

Successful specialization and transaction have two basic prerequisites—security of property and of contract. If property is insecure, people will not improve land, undertake research and development, accumulate capital, or do any of the things that are so important for increasing the productive potential of the economy, for fear that the fruits of their labours and saving will be stolen. Insecurity of contract will jeopardize all transactions except a few trivial ones where one good or service of perfectly known quality is being exchanged for another equally sure good or service or for cash. All but the most primitive economies need institutions to protect property and enforce contracts.

Although security of property and contract is important, I must invoke my mantra in this context too: nothing is 100 per cent secure. The best of democracies take away private property for public purposes under the legal doctrine of 'eminent domain'. This should be rare, the laws and procedures that allow it to happen should be clear and open, and the owners should be given fair compensation. Contracts are not sacrosanct either; under exceptional circumstances beyond control of the parties to a contract, for example in the case of wars, riots, hurricanes, and earthquakes, one or both parties are freed from their contractual obligations and liabilities. Bankruptcy of a party also frees it from contracts; others dealing with it must take their place in the queue of claimants to whatever can be salvaged. Of course powers of eminent domain are sometimes misused, or the compensation is inadequate, and some companies use the threat of bankruptcy to elicit wage contract concessions from their workers. But most modern economies have enough security of property and contract to be able to support high levels of economic activities and transactions.

State and non-state institutions of governance

Most modern economies rely on the state's laws, and the organizations (police and courts) that enforce the laws, to provide the needed security of property and contract. But in many countries, and in all countries at some time in history, the state's institutions and organizations are or have been too weak, slow, inefficient, biased, or corrupt to be reliable. Such societies develop alternative institutions to provide the needed economic governance. Even in modern advanced economies, non-state institutions supplement state ones, and are superior for some purposes.

All voluntary economic transactions promise gain to both parties; otherwise one or the other would have refused the deal in the first place. But one or both can gain by violating the terms of the contract and behaving opportunistically at the expense of the other party. This is a prisoners' dilemma that needs some resolution, and a contract enforcement institution can provide that. Diego Gambetta studied one such non-state institution in his book on the Sicilian mafia. He quotes a cattle breeder he interviewed: 'When the butcher comes to me to buy an animal, he knows that I want to cheat him [by giving him a low-quality animal]. But I know that he wants to cheat me [by reneging on payment]. [W]e need Peppe [the Mafioso] to make us agree. And we both pay Peppe a percentage of the deal.' I will return to Peppe's enforcement methods, for now leaving you in suspense!

The long arm of the law, or the strong arm of the Mafia, is least needed for repeated transactions between family members and close friends. They can resolve their prisoners' dilemmas in favour exchanges because each values continuation of the relationship more than the short-term gain he or she would make by behaving opportunistically. In good relationships the parties don't even keep precise track of who owes the other more favours, relying on the needs to even out over time. Trying to keep an exact score can spell the end of the relationship; asking for or offering money is totally unacceptable. A memorable example in a different 'family' context comes from *The Godfather*. When the undertaker Bonasera, who is unused to the ways of that world, asks Don Vito Corleone how much he should pay for the service of avenging his daughter's rape, the Don replies: 'Some day, my friend, and may that day never come, I will call on you to do me some small favour. Until then, please accept this as a gift.'

In some situations, one person may not have sufficiently frequently repeated interaction with the same other person, but has frequent occasions to deal with *someone* from a relatively small community. Among businesspeople in a small city, for example, A may deal with B only rarely, but has to deal with some others, be they C, D, etc., all the time. Such groups can develop systems of norms, communication, and multilateral sanctions to sustain honesty in contracts among their members. The norm has two parts. The first forbids members from opportunistically cheating another member. If anyone violates this norm, the group's communication network informs all members. The sanction is that no one in the group will in future have any dealings with the miscreant. Thus if A cheats B, in future C, D, etc., will not deal with A, effectively putting him or her out of business. The fear of this multilateral punishment keeps A honest. But what if C, D, etc., are tempted by profitable business opportunities with A? Therefore the norm has a second part: refusal to participate in A's punishment is itself a violation, with the same punishment of ostracism. The fear of this keeps C, D, etc., in line.

This is similar to honour codes at several universities. Students are required to abide by specified standards of academic integrity in their studies and exams. If a student sees another student violating the code, he or she must report it to the honour committee. Failure to report is itself a violation of the code, calling forth punishments similar to those for primary violations like cheating or plagiarism.

As usual, such systems don't work perfectly or 100 per cent of the time, but work well enough to have existed in many places at many times. Here are two examples from very different places and times:

Avner Greif describes and analyses a community of Jewish merchants in the Maghrib (nations in the Mediterranean coastal plain of North Africa) in the eleventh century AD. They sent goods to other markets hundreds of miles away, relying on agents there to sell them at a good price and to remit the proceeds. Merchants' agents could be opportunistic in many ways—not possess the business skill they claimed to have in order to get the job; claim that the goods had arrived damaged; not do a diligent search for the best available price; falsely claim that the goods had to be sold for a low price and pocket the difference; and so on. The merchants also exchanged letters among themselves on various business matters, and in these they would voice complaints about agents' misbehaviour. If enough evidence mounted, the community would ostracize the miscreant.

Lisa Bernstein studies an arbitration forum of diamond merchants in New York to resolve contract disputes that might arise between them. The arbitrators are experienced merchants in that industry, so they know the prevailing practices and norms, and can assess evidence better than a court that lacks the industry-specific knowledge. Therefore arbitration works faster, is cheaper, and more accurate. If the party judged to be at fault defies the arbitration panel's ruling (usually restitution or fine), the miscreant's name and picture is displayed on the bulletin board of the Diamond Merchants' Club, warning other members against dealing with him or her. This punishment, being driven from business and essentially losing one's livelihood, is far harsher than the fines a court could levy, and is therefore a more effective deterrent against opportunism. With some other arbitration forums, their rulings are respected and enforced by the state's courts.

In these examples, members of the trading community provided their own services for the mechanism of contract governance. In other instances they hire the services of an outsider. Gambetta's Peppe is one of these. He provides two kinds of services. In one, he gathers and stores information about past behaviour of traders. If A has found a profitable business opportunity with B, he can for a fee ask Peppe to disclose whether B cheated in any of his past dealings with others. (Of course Peppe may conspire with B and give A a false assurance; Peppe's fee has to be large enough that he would not want to ruin his reputation as an honest informant for sake of the one-time gain he could get by colluding with B.) If a previously honest B nonetheless cheats A in this deal, Peppe in this mode takes no action other than adding B's name to the list of cheats for future reference, and future loss of business is the only penalty B faces. In the other mode, Peppe is not concerned with past actions. If A is his client and B cheats A, Peppe will inflict on B some suitable harm—smashing kneecaps or worse. Not surprisingly, Peppe's fee for the kneecap-smashing mode is higher than that for tracking and supplying information about past behaviour.

Antecedents for Peppe in the information mode go back to trade fairs in medieval Europe. Merchants from faraway countries gathered together for these. The law governing their contracts, known as *lex mercatoria* or *law merchant*, evolved as a system of custom and practice, and formed the basis for formal contract laws in many countries. Private judges administered the law; they had expertise acquired from their commercial background and a reputation for fairness and giving speedy, effective justice. They charged a fee for their services, which included supplying information about the parties' past behaviour, adjudicating disputes, and keeping their information up to date for future use by adding names of new cheats and those who failed to abide by their rulings. This institution also has similarities with arbitration in the Diamond Merchants' Club.

Such private institutions for contract enforcement work quite well because they serve communities whose members all benefit from the security of trade that successful governance brings. Private institutions for property right protection are more difficult to sustain, because they must deter non-members who would benefit if the institution failed. Nonetheless, they can work when the stakes are sufficiently large. For example, California's gold rush started in 1849 before the territory became a state and established a formal law enforcement mechanism, but the prospectors organized to create and enforce a system of rights to mines. But creation of private rights to products of federal timber and range lands in the US's far west in the late nineteenth century were less successful because the number of people involved was larger and they had more heterogeneous interests.

Private institutions of economic governance work quite well in relatively small stable communities. But the transaction opportunities available within such communities may be limited. Benefits of specialization, economies of large-scale production, and consumption of a wide variety of goods require dealing with others far away—geographically, socially, and economically. Such arm's length transactions with strangers require better objective institutions of governance. Intermediaries who set up a market or market-like platform can help. Let us look at some institutions of this kind.

Market design

The needs of some specialized transactions are best met by creating special markets or market-like platforms for the two sides in a transaction to meet. Some of these even create limited-purpose monies for their transactions. Babysitters' clubs are a well-known example, but they are confined to groups of friends, or at least acquaintances, in a small geographic area. The internet has greatly expanded the scope of such markets, and has created what is being termed a 'sharing economy' or 'peer-to-peer economy'.

Airbnb created a private market for rentals of rooms, apartments, or houses, matching hosts and guests. Each party has good reason to worry about entering into the transaction with a stranger. The host worries that the guests may be dirty, noisy, or obnoxious, or may even steal from them; the guests worry about the quality of the accommodation. The owners of the platform carry out some background checks; they also invite ratings from previous users. Hosts without previous record must accept low rents—as they accumulate good ratings they can raise their price. Of course the system is not perfect. For example, you could get your friends to give you good ratings. But on the whole the system seems to be working fairly well for Airbnb. Similar sites exist for rentals of private cars, do-it-yourself tools and equipment, and so on.

Other sites such as eBay, Craiglist, the outside vendors on Amazon, and so on cover a broader range of goods and services. To be successful, all markets or trading platforms must pay attention to several matters. They must facilitate searches for counterparties to the trade each individual using the site wants and match the two sides. They must also facilitate price discovery, helping sellers search for the highest price they can get, and buyers search for the lowest price they must pay (with appropriate adjustment for quality, delivery time, etc.). And they must ensure contractual performance and resolve disputes. Traditional marketplaces—central squares in towns, medieval market fairs, modern malls, stock exchanges, and so on—enabled search and matching by bringing together potential traders at one physical site; on the internet the site is geographically scattered across a million computers or other devices but connected electronically. Smartphones have even facilitated price discovery across markets—for example, fishermen off the southwest coast of India can get information about prices in different coastal towns and decide where to take their catch. All these developments promote economic efficiency by making markets more competitive and making it easier to achieve equilibrium of supply and demand. (These transactions usually avoid the taxes that would be levied on sales in the conventional formal economy; it must be admitted that in some cases that is their raison d'etre.) The needs of contract performance and dispute resolution are met by one of various institutions: the state's machinery of law, industry arbitration, reputations based on peer-reviews and ratings, and so on.

Matching markets

Many transactions involve matching people or objects in pairs, and platforms and institutions exist to facilitate such transactions. People seeking marriage partners and informal or formal matchmaking institutions are the most obvious example, but many others exist: applicants and colleges, students and dormitory rooms, newly graduated doctors and hospitals, organ donors and patients who need transplants, and so on. In some contexts matches must meet certain constraints; for example organs and recipients must be of compatible blood types. In other cases each item on one side could be matched with any of several on the other side, but one or both have preferences among the alternatives: college students have preferences about dorm rooms but not vice versa, but colleges and applicants both have preferences about their matches, as do the prospective bride and groom in marriage. It is important to examine whether existing platforms or institutions achieve matches that are good in some suitable sense, and whether better ones can be designed.

Conventional markets would be problematic in many matching situations. First, items are indivisible and heterogeneous, and numbers of items on each side may be small. Markets may turn into bargaining among pairs, where each member of each pair has significant market power. Second, the use of money is sometimes not customary, and may be abhorrent especially in contexts like organ transplants. Money is sometimes used in disguise; for example, colleges offer better financial aid packages to students they wish to attract, and dowry or bride price payments exist in many cultures. But constraints or prohibition on the use of money complicates matching transactions beyond what is usual in markets.

The theory of matching markets was pioneered by David Gale, Lloyd Shapley, and others; it was extended with several important applications including hospital-doctor matching, organ donation being developed by Alvin Roth and others. Shapley and Roth won the 2012 economics Nobel prize for their contributions. (Gale had died in 2008.) Here is my selective and very short introduction to this work.

What are desirable properties of a matching process? First, of course, comes the economists' obsession: Pareto efficiency. It should not be feasible to devise another matching that leaves all participants better off (i.e. with matches higher in their order of preference). A related property is stability. Label the participants on one side with upper-case letters and those on the other side with lower-case letters. Suppose a mechanism matches A with a, and B with b, but A prefers to be matched with b, and b with A. In the absence of coercion, A and b would be able to get together and do better than they would have done in the outcome of the mechanism, which would therefore be unstable. If no such voluntary exits in pairs are possible, the outcome is stable. When participants' preferences are not known to others, as is often the case, a third desirable property is non-manipulability: no participant should be able to get a better outcome by misrepresenting his or her preferences.

When only one side of the market has preferences over its matches, as with college students and dorm rooms, a simple procedure called top-trading cycle can meet these desiderata. Start with any assignment: this could be the status quo or initial ownership pattern. Each student indicates his or her most preferred room. If the initial pairing is unstable, a set of students can each get their top preferences by swapping rooms among themselves. Let them do this, and remove them from the market. Repeat the process with the remaining students with their preferences over the remaining rooms. Continue until all rooms have been allocated. It has been proved that this method has all three properties—stability, Pareto efficiency, and non-manipulability. Of course, as always with Pareto efficiency, the outcome depends on the initial assignment and need not be equal or fair; if you are not lucky enough to be in one of the early rounds of swapping cycles, your top preferences may be gone before you get your turn.

Things get more complex when both sides have preferences over their matches. As an example, consider four students a, b, c, and d applying to four colleges A, B, C, and D. Table 4 shows the preference using > to indicate a higher place in the preference ranking. For example, college B likes student d best, a second, c third, and b last.

The matching procedure devised by Gale and Shapley, called the deferred acceptance algorithm, works as follows. Choose one side, let us say the colleges, to make offers. Each college makes an offer to the student it ranks highest. In our example, A offers to a, B and D offer to d, and C offers to b. Each student holds on to the offer he or she likes best and rejects the others. Here d has two

Table 4. Example of matching with two-sided preferences

Colleges' preferences		Students' preferences	
A	$a > b > d > c$	a	$D > B > A > C$
B	$d > a > c > b$	b	$D > A > B > C$
C	$b > a > d > c$	c	$D > B > C > A$
D	$d > c > b > a$	d	$A > C > B > D$

offers, from B and D, of which she prefers B, so rejects D. Of the others, a and b have one offer each, and hold on to these; c has no offers and waits for the second round. Importantly, acceptances are not binding yet; hence the title 'deferred acceptance'. In the second round, D (which was rejected by d in the first round) offers to its next preference, namely c. Now c has one offer, and accepts it. Each student has an offer, and the procedure stops. The matches A–a, B–d, C–b, and D–c become binding.

What if students are the side that make the offers? In the first round students a, b, and c make offers to college D, and d to A. Now D has three offers, and accepts c (its top preference among them), rejecting a and b. In the second round, a offers to B and b to A. Now A has two offers, from d in the first round and b in the second round, and rejects the less-preferred, namely d. (Remember that acceptances are not binding until the procedure stops.) In the third round, d offers to its next-ranked college, C. Now we have a one-to-one matching, namely a–B, b–A, c–D, and d–C. The matches are finalized, and the procedure stops.

It can be proved that the procedure leads to stable outcomes, and is Pareto efficient for the side that makes the offers. However, it is manipulable: someone from the side that receives the offer can usually achieve a better outcome by strategically misrepresenting his or her preferences. In the above example, when colleges make offers, acting according to true preferences gets student d college B, which ranks third in her preferences. If she pretended to have preferences A > C > D > B, she would get college C, which is second in her true preferences! The reasoning is lengthy and the procedure takes six rounds; suspicious or diligent readers may wish to construct it for a good mental exercise.

Evolution of the programme for matching hospitals with new graduates of medical schools is instructive. In the first half of the twentieth century this was a largely decentralized market. In the 1940s, US hospitals competed for the best medical students by offering them internships earlier and earlier. This did not work well, because matches were fixed before the quality of the students or their interests in particular specializations became clear. And if an offer was rejected, it became too late to make another offer to an acceptable candidate. In the 1950s the National Resident Matching Program started, and worked like the deferred acceptance algorithm where hospitals made offers. It continues, with some changes, notably applicant-proposing instead of hospital-proposing, and accommodating married couples of doctors who seek joint offers.

The procedure can be generalized to allow for the possibility that some matches are worse than no match at all and therefore unacceptable to one side or the other. It can also be generalized to situations where each item on one side is to be matched with several on the other side, as is the case with colleges and students.

Another important platform matches kidney donors and recipients. These often come in pairs where one person is willing to donate a kidney to a relative or loved one who needs one, but has an incompatible blood type. Situations may arise in which A is willing to donate to a and B to b, but the willing pairs are incompatible, whereas A is compatible with b and B with a. This requires a coordinated set of operations in which A and B donate simultaneously, and the organs are transplanted into b and a, respectively. Even more complex chains of many donors and recipients are being coordinated using centralized clearinghouses.

Auctions

Many transactions are conducted as auctions rather than sales at posted or negotiated prices. An auction brings together all potential buyers for the designated commodity (or package of commodities) to create some form of competition among them. In fact that is why many sellers use auctions. Bidding for supply or construction contracts is the mirror-image, where the buyer brings together potential and competing sellers.

Auctions take many different forms. In a sealed-bid auction, each bidder submits a bid without knowing what any of the others are doing. The seller inspects all bids simultaneously. The highest bidder gets the object and pays what he or she has bid. A similar outcome is achieved if the seller starts a 'price clock' at a very high level and gradually lowers it. At any time any of the bidders can stop the clock and claim the object at that price. In the reverse of this process, the seller starts a price clock at a low level and continuously raises it. Bidders can drop out at any time (but cannot then re-enter). When only one bidder remains, he or she gets the object at the price on the clock, which is the price at which the bidder with the second-highest willingness to pay dropped out. In the familiar ascending or 'open outcry' form where the auctioneer asks 'any advance on' the previous bid, or raises bids in increments and bidders can stay in or drop out, the one willing to pay the most is the last survivor, but pays only a little more than the second-highest willingness to pay. (I said 'a little more' because bids may jump discretely in this form. Suppose A has the highest willingness to pay, offering $120, and B is next at $112. The auctioneer ups the bids in increments of $5. Both bidders are in at $110. B drops out at $115. A is willing to pay $120 but pays only $115, 'a little more' than $112. With a continuously rising clock, B would drop out as soon as the clock crossed $112, and A would pay that; okay, $112.01 perhaps.) This is explicit in a *second-price auction*, where the rules state directly that the highest bidder wins but pays only the second-highest bid. By contrast, the form where the highest bidder wins and pays his or her own bid is called a *first-price auction*.

There even are 'all pay' auctions where the highest bidder gets the object, but all bidders, win or lose, pay whatever they had bid. You may think this very odd, but this is perhaps the commonest form in everyday life. In every four-year cycle for election to the US presidency, numerous politicians spend huge amounts of time, effort, and money; these expenditures are like bids. Only one succeeds every four years, and the losers don't get any refunds on their bids. The same goes for athletes training to win medals at the Olympic games, contestants for lucrative contracts, and so on.

Each bidder formulates a bidding strategy; the seller decides the form of the auction, and perhaps a minimum or 'reserve' price. This makes the auction a game of strategy. It is complicated by asymmetric information. The seller may know things about the object that the bidders don't. Each bidder attaches a value to the object. This may be personal or sentimental (Audrey Hepburn's little black dress in *Breakfast at Tiffany's*) or commercial (an estimate of the amount of crude oil in a tract being auctioned). Any one bidder doesn't know other bidders' value directly, but something may be revealed in the process of bidding, for example how quickly some of the others drop out in an ascending, open outcry auction. The seller does not know the bidders' valuations; if he or she did he or she would simply go to the highest valuer and offer to sell at a price just below that value. The outcome of the auction is an equilibrium of this subtle game of asymmetric information with big practical applications. No wonder research on the topic has burgeoned in economic theory and game theory. I can just begin to touch on a couple of major themes.

In a first-price auction, a bid equal to your valuation of the object will not get you any profit or surplus even if you win. Bidding less than your value decreases your probability of winning, but gets you more profit if you do win. Your bidding strategy should balance these two considerations; the result is that your bid should be somewhat below your value. In a second-price auction, what you pay if you do win is someone else's bid, which is outside your control. Therefore your best strategy is to maximize your probability of winning, namely to make your bid equal to your full valuation. Now look at these strategies from the seller's perspective. If the seller uses a first-price form, bidders will shade their bids below their values; if a second-price form, they will bid their values but the seller will get only the second-highest value. Which earns the seller the higher revenue? In any one instance, the bidders' configuration of values and bids may take the outcome in either direction. But the seller does not know these values in advance. Taking the appropriate probabilistic averages over all configurations, it turns out that under very broad conditions the two effects (underbidding in the first-price form and getting only the second-highest value in the second-price form) exactly cancel out: the two forms are revenue-equivalent! In fact this revenue-equivalence holds for all auction forms under these conditions; this was an amazing early insight of auction theory.

Next consider an auction where the item has an objective or commercial value, but different bidders have different estimates of this value. If their estimation processes are unbiased and there are many bidders (say 100), by the law of large numbers (the wisdom of crowds) the average of their estimates will be close to the true value. But the average bid does not win the auction; the highest bid does. This will be based on the highest estimate of value, which by that very fact is likely to be an overestimate. A truly strategic bidder will recognize this, and think: 'If I win, that means 99 other bidders got lower estimates than I did. What should I learn from that, and how should it affect my bid?' The answer is to shade your bid downward. The mathematics for calculating how much to shade is complex, and in practice many bidders fail to make the correct inferences, with the result that often the winners of rights to mineral and crude oil deposits find that they have paid too much; or sports teams that win the competition for a superstar find that the player does not live up to their expectations. This is known as the *winner's curse*.

Less well-known is a hypothetical phenomenon of a loser's curse. Suppose 99 objects are being auctioned among 100 bidders, and you are the one who loses out. That means you got an exceptionally low estimate of the value. You should have asked yourself: 'If I lose, that means 99 other bidders gave higher estimates than I did. What should I learn from that, and how should it affect my bid?' Here you should raise your bid to correct for the loser's curse.

Now consider a middle range where the ratio of the number of objects to that of bidders is not too lopsided: it is neither too close to 0 (1 object and 100 bidders) nor too close to 1 (99 objects and 100 bidders). Then neither the winner's curse nor the loser's curse has much bite; each bidder can ignore the fact that others have different information and bid based on his or her own valuation. That gives us a really subtle but enlightening way to understand how competitive markets with many buyers and sellers work efficiently, even though the relevant information is widely scattered among all participants. We started out with markets and diverged to consider other platforms and institutions; it is nice to come full circle in closing.

Chapter 7
What works?

If you were hoping for a grand finale, declaring the triumph of the market, or the end of capitalism as we know it, I must disappoint you. In Chapter 4, I showed how competitive markets, when they perform well, yield Pareto efficient outcomes. If you recall the definition: no other feasible outcome can bring greater economic benefit for some people and losses to none. However, a Pareto efficient outcome may have a very unfair distribution of well-being. In Chapter 5, I showed how monopoly, externalities, and information asymmetries can prevent market outcomes from being efficient even in the limited Pareto sense. And, to pile on the bad news, governments often don't deliver any better outcomes. They have their own failures stemming from the nature of political processes, whether democratic or authoritarian. They have their own favourites and clients—existing producers, other organized interests, and campaign contributors—who benefit at the expense of the general public.

Given this long list of defects in markets and governments, the world has fared not too badly. Mixed economies, comprising on the one hand markets and similar institutions that rely on incentives and self-interest, and on the other hand communal institutions and governments to organize collective action, to provide oversight, limit abuses of market power, and deploy taxes or other policies that correct market failures, have achieved reasonable economic outcomes and growth in many countries. I think such muddling through is the most we can hope for.

In my view the biggest risk facing a reasonably good outcome is failure to notice and correct errors before they spiral out of control and do serious damage. This risk is at its worst when one person or one organization controls all pertinent decisions. So long as a competitor can spot the first decision-maker's errors and has a profit or other incentive to correct them, all will be reasonably well. Therefore I am not for or against markets or governments per se, but against monopoly of either kind.

An egregious example of the effects of monopoly over decisions comes from post World War II urban planning and public housing. Influenced by theories of Le Corbusier and others, government agencies designed and built deserts like Brasilia and horrors like the Pruitt-Igoe projects in St Louis. If urban housing had been provided by competitive private builders, at least some of them would have quickly noticed the defects of such developments and offered alternatives. However, government agencies persisted with their plans. Even worse was the horror of McCarthyism in the US, which stigmatized many people with suspicion of treason and barred them from employment in the government and in many, although not all, private firms. Paul Samuelson, surely one of the top five economists of the twentieth century, drew this lesson when describing his life philosophy in a 1983 article in *The American Economist*:

> What I learned from the McCarthy incident was the peril of a one-employer society. When you are blackballed from government employment, there is great safety in the existence of thousands of anonymous employers out there in the market....To me this became a newly perceived argument, not so much for laissez faire capitalism as for the mixed economy.

A mixed economy—where competitive markets or similar institutions generate information about scarcity and create incentives to alleviate the scarcity in a reasonably efficient manner, where antitrust policies keep the markets open to competition, where the government and other social organizations help overcome the inefficiencies of externalities, and where political competition acts as a corrective mechanism against abuses of power and serious errors of judgement—is in my opinion the best way of organizing microeconomic activity.

Further reading

General

In my judgement the best book about markets—how they work, what they accomplish, and why and how they can fail—is *Reinventing the Bazaar* by John McMillan (W. W. Norton, 2002). If you have time to read only one book about economics, make it this one.

At a slightly more technical level, Milton Friedman's *Price Theory*, originally published in 1962 (reprinted in 2001 by Martino Fine Books), is still highly worth reading. I got my own introduction to practically applicable microeconomic theory from it.

Among modern college textbooks, there is an abundance of excellent material. At the risk of doing injustice to numerous others, let me mention two with authors who are my co-authors in other contexts: Robert Pindyck and Daniel Rubinfeld, *Microeconomics* (Prentice-Hall, 7th edition, 2008); and Douglas Bernheim and Michael Whinston, *Microeconomics* (McGraw-Hill/Irwin, 2007).

For historical background, William J. Bernstein's *A Splendid Exchange: How Trade Shaped the World* (Atlantic Monthly Press, 2008) is a sweeping and fascinating tale of world trade and markets through the ages.

Chapter 2: Consumers

The Friedman, Pindyck-Rubinfeld, and Bernheim-Whinston books all analyse conventional consumer choice at an introductory level and in detail far beyond what is possible in this very short introduction. The latter two books also discuss modern behavioural approaches. At an advanced level, in my view the best treatment of the theory and empirics of consumer choice is still Angus Deaton and John Muellbauer's *Economics and Consumer Behavior* (Cambridge University Press, 1980). Readers with good economic and statistical preparation will benefit from reading the survey used in the text: Richard Blundell, 'Consumer Behaviour: Theory and Empirical Evidence—A Survey,' *Economic Journal*, 98(389), March 1988, 16–65.

For behavioural approaches to decision theory, Daniel Kahneman's *Thinking Fast and Slow* (Farrar, Straus and Giroux, 2011) is the best introduction. Richard Thaler's *The Winner's Curse: Paradoxes and Anomalies of Economic Life* (Princeton University Press, 1994) was an early account of the accumulating research that led to changes in economists' thinking. Thaler and Cass Sunstein's *Nudge: Improving Decisions About Health, Wealth, and Happiness* (Penguin Books, 2009) argues the case for, and gives examples of, 'soft paternalism' based on behavioural research. For the application to environmental policies, see Cass R. Sunstein and Lucia A. Reisch, 'Automatically Green: Behavioral Economics and Environmental Protection' (5 April 2013). Available at SSRN: <http://dx.doi.org/10.2139/ssrn.2245657>.

Chapter 3: Producers

More detailed classification and analysis of costs—fixed and variable, average and marginal, sunk and avoidable... and implications for shapes of supply curves can be found in any introductory textbook.

Tim Harford's *The Undercover Economist* (Oxford University Press, 2006, chapters 1 and 2) has an excellent discussion and many examples of screening strategies for price discrimination. It is also great reading for much else about how economics enters our daily lives. Michael Porter's *Competitive Strategy* (Free Press, 1980) is the classic monograph about firms' strategies in competition with rival firms in their industry. Porter himself and many others have written books elaborating, extending, modifying, or challenging its teachings. Interested readers can discover this literature by searching for the book on <http://scholar.google.com>.

Study of strategic competition among firms relies on game theory, which is also useful for elucidating many other political and social strategic interactions. I am biased, but would like to recommend my own (with

Barry Nalebuff) book, *The Art of Strategy* (W. W. Norton 2008) intended for general readership, and my textbook (with Susan Skeath and David Reiley) *Games of Strategy* (W. W. Norton, 3rd edition, 2009). For the fascinating history of the diamond cartel, see Edward Jay Epstein, *The Rise and Fall of Diamonds: The Shattering of a Brilliant Illusion* (Simon and Schuster, 1982). See Austin Ramzy, 'Precious Holdings', *Time*, 18 February 2013, for an account of China's attempt to monopolize the market for rare earth metals, and Paul Klemperer, 'What Really Matters in Auction Design', *Journal of Economic Perspectives*, 16(1), January 2002, 169–89, for a discussion of collusion among bidders in auctions.

The mathematics of screening by self-selection is one of the most subtle and beautiful topics in economic theory. If you are really good at maths—and I mean, *really*: integral calculus and all that—I strongly recommend two articles both of which figured in economics Nobel prizes: James Mirrlees, 'An Exploration in the Theory of Optimal Income Taxation,' *Review of Economic Studies*, 38(2), April 1971, 175–208; and David Baron and Roger Myerson, 'Regulating a Monopolist with Unknown Cost', *Econometrica*, 50(4), July 1982, 911–30.

For detailed statements of the contributions of Ronald Coase and Oliver Williamson that led to a major change in the way economists think about firms, see the Nobel prize web sites: <http://www.nobelprize.org/nobel_prizes/economics/laureates/1991/press.html> and <http://www.nobelprize.org/nobel_prizes/economics/laureates/2009/advanced.html>.

Chapter 4: Markets

My list for this chapter must begin by reiterating a strong recommendation for John McMillan's *Reinventing the Bazaar*. The Bernheim-Whinston and Pindyck-Rubinfeld textbooks cited above offer good detailed and balanced treatments.

Insightful but one-sided accounts include Milton and Rose Friedman, *Free to Choose* (Mariner Books, 1990); and Joseph Stiglitz, *Whither Socialism* (MIT Press, 1996). For the Friedmans, markets are always wonderful and governments should keep away; for Stiglitz, markets, and often even market-based policies, are highly likely to fail and government is the answer.

A classic early analysis of rent controls is Milton Friedman and George Stigler's *Roofs or Ceilings? The Current Housing Problem* (Foundation for Economic Education, 1946).

On market instability, for me the best book is still Charles Kindleberger's *Manias, Panics, and Crashes: A History of Financial Crises* (Basic Books, 1978). Later editions are coauthored with Robert Z. Aliber (Palgrave Macmillan, 2011).

Chapter 5: Market and policy failures

Here I recommend three original books by Nobel laureates that can be read by non-specialists. Ronald Coase's *The Firm, the Market and the Law* (University of Chicago Press, 1995) includes his article on privately negotiated solutions to externalities, as well as his articles on the firm that were mentioned in Chapter 3. Elinor Ostrom's *Governing the Commons: The Evolution of Institutions for Collective Action* (Cambridge University Press, 1990) contains her work on bottom–up management of common pool resources. Remarkably for economics books, these two have no maths at all.

A classic example of Coasian resolutions of externalities is in Steven N. S. Cheung, 'The Fable of the Bees: An Economic Investigation', *Journal of Law and Economics*, 16(1), April 1973, 11–34.

Daniel Spulber has edited a valuable and fascinating collection of articles debunking many popular conceptions about market failures and need for government intervention in *Famous Fables of Economics: Myths of Market Failures* (Wiley-Blackwell, 2001).

Key early chapters of Michael Spence's pathbreaking book, *Market Signaling: Informational Transfer in Hiring and Related Screening Processes* (Harvard University Press, 1974) are highly readable, requiring minimal numeracy. Diego Gambetta's *Codes of the Underworld: How Criminals Communicate* (Princeton University Press, 2011) has many fascinating examples of signalling and screening in organized crime. John Maynard-Smith and David Harper give an excellent overview of biological signaling in their book *Animal Signals* (Oxford University Press, 2004).

Mancur Olson's *The Logic of Collective Action* (Harvard University Press, 1965) and *The Rise and Decline of Nations* (Yale University Press, 1984) are important and readable analyses of how collective action can work or fail in private arrangements, of the importance of concentrated versus diffuse benefits, of how special interests can stifle policy reform that would benefit the economy as a whole and how their power can be broken in a crisis. For an analysis of the political process of economic policymaking, see Avinash Dixit, *The Making of Economic Policy: A Transaction Cost Politics Perspective* (MIT Press, 1996).

In the 1950s and 1960s, Richard Musgrave was influential in establishing the view of government as correcting market failures, and James Buchanan was equally influential in establishing a contrary view of politicians as pursuers of their self-interest rather than larger interests of the country, thereby creating government failures. Therefore it is fascinating to read these two giants in the late years of their lives discuss and debate their opposing views in James M. Buchanan and Richard A. Musgrave, *Public Finance and Public Choice: Two Contrasting Visions of the State* (MIT Press, 1999).

For a general discussion of the economic efficiency costs of monopoly power, see pp. 67–8 of Jean Tirole, *Industrial Organization* (MIT Press, 1991). For the specific example of health care costs in the US, see Steven Brill, 'Bitter Pill: How Outrageous Pricing and Egregious Profits are Destroying our Health Care', *Time*, 4 March 2013. Stephen V. Marks, 'A Reassessment of Empirical Evidence on the U.S. Sugar Program', in *The Economics and Politics of World Sugar Policies*, ed. Steven V. Marks and Keith E. Maskus (University of Michigan Press, 1993), calculates the costs of US sugar import restrictions.

Many instances of policy failure would be outright funny if they were not so costly. My favourite is the Greek ban on banana imports during the 1970s; see Barry Newman, 'The Greeks have a Word for Banana but Lack Bananas', *Wall Street Journal*, July 1983. A Japanese trade official justified their restriction on beef imports by arguing that the Japanese have longer intestines and cannot digest more beef (*New York Times*, 6 March 1988). And France prevented the US multinational Pepsi from acquiring Danone, which makes yogurt and bottled water, on the grounds that it was a national business champion in a strategic industry (*The Telegraph*, 24 July 2005). The US political process of tax reform is brilliantly recounted by Jeffrey H. Birnbaum and Alan S. Murray in *Showdown at Gucci Gulch* (Random House, 1987).

One of the earliest and most perceptive accounts of the financial crisis came in the form of comedy sketches by John Bird and John Fortune on the British television programme, *The South Bank Show*. Some of these are on YouTube; search for 'Bird' and 'Fortune'. Early and perceptive books on the recent financial crisis I recommend are Gillian Tett, *Fool's Gold: How the Bold Dream of a Small Tribe at J. P. Morgan Was Corrupted by Wall Street Greed and Unleashed a Catastrophe* (Free Press, 2010), and Robert Shiller, *The Subprime Solution: How Today's Global Financial Crisis Happened, and What to Do about It* (Princeton University Press, 2009). Among more recent books, Raghuram Rajan, *Fault Lines: How Hidden Fractures Still Threaten the World Economy* (Princeton University Press, 2011) is my favourite. Carmen M. Reinhart and Kenneth S. Rogoff, *This Time Is Different: Eight Centuries of Financial Folly* (Princeton University Press, 2009) is an outstanding study of financial crises through history. Issues of reform are nicely discussed by John Vickers, who chaired the UK Independent Commission on Banking, in 'Some Economics of Banking Reform', Oxford University, Department of Economics, Discussion Paper No. 632, November 2012, available from <http://www.economics.ox.ac.uk/index.php/research/working-papers>.

Chapter 6: Institutions and organizations

For more detailed explanations of the reasons for, and benefits from, specialization in production, see the chapters on trade and growth in any introductory economics textbook, such as Paul Krugman and Robin Wells, *Microeconomics* (Worth Publishers, 3rd edition, 2012, chapter 8). The chapter on growth in their *Macroeconomics* (Worth Publishers, 3rd edition, 2012, chapter 8) is also relevant.

Douglass North's work, exposited in his book *Institutions, Institutional Change, and Economic Performance* (Cambridge University Press, 1990), was important in reviving economists' interest in institutions for property rights and contracts. Oliver E. Williamson started his analysis of firms and broadened it to economic governance more generally; his books *The Economic Institutions of Capitalism* (Free Press, 1987) and *The Mechanisms of Governance* (Oxford University Press, 1996) have been hugely influential. Both of these people won Nobel prizes for their research.

Non-state institutions for property-right protection are studied by Yoram Barzel, *Economic Analysis of Property Rights* (Cambridge University Press, 1989), and Gary D. Libecap, *Contracting for Property Rights* (Cambridge University Press, 1989).

Diego Gambetta, *The Sicilian Mafia: The Business of Private Protection* (Harvard University Press, 1993), is an outstanding ethnographic study of a non-state institution for contract enforcement.

Avner Greif's historical research and game-theoretic modelling of contract enforcement by formal and informal institutions, collected in his book *Institutions and the Path to the Modern Economy: Lessons from Medieval Trade* (Cambridge University Press, 2006) is highly readable. And, if I may be so bold, chapters 1 and 6, and the introductory sections in chapters 2–5 of Avinash Dixit, *Lawlessness and Economics: Alternative Modes of Governance* (Princeton University Press, 2004) are also readable.

A good account of the theory and applications of matching markets is in the advanced information document on the Shapley-Roth Nobel prize: <http://www.nobelprize.org/nobel_prizes/economic-sciences/laureates/2012/advanced.html>.

On auctions, I recommend Paul Klemperer's *Auctions: Theory and Practice* (Princeton University Press, 2004); and Paul Milgrom's *Putting Auction Theory to Work* (Cambridge University Press, 2004). Beginning readers should confine themselves to the introductory chapters.

Peer-to-peer markets are evolving very fast and any description and analysis may get out of date very quickly. But *What's Mine Is Yours: The Rise of Collaborative Consumption* by Rachel Botsman and Roo Rogers (Harper Business Books, 2010) is worth reading.

The concluding point about markets is based on Wolfgang Pesendorfer and Jeroen Swinkels, 'Efficiency and Information Aggregation in Auctions', *American Economic Review*, 90(3), June 2000, 499–525. This is highly mathematical.

"牛津通识读本"已出书目

古典哲学的趣味	福柯	地球
人生的意义	缤纷的语言学	记忆
文学理论入门	达达和超现实主义	法律
大众经济学	佛学概论	中国文学
历史之源	维特根斯坦与哲学	托克维尔
设计，无处不在	科学哲学	休谟
生活中的心理学	印度哲学祛魅	分子
政治的历史与边界	克尔凯郭尔	法国大革命
哲学的思与惑	科学革命	丝绸之路
资本主义	广告	民族主义
美国总统制	数学	科幻作品
海德格尔	叔本华	罗素
我们时代的伦理学	笛卡尔	美国政党与选举
卡夫卡是谁	基督教神学	美国最高法院
考古学的过去与未来	犹太人与犹太教	纪录片
天文学简史	现代日本	大萧条与罗斯福新政
社会学的意识	罗兰·巴特	领导力
康德	马基雅维里	无神论
尼采	全球经济史	罗马共和国
亚里士多德的世界	进化	美国国会
西方艺术新论	性存在	民主
全球化面面观	量子理论	英格兰文学
简明逻辑学	牛顿新传	现代主义
法哲学：价值与事实	国际移民	网络
政治哲学与幸福根基	哈贝马斯	自闭症
选择理论	医学伦理	德里达
后殖民主义与世界格局	黑格尔	浪漫主义

批判理论	德国文学	儿童心理学
电影	戏剧	时装
俄罗斯文学	腐败	现代拉丁美洲文学
古典文学	医事法	卢梭
大数据	癌症	隐私
洛克	植物	电影音乐
幸福	法语文学	抑郁症
免疫系统	微观经济学	